British Military
Service Tribunals,
1916–1918

Manchester University Press

British Military Service Tribunals, 1916–1918

'A very much abused body of men'

JAMES McDERMOTT

Manchester University Press

Manchester and New York

distributed exclusively in the USA by Palgrave Macmillan

Published by Manchester University Press
Oxford Road, Manchester M13 9NR, UK
and Room 400, 175 Fifth Avenue, New York, NY 10010, USA
www.manchesteruniversitypress.co.uk

Distributed exclusively in the USA by
Palgrave Macmillan, 175 Fifth Avenue, New York,
NY 10010, USA

Distributed exclusively in Canada by
UBC Press, University of British Columbia, 2029 West Mall,
Vancouver, BC, Canada V6T 1Z2

British Library Cataloguing-in-Publication Data
A catalogue record for this book is available from the British Library

Library of Congress Cataloging-in-Publication Data applied for

ISBN 978 0 7190 8477 5 *hardback*

First published 2011

Typeset in Warnock Pro with Myriad display by
Koinonia, Manchester
Printed and bound in Great Britain by
TJ International Ltd, Padstow

Contents

Acknowledgements

The present work is developed from my (2009) PhD thesis, *The Work of the Military Service Tribunals in Northamptonshire, 1916–1918*, and so my first and deepest thanks are due to my supervisors, Dr Sally Sokoloff and Professor Ian Beckett, for their invaluable guidance and unflagging efforts to help me make coherent what I had fondly imagined to be so already. My gratitude also to Professor Hew Strachan and Dr Matthew Seligman for further suggestions, and to Barbara Russell for allowing me access to her computer database of Northamptonshire exemption applications. The staff of Northamptonshire Record Office have been unfailingly helpful, not only in supplying a multitude of documents I knew to exist but in pointing me towards other, unsuspected troves. Similarly, I have experienced much kind and energetic assistance at the National Archives, National Library of Wales, the Bedfordshire, Hampshire, Oxfordshire and Warwickshire Record Offices, the Centre for Buckinghamshire Studies, Bodleian Library, Imperial War Museum, Friends' House, Community (Earls Barton) and at numerous local studies departments of public libraries.

Note on the medical grading
of enlisted men

From January 1916 until November 1917, men who passed their army medical examinations were placed into one of three categories: A, B and C (the latter two with sub-divisions). An 'A' man was fit for general service: that is, to serve in the front line. Men certified as B1 or C1 were regarded as fit for support duties, respectively abroad or at home only; B2 and C2 men were allocated to garrison duties on the same basis; those classed as B3 and C3 similarly to clerking or other sedentary work. From November 1917, following the radical reorganization of the examination system and the replacement of military by civilian medical boards, newly enlisted men were allocated levels of fitness as follows: Grade I (old Category A), II (B1, C1), III (B2 and 3, C2 and 3), IV (failed).

1

Introduction

There is this to be said about tribunals: They are a very much abused body of men ... [1]

Military Service Tribunals were the product of legislation that, in venerable British fashion, represented a decisive step taken tentatively. Conscription, though not unprecedented in the nation's history, was sufficiently novel in 1916 to require the expenditure of enormous political energy to introduce in such a way as not to (or seem not to) traduce the principles for which, ostensibly, Britons were fighting. The result was ambiguous: a compulsory system of military enlistment that nevertheless provided a mechanism allowing deferral of, and even release from, the obligation. That mechanism's human face – the Tribunals – comprised thousands of men (and the occasional woman), the vast majority of whom had no judicial expertise, no formal training for their role, no particular insight into Whitehall's precise expectations of their work, and who remained excluded from the slow, tortuous process that sought to create a national manpower policy.

The Tribunals served two masters: one by legislative enactment, one by default. Though part of a wider initiative intended to maintain and replenish the enormously expanded establishment of the British Expeditionary Force (BEF), the logic of their immediate role (almost certainly unintended by conscription's architects) demanded that they should also accommodate the preoccupations of their local communities. The dichotomy ensured that few who had cause to evaluate their work were uncritical. Castigated either for being too sensitive to local concerns (by the War Office and GHQ), or for acting as the unfeeling servants of a voracious war-machine (by almost everyone else), Tribunals were unloved during their lifetimes and unmourned following their demise. Government's subsequent instructions to borough, district, metropolitan and county councils in England and Wales to destroy all files, minute books and other records relating to the Tribunals' work was both a practical measure to expunge the legacy of a politically troubled process and a symbolic repudiation of the process itself. [2]

That deliberate excision has circumscribed dramatically the historiography of the Military Service Tribunals. Expunged from communal perceptions of a local past, and almost unmarked in official histories of the war, their work has been viewed largely from the perspective of contemporary observations, reproduced in press reports of proceedings or in personal memoirs. Few offer a balanced perspective. Newspapers of the period, while often carrying verbatim reports, naturally sought out the atypical or remarkable story, while critics of the system invariably identified and advertised its least attractive manifestations. Given the controversial nature of the encounters, early commentaries overwhelmingly addressed the Tribunals' treatment of the relatively few conscientious objectors who came before them. Supported by documentary evidence from the No-Conscription Fellowship's *The Tribunal* newssheet, *The Labour Leader* and *The Friend*, all of which detailed occasions of abuse and unyielding judgements visited upon cases of conscience, they established an abiding image of tribunalists as middle-class, reactionary servants of the Establishment, instinctively antagonistic towards pacifist sentiments.[3] A number of more recent works have buttressed this perspective, allowing, at most, the mitigations of ignorance and incomprehension.[4] A few commentaries provide more balanced views, noting both the difficulties imposed by ambiguous legislation and the often-confrontational demeanour of conscientious objectors whose principles denied the moral validity of the process they were obliged to undergo.[5] Nevertheless, enduring negative opinions of the Tribunals have been sustained largely by reference to the matter of conscience and its (lack of) accommodation.

Other aspects of the Tribunals' work have received far less attention. Some monographs, examining official policy with regard to manpower allocation, assess their impact with specific reference to the expectations of the War Office. However, while broad overviews of the exemption process are offered, only the occasional illustrative reference illuminates the work of individual Tribunals.[6] Indeed, a limitation common to all is that they consider the system only as an auxiliary issue. Shorter pieces that focus specifically on the work of named Tribunals necessarily lack depth, relying either upon fragmentary records, or in the case of the very few personal memoirs available to us, upon the recollections of individual tribunalists.[7] As yet absent from the historiography is a detailed, discrete analysis of Military Service Tribunals based upon substantial documentary evidence. The present work is intended to provide that analysis.

In ordering the destruction of Tribunal records (both of local Tribunals and of Appeals or county Tribunals), the Ministry of Health decreed two exceptions: all papers compiled by the Middlesex and Peebles and Lothian County Appeals Tribunals were retained as benchmark models for future reference. These are held, respectively, at the National Archives, Kew, and the Scottish Record Office, Edinburgh. Elsewhere, there remain a number of unauthorized 'survivals'. No formal, standardized method of maintaining Tribunal records was laid down by Whitehall, and, consequently, their disposal was undertaken with varying degrees of efficiency. Many counties' archives retain no trace of their Tribunals' documented business; a few hold considerable fragments still, the result of oversight or deliberate efforts to preserve some token of a recent and substantial commitment.

In the case of one county, Northamptonshire, all urban and rural councils appear to have followed Whitehall's directive faithfully, as no original records relating to the proceedings of the county's local Tribunals are known to survive. In contrast, a decision was taken at some point to disregard official instructions and to preserve the Appeals Tribunal's paperwork almost in its entirety. If upon a sole initiative, it was most likely that of Herbert Millington, secretary and clerk to the Tribunal, though his culpability may only be assumed.[8] At his or another's decision, some 11,200 individual appeals forms were preserved, each giving an appellant's name, address and occupation, the ground(s) for his appeal, the decision of the local Tribunal that heard his original application and the confirming or dissenting decision of the Appeals body. Additionally, Millington's working notes of the Appeals Tribunal's sittings (rough and fair-copied) survive. In the case of sessions held at County Hall, Northampton, these date only from 1 January 1917 until the end of the war, but notes of their less frequent Peterborough sittings cover the entire conscription period. Too terse to represent a full record of the Tribunal's business, they nevertheless record appellants' case references, brief details of issues considered and decisions reached, with, very occasionally, supplementary information attached.[9] A large, though not comprehensive, selection of circulars and instructions from government departments was retained also.[10]

The Appeals Tribunal files and supplementary material, now held at Northampton Record Office, constitute the principal primary sources for this study.[11] Additionally, Northampton's press paid much attention to local Tribunals' proceedings. Three of the town's newspapers, the *Northampton Mercury*, *Northampton Herald* and *Northampton Independent*, carried 'Tribunals' columns, with the first-named assuming, for the purpose of this work, the role of medium of record.[12] These reports, revealing the political and social dynamics of the Tribunal Chamber and setting the context of appeals made against judgements therein, constitute a further major source for the following analysis.

Comparative data are drawn principally from the comprehensive records retained in the National Archives, comprising all Middlesex Appeals Tribunal files, minute books, registers and correspondence.

Central Tribunal minute books, correspondence with local and appeals Tribunals, and postwar reports are held in the same division.[13] The Peebles and Lothian Appeals Tribunal files – held at the Scottish Record Office – are in fragile condition and cannot be accessed at present. However, many surviving files and supplementary material from Cardiganshire's Appeals Tribunal are held at the National Library of Wales, and, where appropriate, reference has been made thereto.[14] Finally, fragmentary material contained in a number of regional record offices has also been examined and utilized where useful comparisons may be made with the work of the Northamptonshire Tribunals.

Drawing upon these sources, this book examines the character, functions and developing policies of the county's Tribunals, and of the Appeals body in particular. Certain themes will emerge strongly. The impact of ambiguity in legislation is analysed, particularly in areas where it allowed (or obliged) Tribunals to place their own interpretations upon what was required of them. Few tribunalists were entirely new to aspects of local administration; however, the particular nature of their task, was, in early 1916, beyond the experience of any contemporary Briton. It will be proposed that legislation defined their role in broad terms yet failed to provide meaningful preparation for the minutiae of adjudging claims for exemption. This lack of precision had important consequences. As constituted, Tribunal were, in effect, sovereign entities, duty-bound to consider cases judiciously and impartially, but with no *de jure* obligation to answer for their decisions. They received occasional, non-binding advice on specific issues from the Local Government Board, and amending legislation sought to close off their perceived misinterpretations, once apparent. Decisions contested either by the applicant or military representative were appealed at the County Tribunal and, ultimately (with leave), to the Central Tribunal at Westminster. Yet the 'policy' of each Tribunal grew entirely from within, not as a product gifted by a higher authority. Accordingly, individual bodies exhibited discrete and even divergent tendencies that were only slowly, and partially, corrected by the intervention of Whitehall.

This book examines how these idiosyncrasies impacted upon the consideration of cases, and, in consequence, upon local Tribunals' relationships with the Appeals body, in whose hands laid responsibility for the correction of aberrant decisions. It also, and particularly, considers the degree to which the latter were willing to define their own role independently of government direction – where lacking or ambiguous – and expectations. In evaluating these issues, reference is made to applications made in a purely personal context (conscientious objection, domestic hardship), to those reflecting local occupational and industrial issues (agriculture, boot and shoe, one-man businesses), and to what might be termed functional complications of the exemption process (medical examination and re-examination of applicants, imposition of the Volunteer Training Corps requirement).

More than any other issue, the social impact of conscription highlighted differences of approach between individual Tribunals. Some exhibited relatively little awareness of (or, perhaps, concern for) the personal and domestic consequences of their decisions, regarding their role as essentially identical to that of the defunct 'Derby' Tribunals, which existed merely to process postponement applications from voluntarily attested men. Others adopted notably progressive policies with regard to such issues as the sole child – and support – of a widowed parent, the last remaining sons of families who had already contributed creditably, and, in the case of one Tribunal at least, conscientious objectors who had been misled into attesting their willingness to serve with the Colours. Occasionally, the degree to which a Tribunal might accommodate extraordinary personal circumstances placed them directly at odds with the spirit of legislation and firmly within the mainstream of local sentiment.

If Tribunals' attitudes towards personal applications often reflected their localist concerns, decisions on claims for exemption by reason of occupation were often regarded as having implications at both community and national level. It was in the consideration of these cases that different interpretations of what constituted the 'indispensable' man were most pronounced. Other than ironstone quarrying, which had been brought within the jurisdiction of David Lloyd George's 'Super-Ministry' of Munitions and therefore lay outside the Tribunals' remit, Northamptonshire had two principal industries: agriculture and footwear (or 'boot and shoe'). Each had assumed a transcendental importance to a nation at war, yet enjoyed only partial – and, in the case of boot and shoe, declining – protection from manpower dilution. The necessity of maintaining production was recognized by most Tribunals from their earliest sittings, and several developed robust policies that placed them in direct confrontation with recruiting officers and their representatives. Agriculture's 'corner' was fought also by the Board of Agriculture, which negotiated temporary freezes upon recruitment from the land in every year of the conscription period. Boot and shoe had only its presence on the Tribunals (from both management and the unions), yet used these with great effectiveness. As discussed, large-scale arrangements were negotiated and implemented in 1916–1917 that both contradicted Local Government Board instructions and directly resisted efforts by the War Office to control the rate of manpower depletion in the industry.

Applications made by sole proprietors and directing heads of business were, as Government recognized, among the most difficult to adjudge.

Tribunals faced conflicting imperatives here: they felt keenly the necessity of demonstrating equity of treatment, yet increasingly were sensitive to the implications of over-dilution of key men, particularly in the food production and distribution trades. Prompted constantly by Whitehall to consider one-man businesses on a trade-wide basis, most Tribunals, it will be proposed, employed a 'strategy' of prevarication that contrasted strongly with their energetic policies towards agriculture and boot and shoe. In the few cases where a collective policy was attempted, the resulting decisions almost always reflected an unwillingness to weaken local commerce further. To many Tribunals, the value to the Army of these relatively few men was greatly outweighed by the potential loss to their communities.

Regarding the fraught issue of conscience, the county's Tribunals largely reflected contemporary prejudices. However, following an early period of relative harshness (due in part to a peculiar degree of ambiguity in the relevant legislation), many exercised a marked degree of circumspection in the treatment of men seeking exemption on this ground. Applicants continued to be subjected to heated interrogations regarding their willingness to defend their mothers and wives against marauding Germans, but the certificates they were offered thereafter were not notably more circumscribed than those provided on other grounds. Indeed, it will be argued that several Tribunals in Northamptonshire recognized the futility of sending such men into the Army from a relatively early stage in their proceedings: one went so far as to indicate a willingness to re-open the cases of former 'absolutists' who had expressed a change of attitude, and examined the possibility of returning them from military to civilian life. Preconceptions and prejudice, however strongly expressed, did not always reflect policy in these cases.

Having been gifted a degree of discretion, Tribunals did not shy from exercising it, and often resisted pressures from government where they felt that inequitable or unsustainable decisions would result. Occasionally, they drew lines in the sand and refused outright to participate in what they considered to be blatantly unjust processes. The quality of medical examinations of recruits, carried out at Northampton Barracks under a particularly idiosyncratic regime, became a cause for concern from late 1916. As pressures to replenish depleted front-line divisions grew, men with a variety of serious ailments or physical handicaps were passed fit for general service. The Tribunals, choosing to believe the evidence of their own eyes in preference to that of Army medical certificates, increasingly refused to accept a passive role in processing unsuitable men. Country-wide, similar resistance to the existing system led to its abolition in 1917, following which the medical examination process was removed entirely from military control.

Similarly, the option of requiring exempted men to drill with the Volunteer Training Corps, urged by the War Office, made unrealistic demands upon men working long hours in important industries and excited local tensions as widespread evasion effectively penalized the assiduous man. The Tribunals, initially applying the requirement diligently, gradually came to regard official policy as misguided and acutely under-resourced, resulting ultimately (in the words of one tribunalist), in 'an exhibition of colossal stupidity'.[15] Again, it will be proposed that the principle of equity of treatment was paramount in the Tribunals' concerns, however disparately they viewed their roles. Where official policy undermined that principle, sovereignty asserted its rights strongly.

'Sovereignty' is the unifying theme of this book. Its expression within the Tribunal process allows us to evaluate the interplay of government intention, the practical application of legislation and the Tribunals' appreciation of their relative responsibilities to nation and community. Occupying the only non-military staging post between the hearth and front line, most tribunalists were, or swiftly became, sensitive to the inherent contradictions of their task. In the first year of the war, a vast Army, fed by a tide of enthusiastic voluntary recruitment, had been created almost from scratch. Once that enthusiasm faded, compulsion became necessary. The War Office's abiding (though untested) assumption was that the workforce of non-military age was infinitely pliable, able to expand and be re-shaped to fill every gap created by the transfer of younger men to the Colours. When realities proved otherwise, the military's sense of betrayal was palpable. To Sir Henry Wilson, the Tribunals – bodies, it should be recalled, who were charged with deciding who should *not* go to war – comprised 'local men who owed their position to local popularity and local influences and who have had neither training in judicial or imperial matters nor that experience in official administration which develops the judicial facility and the instinct of placing the affairs of the Nation first'.[16] Undoubtedly, much evidence may be cited to support that view, but it is useful to recall the wider implications of what these men (and occasional woman) were being asked to do.

They commenced their work with the uneasy knowledge that the discretion allowed to them was, in a very real and immediate sense, of fateful proportions. Each of them would have had in mind (if not necessarily at heart) the most fundamental requirement of their role: that they should discharge their duties judiciously and impartially, and to keep 'clearly in mind the urgent requirements of the State at the present time'.[17] The last was the nub, for what comprised 'urgent' to one tribunalist may have been a lesser quality to another. Some, recalling their former roles on the Derby Tribunals, or having an overarching sensitivity to the national crisis, would have felt themselves impelled to adjudicate cases with the Army's needs foremost in their minds. Others, if not instinctively attuned to local needs, were about to be reminded that their responsibilities extended further than from the tribunal chamber to the barracks gate. Northamptonshire was at war no less than England, and perceptions of (and within) the community were being altered irrevocably by the conflict's profound material intrusion into the home, the workplace and the dialogue of everyday life. The State's 'urgent requirements' were fully appreciated already, but the advent of conscription introduced more than just a rationalization of the process of recruitment. Its exemption process – almost certainly unintentionally – provided a public forum in which the human cost of meeting the State's demands was to be comprehensively aired.

The first of these voices was heard almost immediately. On 25 February 1916, a matter of weeks after Northamptonshire's Tribunals had begun their deliberations, the *Northampton Mercury* reported Lord Derby's strongly worded circular, 'necessitated by the enormous number of exemptions granted to Derby recruits and single men who come under the Compulsion Act'. The newspaper's editor responded in the same issue, with an admonishment to the Tribunals that Derby was not, nor should be, their only concern:

> the Tribunal is also under obligation – that, indeed, is the main reason for its existence – to safeguard, as far as possible, legitimate business interests. It was never intended by Parliament or Government that established trading firms shall be so deprived of labour that they cannot be carried on. The indispensable and irreplaceable man must remain in industry.[18]

It was a timely reminder that the role of the new Tribunals involved more than filling the trenches. They were being required, in effect, to implement a manpower policy that the government had yet to conceive.

Notes

1 Sir Donald Maclean to the Commons, 10 April 1918 (5 H.C. 104:1494).

2 Ministry of Health Circular R.293 (27 March 1922). The Local Government Board, under whose authority the Tribunal system had functioned, was disbanded in 1919.

3 For example, Graham, *Conscription and Conscience: A History 1916–1919*, pp. 66, 76; Chamberlain, *Fighting for Peace: The Story of the War Resistance Movement*, pp. 47–58; Stephen, 'The Tribunals', in Bell (ed.), *We Did Not Fight: 1914–1918 Experiences of War Resisters*, pp. 381–382.

4 Boulton, *Objection Overruled*, p. 124; Moorhead, *Troublesome People: The Warriors of Pacifism*, pp. 31–34.

5 Ceadel, *Pacifism in Britain, 1914–1945: The Defining of a Faith*, pp. 38–40; Rae, *Conscience and Politics: The British Government and the Conscientious Objec-*

tor to Military Service, 1916–1919, pp. 105–111, 131–133; Kennedy, *The Hound of Conscience: A History of the No-Conscription Movement*, pp. 89–105 *passim*; Robbins, 'The British Experience of Conscientious Objection', pp. 691–706.

6 Hayes, *Conscription Conflict*, pp. 209–212; Grieves, *The Politics of Manpower, 1914–1918*, pp. 26–27, 54–56, 188–189. Rae and Kennedy also provide detailed overviews of the Tribunals.

7 Shorter articles: Beckett, 'The Local Community and the Great War: Aspects of Military Participation'; Grieves, 'Military Tribunal Papers: The Case of Leek Local Tribunal in the First World War'; Pierce, 'A Community of Resistance: The Anti-War Movement in Huddersfield, 1914–1918'; Slocombe, 'Recruitment into the Armed Forces during the First World War: The Work of the Military Service Tribunals in Wiltshire, 1915–1918'; Spinks, '"The War Courts": the Stratford-upon-Avon Borough Tribunal 1916–1918'; Gregory, 'Military Service Tribunals: Civil Society in Action, 1916–1918'; Housden, 'Kingston's Military Tribunal, 1916–1918'. Memoirs: Armitage, *Leicester 1914–1918: The War-time Story of a Midlands Town*; Cartmell, *For Remembrance*; Scott, *Leeds and the Great War*. The only modern monograph devoted entirely to a Tribunal for which substantial records survive (Slocombe, *The First World War Tribunal in Swindon*) is predominantly a statistical survey.

8 A possible abettor was Joan Wake, first honorary secretary (from 1920) of Northamptonshire Record Society, whose tireless (and, usually, irresistible) determination to preserve the documentary heritage of her county may have confounded government's efforts to excise one element of it.

9 Surviving Tribunal minute books reveal a remarkable lack of consensus regarding what constituted an adequate level of detail. Banbury Urban Tribunal, for example, merely recorded the dates of meetings, the names of those attending, and, of the cases they heard, only the bald statement: 'applications considered as per the clerk's register' (Oxford Record Office (hereafter ORO), BB/xxiv/i/i, *passim*). That of Cardiganshire Appeals Tribunal, except where it (very) occasionally notes an individual decision, is similarly unhelpful (National Library of Wales (hereafter NLW), CTB 2/1, *passim*). In admirable contrast, Eton Rural Tribunal not only used the alphabetical section at the start of their minute book to record the names of all applicants but also constructed therein a fairly comprehensive subject index with which to reference their copious and detailed minutes (Centre for Buckinghamshire Studies (hereafter CBS), DC/10/38/1, *passim*).

10 Copies of all departmental circulars and instructions cited in this study are retained in Northamptonshire Record Office (hereafter NRO) Quarter Sessions/368, the National Archives (hereafter TNA) MH47/142 and/or MH10/79–84.

11 See Appendix 1 below for file sequences under which the NRO material is held.

12 In the early conscription period, the *Herald* and, to a lesser extent, the *Independent* carried detailed reports, but these became occasional from mid-1916. The *Mercury* continued to run substantial weekly coverage of sittings; in part, perhaps, because the paper's proprietor was himself a tribunalist (below, p 32, n.24).

13 TNA MH 47/1–163.
14 NLW CTB1–4.
15 Below, p. 212.
16 TNA NATS/1/876: Wilson to the Secretary of the War Office, 27 October 1917.
17 LGB Circular R.36, p. 12, para 39.
18 Editorial, p. 3.

2

The Tribunal system: provenance, characteristics and issues

> It took some time ... before Local Authorities and the public generally were able to understand the machinery of the scheme, and it was not surprising, therefore, that applicants, and at times the Tribunals, failed to interpret rightly the regulations and instructions.[1]

The overwhelming response to the call to arms during August and September 1914 represented the high-water mark of British voluntarism. Thereafter, with the German retreat from the Marne and the coalescing of semi-permanent front lines, the pace of recruitment fell steadily. By mid-1915, enlistments averaged approximately one hundred thousand per month, by which time just over two million men had gone to the Colours.[2] In the same period, government's calculation of the resources necessary to prosecute the war successfully had moved from envisaging the creation of a thirty-division army to one of seventy.[3] Given the scale of battlefield losses to date, it was becoming increasingly evident that the New Armies could not be brought to, much less maintained at, their proposed strength without significant modifications to methods of recruitment.

Calls for some form of compulsory military service for single men had been heard in Britain since the end of the South African War. Periodic war scares, the perceived physical deficiencies of the average working-class British male and fears for the survival of traditional social mores had prompted prominent individuals and organizations such as the National Service League to press for models which emulated, to a greater or lesser degree, existing European systems. Juvenile 'improvement' organizations such as the Boy Scout movement and various lads' drilling associations resulted from these initiatives; conscription, in any form, did not. All initiatives to introduce some measure of compulsory military service faced, and failed before, widespread distrust of what was seen to be a fundamentally un-British and socially intrusive device.[4]

From August 1914, the unanticipated demands of industrial-scale warfare weakened but did not expunge this resistance to compulsion. Some in government, who fully recognized the need to create and maintain a larger army, continued to insist that refinements to the voluntary system would meet this challenge. However, the developing military debate, which increasingly looked to a strategy of attrition to wear down the Central Powers' will to prosecute the war, posed questions which the voluntarists found difficult to answer.[5] Further momentum towards compulsion was provided, paradoxically, by the implications for wartime industry of the wholesale loss of men to the Army during the voluntary period. Most famously, Sir John French's claim that munitions shortages had doomed the offensive at Neuve-Chapelle during May 1915 (resulting in the so-called 'shells-scandal'), encouraged efforts to impose greater control over, and direction of, the production of war materials. In the following month, Lloyd George's Munitions of War Act established a super-ministry with powers to assess, allocate and direct the resources necessary to arm Britain's war machine. Ostensibly, these measures provided protection against further dilution of the munitions workforce. In a broader sense, however, they accelerated the appreciation in government that management of the nation's manpower assets required more than the traditional reliance upon individuals' sense of duty.

Walter Long, President of the Board of Trade and himself a committed compulsionist, pressed for a canvass of the nation's manpower reserves to complement the industrial census that had facilitated the Munitions of War Act. On 8 July 1915, his bill, the National Registration Act, providing for a labour census of the entire British population, passed its third reading. Lord Curzon, sponsoring the bill in the Lords, urged it as a necessity if the government were to allocate efficiently the resources to satisfy the needs of both the Army and industry. But Curzon, like Long, was known to be a fervent supporter of compulsion, and few on either side of the debate were misled as to the real motives for the initiative.

On Sunday 5 August 1915, some forty thousand canvassers visited British households to record the names, addresses and occupational details of men and women between the ages of 15 and 65. The results indicated that slightly more than 5.1 million men of military age lived in England and Wales, of whom 1.5 million were in reserved or war-essential occupations. Of those remaining, it was assumed that some 15–25 per cent would be physically or medically unsuited for service, leaving a potential recruitment pool of 2.7–3 million men. This information became widely available in October 1916, with the release of the Registrar-General's Committee report.[6]

While the census itself gave further momentum to the conscriptionists' cause (as their opponents had feared), events elsewhere were also beginning to shift opinion, both in Parliament and in the country, towards the acceptance of some form of compulsion. On the day the census was taken,

Warsaw fell to the Germans and news of the stalled Suvla Bay landings in the Dardanelles reached London. In September, the Loos offensive commenced; in little more than a month, almost fifty thousand British lives would be lost for no appreciable battlefield gain. On 8 October, presenting his own proposals for a hybrid, compulsory/voluntary system, Kitchener – formerly a resolute voluntarist – reported to Cabinet that existing recruitment arrangements were breaking down, and that 130,000 men were needed each month to cover 'wastage' (his calculation was later said to be an underestimate, covering only infantry losses). It appeared to be a matter no longer of compulsion or not, but of what form compulsion should take.[7]

Ostensibly, Asquith was not willing to abandon the voluntary system until public opinion moved clearly in favour of the alternative. Yet, even before the results of the August census were known, he had agreed to the establishment of a War Policy Committee under Lord Crewe (with a majority in favour of conscription thereon), to examine viable options for future recruitment. A – rather premature – supplementary report, issued by a minority of committee members on 3 September, stated unequivocally that conscription was the only mechanism that could bring the necessary numbers of men into the Army.[8] Nevertheless, voluntarism was to be given one last chance, if only so that its failure should make conscription more palatable. At Asquith's urging, Kitchener had already asked his friend, the Earl of Derby, to take over responsibility for national recruiting. A strong supporter of conscription and an exemplary amateur recruiter, Derby made it a condition of his participation that, if a revived voluntary scheme failed to deliver the necessary manpower, government would commit to introducing compulsion.[9]

Derby became Director-General of Recruiting on 5 October. Two weeks later, the 'Derby Scheme' was announced; utilizing data gathered in the August census, forms were sent out to households in England, Wales and Scotland, asking all men between the ages of 19 and 41 to enlist immediately or attest their willingness to serve when required. Those attesting were allocated to one of 46 groups, according to age and marital status, with single men (groups 2–23) to be called up before their married compatriots (groups 24–46). As part of the push to make the scheme succeed, the King made a national appeal for volunteers; it was announced also that all men attesting were to receive a bounty of 2s. 9d. and an 'attested' armband, the latter, presumably, to deter unsolicited white feathers.[10]

The scheme proved to be the failure that Lord Derby – and, probably, Kitchener and Asquith – had anticipated, despite a late rush of attestations in the days before 11 December, the close-off date.[11] Of some 2.2 million single men identified by the household census as potentially available, only 840,000 attested. Of these, more than half a million were employed in reserved occupations and almost 200,000 rated as unfit for service. Of an estimated pool of 2.8 million married men, approximately 1.35 million attested, though 450,000 of these were reserved and 220,000 rejected. The logic of the statistics was irrefutable: if the Army were to make good the losses of the year and fulfil Kitchener's commitment to the French government, some form of compulsion would be mandatory.[12]

Asquith prevaricated for a few days more, but the momentum for innovation was now irresistible. Unwittingly, the Prime Minister had committed himself implicitly to conscription as early as 2 November 1915, when he made a straitjacket pledge to the Commons that no married man attesting under the Derby Scheme would be called up until all single men had been 'considered'.[13] On 6 December, at the Allied conference at Chantilly, it was agreed that the British Army would bear a greater share of wearing-down operations against the enemy during the coming months. Eight days later, a Cabinet Committee, chaired by Long, was established to consider a compulsion bill. By 20 December, Curzon and Leo Amery were working on a draft; on 5 January 1916, the Prime Minister introduced it to the House. Twenty-two days later, the Military Service Act, 1916 (or 'Bachelors' Bill') was placed on the statute books.[14] Every single man, ordinarily resident in Great Britain, who had reached the age of 18 but was not yet 41 on 15 August 1915 (and every similarly aged widower without dependent children) was deemed 'to have been duly enlisted in His Majesty's regular forces for general service with the Colours or in the reserve for the period of the war, and to have been forthwith transferred to the reserve'.[15]

Conscription had been implemented, but only partially. Despite its promoters' decisive parliamentary victory, Asquith and his government remained extremely sensitive to the political pitfalls of a compulsory system. The introduction of militia ballots in the eighteenth and nineteenth centuries had brought widespread agitation and riots, necessitating the suspension of the ballot in some districts. Government's reaction then had been to ameliorate the social burden of non-voluntary enlistment by allowing exemptions based upon remittance payments and substitutions, with further exemptions allowed subsequently to poor men with more than one (legitimate) child, and to those with prior militia service.[16] Absorbing the lessons of these earlier experiments, the new Act contained a number of provisions intended to placate potential resistance. Already, the Derby Scheme had established the principle of appeal against its grouping system, allowing postponements (that is, by re-allocation to later groups) for attested men whose personal or business circumstances were such that their immediate transfer into the Army would have been inequitable. The Military Service Act 1916 went further, allowing for actual exemption from its measures. Such exemption might be temporary, to allow a man to order his personal affairs, or to make arrangements so that his business or professional interests were not unduly compromised. Alternatively, exemption might be offered for the longer term, and remain in force while existing or stipulated conditions continued to be met by someone so exempted. Finally, in exceptional circumstances, an exemption might be absolute, recognizing that any future removal of a man from civilian life would be unjust, unnecessary or against the country's interests (though the legislation also provided for review and adjustment of individual certificates of any duration).[17]

Similarly, the grounds for exemption from conscription were broader than those allowing for postponement under the Derby Scheme. Any of the above forms of exemption could be offered in one or more of the following circumstances:

a. that it was expedient in the national interests that the man should, instead of being employed in the military service, be engaged in other work in which he was habitually engaged; or
b. that it was expedient in the national interests that the man should, instead of being employed in military service, be engaged in other work in which he wished to be engaged; or
c. if the man was being educated or trained for any work, on the ground that it was expedient in the national interests that, instead of being employed in military service, he should continue to be so educated or trained; or
d. that serious hardship would ensue, if the man were called up for Army service, owing to his exceptional financial or business obligations or domestic position; or
e. by reason of ill-health or infirmity; or
f. by reason of a conscientious objection to the undertaking of combatant service.[18]

Someone had to apply these criteria in deciding who should be exempted and who should go into the Army, and, as such decisions necessarily had to be based upon consideration of personal circumstances, the process could not be centralized. Nor did government intend to bear the political cost of supervising an (almost inevitably) unpopular mechanism directly through existing local government structures. Ironically, responsibility for implementing legislation that effectively buried a venerable British tradition of voluntarism was to be devolved entirely upon a group of volunteers.

To hear applications for postponement under the Derby Scheme, Long's Local Government Board had established a network of some two thousand local Tribunals, comprising up to five members, drawn predominantly, though not exclusively, from the local registration authorities that had organized the August census (that is, the metropolitan and municipal boroughs, urban and rural district councils). Additionally, a Central Tribunal, sitting at Westminster, was established to adjudicate contested or technically difficult cases arising from the formers' deliberations.[19] Decisions made by a Tribunal could be challenged by a military representative, usually a retired soldier or serving Territorial officer, who attended sittings on behalf of the local recruiting officer.[20] In preparing his case, he was able to draw upon the expertise of an advisory committee, a War Office-appointed group of local men with knowledge of a district's industry and economic conditions, whose role was to provide advice and recommendations on individual applications. Though designed ostensibly to balance the needs of the Army and the vagaries of personal circumstance, the Derby tribunal system overwhelmingly served the former. Every man appearing before the Tribunals had attested his willingness to serve, and so proceedings commenced with the assumption that at some point he would join the Colours. Applications for re-grouping were heard in many cases by tribunalists who, prior to the Derby Scheme, had been prominent recruiters in their communities and who enjoyed a close working relationship with local barracks. Disagreements might arise as to the length of postponement an applicant should obtain, but otherwise the system was not intended to be adversarial.

The Military Service Act introduced compulsion, but also a statutory right to avoid that compulsion. Furthermore, it established a new level of Tribunal, one serving each county, to which applicants dissatisfied with the decisions of their local Tribunals had the right to appeal.[21] Otherwise, however, the mechanism processing applications for exemption was largely the same as that which had administered the voluntary scheme (though the new Act specifically abolished the old 'Derby' Tribunal and instituted the Military Service Tribunal in its place). A Local Government Board circular was issued to all Local Registration Authorities on 3 February 1916, outlining the constitution, functions and procedure of the new, post-Derby local Tribunal system.[22] Prefacing the instructions, Long recommended that former members of the now defunct Derby Tribunals should be invited to form the core of the new Military Service Tribunals, which, to reflect the increased complexity of their role and brief, might be expanded to a maximum of 25 members. Almost without exception, the recommendation was followed, and the same tribunalists whose principal role had been to consider re-grouping applications were now faced with a more complex responsibility.

For the purposes of the August census, local registration districts in Northamptonshire, as elsewhere, replicated existing urban and rural council boundaries, and a 'Derby' tribunal was established in each of these. With the implementation of the Military Service Act, thirteen urban Tribunals were appointed at Northampton, Brackley, Daventry, Finedon, Higham Ferrers, Irthlingborough, Kettering (with Desborough and Oundle), Raunds, Rothwell, Rushden, Towcester, Wellingborough and Peterborough, and a further fourteen rural bodies at Northampton, Brackley, Brixworth, Crick, Daventry, Easton-on-the-Hill, Gretton, Hardingstone, Kettering (with Oundle), Middleton Cheney, Oxendon, Potterspury, Thrapston and Wellingborough.[23] Once active, Tribunals would sit from time to time at other locations within their registration area: hence a newspaper might refer to the proceedings of 'Badby' Tribunal, when in fact it was reporting a rare Badby sitting of Daventry Tribunal.

As noted, the men who sat upon these Tribunals (Northamptonshire's local Tribunal network was an exclusively male preserve) were volunteers. Asked to serve by their town, district or county council, most had a degree of managerial experience in municipal administration, industry, agriculture or the professions. Many were already engaged in voluntary war work in their communities, sitting upon funding, recruitment or charitable committees to support local regiments abroad or their wounded at home. Their experience, together with their standing and understanding of local economic and social issues, made them natural choices for Tribunal service.

As elsewhere in the country, town councillors, justices of the peace and other officers of local government featured prominently. Upon Northampton Borough Tribunal sat four councillors, three of whom were also JPs (a fourth JP, J. Bingley, resigned from the Tribunal after a month because it 'took up too much of his time').[24] The relatively small Brixworth and Wellingborough Rural Tribunals had three JPs each from total complements, respectively, of seven and five. At Daventry, the municipal hierarchy transferred itself seamlessly into the business of deciding which of its citizens should go to war: the town's mayor, J. Gardiner, was elected chairman, sitting with a former mayor, Councillor W. Edgar, Alderman T.H. Marriot and Dr (also Councillor) C.E. Oldacres, while the town clerk, W. Murland, assumed the role of military representative. At Thrapston, seven of nine tribunalists were members of the rural district council. In the smaller rural Tribunals, justices of the peace filled almost all the chairs, notable exceptions being at Oxendon and Crick, where local clergymen presided. At the latter, the Reverend R.S. Mitchison took on the role very reluctantly, observing at his Tribunal's inaugural sitting 'it was not a very attractive position, and the duties they had to perform were not very attractive either'.[25]

The slight preponderance of rural Tribunals was a consequence of Northamptonshire's largely agricultural landscape. The county's only other significant industry outside the urban areas was ironstone quarrying, overseen by the Ministry of Munitions and therefore outside the Tribunals' remit. The latters' business, overwhelmingly, would comprise applications from farmers, farm labourers and those in the many ancillary occupations supporting agriculture. Accordingly, many of their members were farmers and landowners, intimately familiar with (if not always sympathetic to) the preoccupations of men who appeared before them. To assist their deliberations, and to counter the efforts of the military representatives, the Board of Agriculture appointed a representative to each rural Tribunal to resist further dilution of the agricultural workforce by stressing the necessity of maintaining food production.

In the early part of the twentieth century, Northamptonshire was the world capital of footwear manufacturing, and the county's urban Tribunals, particularly those of Northampton, Wellingborough, Kettering, Rushden and Raunds, were inundated by applications from the industry's employees and employers. Inevitably, therefore, many local manufacturers were invited (or volunteered) to join the Tribunals. Northampton Borough had three footwear-magnate tribunalists: Councillor E. Lewis, Albert E. Tebbutt and F.O. Roberts; Wellingborough Urban also had three: Alderman George Henson, C. Forscutt and W. Sharman; while Rushden Tribunal had two: Fred Knight (also a JP) and C. Bates.[26]

Long's instructions had stressed that it was of 'the utmost importance that the Tribunals should be constituted so as to command public confidence'. In that respect, 'a fair and just representation of labour' was regarded as mandatory, and as much had been promised in the House. Almost certainly, this was intended to defuse continuing political resistance to conscription by associating labour organizations with the exemption process. It has been noted elsewhere that many registration authorities, mistrustful or contemptuous of local union officials, simply ignored Long's exhortation.[27] However, Northampton Borough Council took it to heart. They appointed as one of their tribunalists 'General' James Gribble, vice-chairman of the Northampton Trades Council and leader of the famous Raunds March to London in 1905, at the culmination of which he had led an invasion of the floor of the House of Commons in an attempt to beard the Minister of War for his refusal to agree minimum prices for boot orders for the Army (even in peacetime, Raunds' boot and shoe industry was devoted almost exclusively to military orders).[28] Upon his return to Raunds, and until the outbreak of war, Gribble managed the Pioneer Boot Company, a taste of the capitalist perspective that did nothing to quench his ardent belief in labour rights. As recently as 10 January 1916, he had roused a packed Trades Council meeting in Northampton to reject the principle of conscription, condemning it as a Tory-inspired device to set workers at each other's throats.[29] Garrulous, industrious and humane,

Gribble was to become one of the leading voices on Northamptonshire's busiest Tribunal (and, invariably, the drafter of irate resolutions expressing their dissatisfaction with Local Government Board directives). A fellow tribunalist, W.P. Townley, was vice-President of Northampton no. 1 branch of the National Union of Boot and Shoe Operatives (and President after March 1917).[30]

The county's Appeals Tribunal, a creation of the new Act, came into existence several weeks after the local Tribunals commenced their consideration of re-grouping applications.[31] The precise circumstances of individual tribunalists' recruitment were not committed to record; however, we know from surviving correspondence from the Local Government Board to Bedfordshire County Council that Walter Long asked each council to approach men (and, occasionally, women) of 'judicial and unprejudiced mind [who would] command the confidence of the community'.[32] Northamptonshire's County Council commenced its search at home, appointing as chairman of its Appeals Tribunal Colonel (ret.) Sackville George Stopford-Sackville, JP, of Drayton House, Thrapston: formerly one of two Conservative MPs for North Northamptonshire, currently vice-chairman of the County Council, and, eventually, their longest serving chairman. The Tribunal's deputy chairman was Stopford-Sackville's erstwhile political adversary on the Council, Sir William Ryland Dent Adkins, KC, DL, JP: barrister, poet, wit, recorder for Birmingham and Nottingham and Liberal MP for Middleton, Lancashire. Adkins had once expressed his pale appreciation of serving as a councillor with Stopford-Sackville, 'whom to know was a liberal education'.[33] Despite their disparate political views, both Stopford-Sackville and Adkins had been active in manpower issues prior to the advent of conscription: the former chairing a sub-committee examining options for employing women in agriculture, the latter as a member of the Commons Committee considering amendments to the draft Military Service Bill, and as chairman of the Northamptonshire Territorial Recruiting Committee.[34] The Tribunal's third MP was Sir Richard Winfrey, co-founder of the National Union of Agricultural Workers, former mayor of Peterborough (1914), and now representing the town in the Liberal interest, appointed to consider appeals from local Tribunals in the Soke of Peterborough.[35]

The county's landed interests were represented on the Tribunal by Luke White, third Baron Annaly, master of the Pytchley hunt and lord-in-waiting to George V, and by Sir Charles Valentine Knightley, Bart, final scion of the Fawsley dynasty.[36] Much later, in June 1918, the Tribunal co-opted Alfred William Maitland Fitzroy, Earl of Euston (and soon to be Eighth Duke of Grafton), successful libel suitor in the infamous Cleveland Street Scandal.[37] There was also a strong municipal presence on the Tribunal: two Northampton councillors, George Wilson Beattie and Frederick Ellen (the latter had been mayor of Northampton in 1893), were enlisted, and also, notably, the county's only female tribunalist, Beatrice Cartwright, the first of her sex to become a (Conservative) county councillor (1919), county alderman (1940), and eight times mayor of Brackley.[38] Notwithstanding the presence of a barrister and several justices of the peace to provide the 'judicial and unprejudiced mind(s)' envisaged by Walter Long, the Tribunal also recruited a solicitor, Christopher Smyth, future chairman of the county's quarter sessions.

Unusually, the Appeals Tribunal included from its establishment two representatives of labour – Samuel Thompson and Charles Mayes: officials of, respectively, the Northampton and Kettering branches of the National Union of Boot and Shoe Operatives (NUBSO). There was no corresponding representation of footwear management until January 1917, when A.E. Marlow, President of the Northamptonshire Boot and Shoe Manufacturers Association (a leading voice in the struggle against further depletion of the county's boot trade workforce), was invited to join the Tribunal. Three months later, Owen Parker, President of the Incorporated Associations of Boot and Shoe Manufacturers of Great Britain and Ireland, also became an appeals tribunalist.[39] Their expertise, and that of their union counterparts, would be tapped repeatedly during 1917 and early 1918, when mass appeals by manufacturers constituted by far the heaviest element of their Tribunal's workload.[40]

In total, seventeen tribunalists were appointed to the appeals body during the conscription period. No more than nine ever attended a single sitting, and a quorum of three was deemed sufficient from an early stage. Their complement appears to be broadly in line with practice elsewhere. Middlesex Appeals Tribunal's two divisions, who, as will be noted, considered approximately the same number of cases as Northamptonshire during the conscription period, usually comprised between five and eight sitting tribunalists (from a pool of ten), while Cardiganshire, with a population of only 54,000 (1911 census), appointed 11 tribunalists, of whom a maximum of seven sat at any one time.[41]

These men (and solitary woman) were charged with a novel and onerous responsibility, but its day-to-day mechanisms were reassuringly bureaucratic. Those applying for exemption under the Act were required to complete and submit form R.41 (form R.53 for attested men), obtainable from the local Tribunal or recruiting office, before 2 March 1916. For men who became eligible for service after this time – principally those coming of age, or falling out of reserved occupation status – applications were to be submitted within fourteen days of receipt of their call-up papers. The form required the applicant's basic details: name, address, age and occupation, the ground(s) of the application and its (their) nature, and argument(s) in support of the application. On the final page was a section reserved for the Tribunal's decision.

The applicant could submit a written representation if unable, or unwilling, to appear before the local Tribunal personally, though those who chose not to attend in person almost always compromised their chances of success (tribunalists much preferred to 'look their man in the eye' to gauge the veracity of what they heard). An attending applicant might speak for himself or be represented by his employer, who, on occupational grounds, had the right to enter the application on his behalf, or a relative or legal counsel – the latter being permitted though explicitly frowned upon in Long's instructions (many solicitors, willing to state their client's case upon one or more of five grounds, would often avoid the sixth – that of a conscientious objection to military service – and leave its statement to the appellant).[42] Usually, the applicant or his representative would be invited to make a short statement in support of the application, following which the Tribunal and/or the military representative might ask questions or challenge the facts as presented. After a brief discussion (very rarely, tribunalists would withdraw to discuss a particularly abstruse or potentially sensitive point of procedure *in camera*) a decision would be given. If this were not acceptable to the applicant or the military representative, a notice of appeal had to be lodged by either party within three days.[43] This required completion of form R.43 (with duplicate form R.44), recording the same basic personal information as R.41, plus the identity of the appellant (whether the man himself, his employer or the military representative), the grounds of the appeal and decision of the local Tribunal. The form was then submitted to the clerk of the Appeals Tribunal, who allocated the appeal to the next available sitting.

Broadly, procedures followed at the latter were similar to those at local hearings, though the appellant, in making a case as to why the decision previously given was unjust or inappropriate, was allowed to introduce further evidence, if available. Occasionally, a local Tribunal might send one of their members to expand upon reasons for their decision, though the Appeals Tribunal were under no obligation to hear him (it was the policy of Northamptonshire's to refuse all such approaches on the basis that unfair emphasis might be gifted to one side of the argument).[44] Again, an appellant might present his own appeal or have it stated by a relative, an employer or legal counsel. Once the Appeal Tribunal's determination was made, the appellant's local Tribunal would be notified. In the case of an outright dismissal, the man would go to the Colours within fourteen days (or two months if, previously, he had been exempted on occupational grounds). If an earlier exemption was confirmed or varied, it was the responsibility of the local Tribunal to issue exemption certificate R.39 (the

Appeals Tribunal did not itself issue certificates), which bore the exempted man's name, age, address, occupation and form of exemption.[45] Exceptionally, and solely at the discretion of the Appeals Tribunal, the unsuccessful appellant might appeal further (on a point of law or principle) to the Central Tribunal at Westminster. Northamptonshire's gave such leave upon only fifteen occasions.[46]

It was intended that the judicial nature of these procedures should reassure applicants and appellants that they had been given a fair hearing, but not at the expense of brevity. Government's primary aim – certainly during the first year of the conscription period – was to get men into the Army as quickly as possible. As with any system, however, its architects could not fully anticipate every potential weakness prior to implementation. Nor, given Whitehall's intentionally 'hands-off' approach, could such weaknesses, once apparent, be corrected except by suggestion, recommendation, 'clarification' or an eventual legislative adjustment. The timeliest technical assistance provided to the Tribunals comprised the series of notes of cases considered and determined by Central Tribunal, which were distributed by the Local Government Board on an occasional basis. However, as with many other directions from the LGB, the decisions recorded in these circulars were offered for guidance only, and not binding upon their recipients. The effect of government distancing itself from the day-to-day operation of the Tribunals was to ensure that, during early sittings, debates upon points of law, interpretation, procedure and jurisdiction would constitute a significant proportion of the latters' business.

They were also to be burdened by a number of systemic anomalies and ambiguities. Though a landmark piece of legislation, the Military Service Act did not represent a clean sheet as regards recruitment, being intended to operate in conjunction with, rather than supersede, the existing Derby Scheme of attestation. This not only burdened the Tribunals' schedules (as early as 10 March 1916, Councillor Parker, chairman of Northampton Borough Tribunal, noted that some nine hundred applications from attested men had been received, of which, to date, they had managed to process just 136),[47] but required also that tribunalists should apply two sets of – as yet unfamiliar – regulations. The result, to cite the pithy opinion of Crick Tribunal's military representative, was 'a most stupid arrangement' that further complicated the work of the Tribunals, and, consequently, slowed the rate of recruitment.[48] Additionally, the unexpected volume of attested men's re-grouping applications made it inevitable that the new County Tribunals would hear their subsequent appeals, rather than Central Tribunal (as had been intended originally).[49]

Furthermore, Derby voluntarism, if we are to believe the testimony of many attested applicants who came before the Tribunals, had not been explained adequately to those it sought to mobilize. Some men claimed that they had misunderstood the implications of attestation (at least one Northamptonshire applicant admitted frankly that he had attested only because 'I didn't think for a minute that I should have to go'[50]); others, that they had been misled as to the consequences of not attesting. One of the more prevalent – and sustainable – complaints, made by men who had a conscientious objection to fighting, was that they had been told by recruiting officers that they would not be entitled to appeal under any subsequent compulsory scheme unless they had first attested.[51] As conscience was not a ground for exemption for attested men, those who accepted this advice found themselves not only excluded from consideration but condemned for having elastic or disingenuous principles.[52] Many attested men were also to resent the tighter criteria applied to their certificates (particularly the absence of a two-month 'grace-period' following the expiration of their exemptions) as compared to those offered under the Military Service Act – in effect, it was believed that their patriotic gesture in attesting a willingness to serve was being penalized. Consideration of all these issues further slowed the Tribunals' business during the early months in which unfamiliarity with their role was most pronounced and the volume of applications at its greatest.

One further, and cardinal, point of confusion arose upon the provision for 'absolute' exemption. There is a case to be made that government, in allowing even the possibility of total exemption from military service, drafted its legislation poorly. In Northamptonshire, as elsewhere, a number of exemptions of this type were offered during early sittings – among others, to a man who wore a metal brace to support the curvature of his spine, to another with a wooden leg and to two men who had been diagnosed as mentally ill.[53] These seem to have been the sort of exceptional circumstances envisaged by the Act's architects: circumstances that, at the moment of consideration by a Tribunal, were demonstrably incapable of changing thereafter. Men so qualifying might be removed from potential future recruitment without controversy; as for the rest, the fact that legislation provided for reviews and variations of certificates at any time suggests that the very term 'absolute' was a misnomer.

Initially, however, many Tribunals misunderstood the intention because it was not represented clearly to them. The wording of the Act suggested that absolute exemption might apply across all the available grounds for exemption, subject to 'exceptional' circumstances being present. Yet, as government's reaction to the early spate of such exemptions shows clearly, the principle had not been thought through sufficiently. An exemption upon business or occupational grounds – by far the most prevalent application to the Tribunals – addressed, by definition, circumstances which could be neither everlasting nor immutable. A man's domestic situation or health (long-term mental or physical degeneration apart) was equally capable of change. Someone wishing to complete a course of study – another ground for exemption – would do so, at some point. A sincere moral imperative might be a less fluid quality, but as will be seen, applications on conscientious grounds generated their own rationale for resisting the absolute option.[54] In formulating the various grounds for exemption, Curzon, Amery and others had intended that none, in itself, should be capable of removing the exempted man entirely from future consideration. The wording of the Act, however, did not reflect that intention unequivocally.

Thus, at their inception, the Tribunals were armed with an option that government had omitted to stress should not, barring truly exceptional circumstances (whatever they might be), be used. Like so much else concerning the system, they were left to discover the 'correct' answer by trial and error. From their first sittings, some offered only temporary or conditional exemptions whatever the applicant's circumstances.[55] Conversely, other Tribunals were willing to offer absolute certificates to men whose circumstances made their eligibility for exemption from military service obvious on the day itself, and leave the matter of any subsequent change in circumstances to future review. Lord Derby's urgent remonstration in late February 1916 regarding absolute certificates seems to have encouraged the more 'lenient' Tribunals to halt or even revise the latter practice; however, as late as 30 April 1917, 40,146 men in England and Wales still held 'absolute' certificates.[56]

With regard to all forms of exemption, it is fair to say that the Tribunals disappointed their parents from the start. Confusion regarding government intentions, widely varying local demographic conditions and the personal inexperience of tribunalists produced many inconsistencies in policy and practice during the early months of military conscription. Unsurprising, therefore, the net cast by the first Military Service Act produced an unsatisfactory 'catch' for the Colours. Of almost 1.2 million single men deemed now to be enlisted, some 750,000 applied for exemption.[57] Results for the first month following the establishment of the Appeals Tribunals were particularly shocking to government: a grand total of 25,941 unattested men were secured for the Army, while 58,947 received exemption certificates (22,919 being of the 'absolute' variety). The proportion of attested men applying to the Tribunals also continued to be higher than expected, this being due in no small part to the acceleration of their groups' call-up to compensate for the shortfall in conscripted recruitment. In the first three months of 1916, some 190,000 attested men went to the Colours, but a further 839,000 variously received postponements, were variously excused by reason of being in badged or certified occupations, rejected as unfit for service or simply failed to appear at barracks.[58]

The persisting recruitment shortfall, and further manpower pressures on the Army resulting from the Easter Rising, brought universal conscription a step closer in May 1916, when the Military Service (Session 2) Act, 1916, extended the scope of compulsion to married men between 18 and 41 years of age.[59] This removed one perceived inequity between attested and conscripted men, but broadened resentment at the prospect of even more fathers being obliged to go to war while single men demonstrating sufficient grounds for exemption remained at home. The new legislation also removed several exceptions provided for in the principal Act – now allowing, for example, the re-examination of men previously discharged or rejected as medically unfit – and gave Tribunals the power to impose 'finality' upon their certificates: in other words, to specify that a period of exemption was granted with no possibility of extension thereafter.

Inevitably, the manpower crises of late 1916 further impacted upon the Tribunals' business. Growing awareness that many French divisions were physically or psychologically exhausted, and that the BEF would be obliged to bear the brunt of offensive operations in 1917, led the Army Council in November 1916 to conclude that 940,000 new recruits would be required in the coming year. In that respect, they noted that recruitment was falling short of current requirements by 20,000 men each month (during the first year of military conscription, a total of 809,272 men of all categories – including those re-enlisting – had been secured for the Army).[60] Clearly, existing legislative measures (or, rather, their implementation via the Tribunal system) were not working. In December, the fall of Asquith's administration and Lloyd George's succession brought urgent efforts to formulate a longer-term, national service policy to allow the mobilization of the entire industrial workforce, but no formal new measures to secure men for the Army directly. Instead, efforts to access the 'slack' of military-age men in non-vital industries resulted in a series of instructions to Tribunals that tightened definitions of certified occupations and urged the release of younger 'general service' men in all employments, subject to their substitution by older or lower category men.[61] On 1 December, the Local Government Board instructed Tribunals to assume, when hearing applications made on employment or business grounds, that all men under 26 years of age rated fit for general service were of more use in uniform than in their civilian occupations. Little more than a month later, the Board's new President, Lord Rhondda, extended this instruction to encompass men up to 31 years of age in Categories A or B1, while further instructions issued in March 1917 hinted more at a mood of panic than urgency: 'It is imperative that more young men should be obtained for the Army ... it becomes the duty of the Tribunal, without any further application, to review the certificates of all the men covered by the instruction.'[62]

With regard to one of Northamptonshire's two principal employers – the boot and shoe trade – these measures placed great pressures upon the Tribunals to consider methods of applying industry-wide policies to allow the release of younger men while preserving indispensable operatives within an already much-depleted workforce. Their resulting initiatives were to be resisted strenuously by many military representatives, who had no authority to act independently of Army Council Instructions.[63] The county's other principal industry – agriculture – was specifically exempted from Lord Rhondda's instructions; however, in late January 1917, the War Cabinet decided that thirty thousand men in medical Category A not currently holding exemption certificates should be taken from the land.[64] While agriculture was less amenable to consideration 'globally', increased pressures upon the industry during the first half of 1917 were to test further the Tribunals' resolve to meet the needs of both the Army and the Board of Agriculture.[65]

By April 1917, the continuing gap between expectation and delivery in recruitment caused government to try a different approach with the Military Service (Review of Exceptions) Act, which, rather than extend the scope of conscription, gave the Army a second 'go' at some exempted men. Subject to notice being issued by the Army Council, those previously rejected or discharged on medical grounds, and members of the Territorial forces who had been medically assessed as unfit to serve overseas, were required to present themselves for medical re-examination. Men upwardly regraded thereafter would then be called to the Colours. The copious evidence of incompetence and deliberate misdiagnoses that marked this process did much to hasten the demise of the unloved Army Medical Boards and represented a significant self-inflicted wound on the part of the War Office (recruitment actually fell from a high of 95,900 in March 1917 to 70,896 in May and fewer than 60,000 in July).[66] Equally, it brought a marked deterioration in the relationship between Tribunals and the military, who were already far apart on their respective appreciation of the quality of medical examinations. The former largely regarded the new process as odiously dishonest, and were very receptive to applicants' complaints that their ailments had been declared non-existent or miraculously cured. Conversely, the conviction of the Army Council and its medical officers that the Tribunals existed only to confound their work was strongly reinforced. [67]

In July, the government's barrel-scraping strategy was supplemented by the Military Service (Convention with Allied States) Act, 1917, which provided for the conscription of British subjects living abroad and of Allied citizens resident on Britain. It had been claimed in the House that many of the latter, and Russians in particular, were busily buying up the going concerns of Englishmen who had gone to the Colours and supplanting native businessmen in their communities (though in Northampton, it would appear that Jews and Belgians were discharging this contemptible role).[68] The measure was therefore uncontroversial, and in any case had little impact upon inland, largely rural Northamptonshire (interestingly, it did not result in the withdrawal of a long-standing certificate from one of the county's few 'allied' but exempted residents, a Canadian national based in Northampton).[69] Otherwise, the only other substantive measures to increase the monthly recruitment rate in this period were further revisions – that is, substantial cuts – to the certified occupations lists in June and September 1917.[70] In this, the middle period of the Tribunal system, the volume of new applications for exemption (industry-specific dilution initiatives aside) fell to a relatively low level compared to the previous year and to early 1918, when new legislation and short-term emergency measures to meet the German spring offensives would create brief surges in the rate of conscription.

Broadly, government initiatives during 1917 had picked at the edges of the recruitment problem without delivering the recruits that the Army regarded as necessary to maintain front-line strength. In December of that year, monthly recruitment fell to a new low of just under 25,000 men. Having demanded 940,000 recruits for 1917, of whom 800,000 were to have been Category A men, the Army had in fact received just over 800,000 men of all categories, and fewer than 100,000 had been made available during the final three months of the year.[71] Despite this, the balance of government manpower priorities was about to move even further from the once predominant 'Army first' philosophy. In November 1917, responsibility for recruitment and labour resource allocation was removed from the War Office and placed with the newly constituted National Service Ministry, headed by Sir Auckland Geddes. While he was by no means sympathetic to the Tribunals (indeed, by early 1918 he had come to regard their extinction as a desirable goal), Geddes's aim was to ensure that the maintenance of war production – particularly in munitions, food and shipping – ranked at least equally with the Army's need for men.

Government manpower policy in the final twelve months of the war may be characterized as resistance to further large-scale recruitment (anticipating instead that growing American participation would address the shortfall), while meeting short-term military necessities via scheduled releases of men from formerly protected industries. Several legislative measures assisted the latter. The Military Service Act 1918, receiving royal assent on 19 February 1918, provided for the cancellation of any exemption offered by reason of a man's occupation, allowing, as Geddes explained to the Commons on 14 January, 'clear-cut' or bulk-release recruitment of most able-bodied men below a certain age, should military exigencies demand it. The Act also abolished the two-month grace period allowed to men upon the expiration of occupation-related exemptions.[72] Also in January, the list of certified occupations was again, and significantly, revised to remove protection from younger, higher-grade men: an initiative that resulted in higher levels of recruitment during the following two months without recourse to the clear-cut provisions. However, the German Army's 'Michael' Offensive, commencing on 21 March, necessitated a royal proclamation (20 April) cancelling all exemption certificates held by men under 23 years of age rated fit for general service, and accelerated government's consideration of ways to further expand the conscription net.

The result of their deliberations was the Military Service (No. 2) Act, 1918, effective from 2 May. This hastily conceived piece of legislation raised the military age to 51 years (with further potential extension to 56 years, subject to an activating Order in Council), intending thereby to release younger garrison and support troops for front-line service. It also provided for (without yet triggering) the conscription of Irishmen: a measure that, for obvious political reasons, was not implemented subsequently. The power to cancel all existing exemptions without recourse to the Tribunals was also built into the Act: again, subject to an enabling Order in Council (a proclamation of 4 June, effective four days later, duly withdrew certificates from all 18-year-olds except for those graded III, coal-miners, port workers or men exempted upon grounds of ill-health). A still-born provision, urged by Geddes at the drafting stage but dropped before the Bill went to the House, would have abolished the Tribunals entirely, replacing them with modified county advisory committees that would be far more amenable to official direction. Similarly, a proposal to deny legal representation to applicants to the Tribunals passed the Bill's Third Reading but was withdrawn subsequently by amendment.[73]

Notwithstanding the pared-down nature of the new legislation, it is apparent that most Tribunals regarded it as a step too far, and they proved extremely reluctant to deny exemptions to married men falling within the new age-limit.[74] Conversely, the measure further highlighted and encouraged efforts to address the problem of younger men remaining within protected occupations (particularly sensitive issues for Northamptonshire Tribunals were local ironstone quarries and the Wolverton Rail Carriage Works, just across the Buckinghamshire border, which were said to represent safe havens for many single, Grade I men).[75] That sole goad apart, the impact of the final Military Service Act was limited beyond the brief period during which the BEF's cohesion seemed threatened. On the Marne, the last of the German offensives was halted definitively in June; thereafter, British counter-offensives began to realize significant results, and pressures on manpower were further eased as significant numbers of American troops arrived on the Western Front. Though the nation remained in a state of war, there was from this time a discernible sense within the Tribunals that the final crisis had passed. Already, some had responded to the 'clean-cut' provisions by offering long exemptions to men over the proclamation age in industries where the emergency provisions hit hardest.[76] As the apparent crisis receded, the peace economy, if only anticipated, began to command greater attention in their deliberations, with the core of indispensable men in certified occupations almost automatically protected whatever their age, marital status or medical category.[77]

Beyond the impact of legislation, formal instructions and official guidelines, a further point should be made regarding a 'system' that exhibited many of the worst characteristics of the British tradition of extemporization. Conscription, which was intended to secure more men for the Armed Forces, clearly hindered the search for a structured manpower policy because it provided inordinate access to a finite pool of resources to the War Office. Yet other great departments of state needed manpower also, and were extremely reluctant to allow excessive dilution within their industrial provinces. Until responsibility for manpower policy was placed with the Ministry of National Service in November 1917, these departments sought or protected resources on an adversarial basis; thus, lines of communication from the Centre to the Tribunals were often both separate and contradictory. The Board of Agriculture, for example, applied a very liberal understanding of legislation when instructing their representatives to press the paramount importance of maintaining food production.[78] Similarly, at times when the recruiting shortfall was particularly pronounced, the War Office attempted to correct the Tribunals' apparent leniency by methods which were not only extra-legislative but introduced solely upon departmental initiative. Repeatedly, orders were issued to military representatives to appeal exemptions given to men of a certain age group or category regardless of the circumstances thereof, which had the effect of both overturning carefully crafted compromises negotiated at local level and damaging the surviving bonds of trust between the Tribunals and the military.[79] Almost all of these initiatives were resisted or challenged by tribunalists, and quickly reversed thereafter when military representatives complained of their poor results and significant collateral disadvantages. Finally, with respect to the boot and shoe trade (whose status within war production lay uncomfortably between 'vital' and 'important'), the War

Office occasionally indulged in internecine strife, with the Army Contracts Department resisting strongly the Recruitment Office's efforts to secure more men and compromise thereby the supply of army boots not only to the BEF but to most of the Allied armies also.[80]

Although we should not necessarily infer from the above that the Tribunals' business was habitually conducted in a gladiatorial atmosphere, it will become apparent that the system had in-built tensions. The contradiction between the urgent aims of successive Military Service Acts and the judicial independence they provided to the Tribunals, the contrast between the rigidly bureaucratic nature of sittings and the amateur spirit in which they were enacted, and, not least, the failure of government to come fully to terms with what it required of the Tribunals, ensured that the process rarely operated to the satisfaction of its many architects. Consequently, charges that Tribunals were too 'lenient' with applicants, or that they represented the civilian face of an unpitying war machine, are equally unsatisfactory. Both perspectives fail to acknowledge that, at various stages during the period of conscription, tribunalists faced different and often contrary pressures that had the effect of modifying, altering and even reversing existing practices. Thus, it will be seen that the policies of individual Tribunals were not, nor could be, constant qualities. Indeed, any broad critique of the system's performance as a whole is otiose, because a 'system', as such, hardly existed. Rather, some two thousand near-independent bodies, in receipt of the same instructions, suggestions and proscriptions, applied their idiosyncratic understanding of the responsibilities their role entailed, in most cases with the peculiar demographic circumstances of their towns and villages firmly in mind. What resulted cannot be measured upon a single yardstick.

Notes

1 *Report of the Central Tribunal Appointed under the Military Service Act, 1916*, p. 3.
2 *Statistics of the Military Effort of the British Empire during the Great War*, p. 364.
3 Kitchener pledged the latter figure in discussions with the French High Command at Calais in July 1915; two months later the War Policy Cabinet Committee was using it as the basis for discussions on the future of the voluntary system (TNA CAB 37/134/7).
4 In 1908, T.M.H. Kincaid–Smith, MP for Stratford-upon-Avon, attempted unsuccessfully to amend Haldane's Territorial and Reserve Forces Act to make compulsory training in the Territorial Forces. Other abortive efforts to introduce some form of conscription included Lord Roberts's National Service (Training and Home Defence) Bill (1909); G. J. Sandys's National Service (Territorial

Force) Bill (1913) and Lord Willoughby de Broke's curious 'gentleman's bill', the Territorial Forces Amendment Bill (1914).

5 For example, Curzon's somewhat pitiless memorandum of 21 June 1915 (TNA CAB 37/130/19): 'one man seems to me about the equivalent of another, and one life taken to involve another life. If then two millions (or whatever figure) more of Germans have to be killed, at least a corresponding number of Allied soldiers will have to be sacrificed to effect that object.' Curzon had been a compulsionist since at least 1909 (Howard, *Continental Commitment*, p. 38; Hayes, *Conscription Conflict*, p. 95).

6 Adams and Poirier, *Conscription Controversy*, p. 98; Grieves, *Politics of Manpower*, pp. 21, 212.

7 Douglas, 'Voluntary Enlistment in the First World War and the Work of the Parliamentary Recruiting Committee', p. 579; Simkins, 'Kitchener and the Expansion of the Army', pp. 103–104; TNA WO 106/368.

8 CAB 37/134/3 (supplementary). Curzon and two other committed conscriptionists, Austen Chamberlain and Winston Churchill, jointly authored the report.

9 According to Derby himself, his fellow compulsionists Lansdowne, Curzon, Chamberlain and Churchill were 'perfectly furious' that he had accepted the appointment (quoted in Churchill, *Lord Derby, King of Lancashire*, p. 192).

10 Grieves, *Politics of Manpower*, p. 22; Adams and Poirier, *Conscription Controversy*, pp. 120–121; Hayes, *Conscription Conflict*, pp. 194–195.

11 As early as 16 October 1915, the Prime Minister acknowledged that, if the Derby Scheme failed, voluntarism would have proved to be inadequate to the Army's needs (Kitchener Papers, WO 30/57/73).

12 Lloyd George, *War Memoirs*, II, p. 726; Adams and Poirier, *Conscription Controversy*, p. 135; Beckett and Simpson, *A Nation in Arms*, pp. 12–13.

13 5 H.C. 75:520.

14 The Act came into force on 10 February.

15 Military Service Act, 1916, section 1. The maximum age cut-off date for widowers was 2 November 1915.

16 Beckett, *The Amateur Military Tradition, 1558–1945*, pp. 64, 84, 98.

17 Military Service Act, 1916, paras 2 (3), 3 (1).

18 In the original text of the Act (para 2.1), four grounds for exemption were given, the first being a composite of grounds a, b and c above. This was sub-divided for reasons of clarity in the Orders in Council of 3 February 1916 (circulated to registration authorities as Local Government Board (hereafter 'LGB') Circular R.36).

19 LGB Circular R.1 (26 October 1915). The Central Tribunal's first chairman was Lord Sydenham, former Governor of Bombay; Lord Salisbury succeeded him seven months later.

20 In Buckinghamshire, Bletchley Urban Tribunal occasionally allowed the recruiting officer and his assistant to attend hearings and consult with the military representative as cases were considered (CBS DC/14/39/1: Tribunal minute book, *passim*). This was not permitted by legislation, and almost certainly would have been discouraged by the Local Government Board (had they been aware of it) as prejudicial to proceedings. Another local Tribunal,

Sutton Coldfield, were subject to a Commons censure on 10 August 1916 merely for allowing two military representatives to attend their sittings simultaneously (5 H.C. 85:1255).

21 In some counties, the Appeals Tribunals were constituted in permanent divisions to reflect local demographic conditions. In Warwickshire, for example, 18 tribunalists were appointed, six each to sit for the Birmingham, Coventry and Warwick districts (WRO CR1520, 64: LGB to Warwickshire County Council, 10 February 1916). Middlesex Appeals Tribunal sat in two divisions (TNA MH 47/5, Minute Books, *passim*).

22 LGB Circular R.36.

23 NRO Quarter Sessions, Misc., 368, file: 'Tribunals, 1916', 2/2.

24 *Mercury*, 24 March 1916. Names and titles of local tribunal members have been derived predominantly from the *Mercury* and *Herald*. The *Mercury*'s proprietor, Alderman Samuel Smith Campion, was one of the four town councillors sitting on Northampton Borough Tribunal.

25 *Mercury*, 25 February 1916, 9 September 1917; *Herald*, 25 February, 17 March 1916. The Reverend A.W. Pulteney chaired at Oxendon.

26 NRO, Quarter Sessions, Misc: Boot and Shoe/16, 17; *Herald*, 25 February 1916; *Mercury*, 26 June 1916.

27 LGB Circular R.36 (para 5). On the reluctance of Tribunals to appoint labour representation, see Rae, *Conscience and Politics*, pp. 56–57.

28 *Statistics of the Military Effort of the British Empire*, p. 536. Apparently, Gribble's invasion of the Commons' floor lasted all of two seconds; he was bundled out by police as he opened his mouth to deliver an impromptu speech (Kirby, Thomas and Turner, *Northampton Remembers: Boot and Shoe*, pp. 67–69).

29 Crick, *History of the Social-Democratic Federation*, p. 305; *Herald*, 14 January 1916. Gribble was not, however, a pacifist. He had served in the Army from 1885 until 1893, and was organizer of the Northampton Allied War Fund, for which he was honoured for his part in having raised more than £10,000 in the year to July 1916 (NUBSO Monthly Report, as dated; *Northampton Independent* (hereafter *Independent*), 1 July 1916).

30 NRO Quarter Sessions, Misc., 368: 'Tribunals, 1916', 2/1; *Mercury*, 20 October 1916; NUBSO Monthly Branch Report, March 1917, p. 225.

31 Northampton Borough Tribunal had their first sitting on 10 January 1916 to consider applications from men in groups 2–5, who had been directed to report to barracks by 20 January (*Mercury*, 24 December 1915). The Appeals Tribunal, after a preliminary administrative meeting on 16 March, heard their first appellants on 23 March (NRO, Quarter Sessions, misc., 368: 'Tribunals 1916': 2/1).

32 Bedfordshire Record Office, AT/1; quoted in Gregory, 'Military Service Tribunals in Action', p. 181.

33 *Mercury*, 16 March 1913; Bradbury, *Government and County: A History of Northamptonshire County Council, 1889–1989*, p. 14. Of Stopford-Sackville's alleged social pretensions, Adkins observed 'If his mother had been a man he would have been Duke of Dorset' (ibid.).

34 5 H.C. 78:645; *Mercury*, 10 December 1915, 21 January 1916.

35 Mansfield, *English Farmworkers and Local Patriotism, 1900–1930*, p. 100.

Winfrey also attended one of the Appeals Tribunal's rare Kettering sittings, on 7 April 1916 (*Mercury*, 14 April 1916).

36 Knightley sold Fawsley Hall, the ancestral home, in 1921 (*Washington Post*, 16 May 1921). His family had resided there since 1415.

37 Euston, with Alfred, Lord Somerset, had been accused in *the North London Press* of 'the abominable crime of buggery' in a male brothel at 19 Cleveland Street, London, where Post Office telegram delivery boys were corrupted, allegedly, 'at four shillings a time'. Somerset fled to Hamburg; Euston faced and defeated his accusers. In 1918, he joined Northamptonshire's Appeals Tribunal just two weeks following the death of his son, Viscount Ipswich, in an RFC training flight (*Guardian*, 20 September 2002; Potterspury Roll of Honour).

38 Bradbury, *Government and County*, p. 19.

39 NRO Quarter Sessions, Misc., 368, file: 'Tribunals, 1916', 2/1; 'Boot and Shoe Trade', 1–11. Marlow's company was praised effusively in a trade magazine of the period as: 'simply an unrivalled economic machine, in which the machine proper and the human agent are component parts' (*Footwear*, February 1909; reproduced in Brown, *Northampton 1835–1985*, p. 69).

40 Below, pp. 76–80, 83–85.

41 NLW CTB2/1: Cardiganshire Appeals Tribunal Minute Book.

42 LGB Circular R.36, p. 3, para 8: 'this practice should certainly not be encouraged, and it is desirable that the parties should be so represented only where there are special reasons for this course'. On the matter of the legal profession's reluctance to touch the issue of conscientious objection, cf. the case of Frederick George Cooper (NRO X181/759), whose solicitor, A.J. Darnell, stated explicitly that he would not represent him on conscientious grounds (*Mercury*, 4 August 1916). Local newspapers often carried similar statements in their Tribunals reports, possibly at the request of solicitors who, for professional reasons, wished to distance themselves publicly from unpopular moral stances.

43 LGB Circular R.36, para. 28.

44 This policy was most notably criticized by a local Tribunal in the aftermath of the Michael Verrachia case (below, pp. 164–165).

45 Subsequently form R.200. Regulations issued with the Military Service (No. 2) Act, 1918, provided that, from May 1918, Appeals Tribunals might (at their discretion) issue certificates themselves, though their power to require local Tribunals to do so remained intact (LGB Circular R.185, para. 49). The first Military Service Act (section 3(3)) provided that a man whose exemption certificate had expired should not be taken to the Colours for a period of two months following the expiration date. This period was shortened to two weeks by the Military Service (Session 2) Act, 1916, section 6, except in the case of men formerly exempted by reason of their (certified) employment, who continued to receive the longer 'grace' period, largely to forestall the threat of dismissal – given its implications during wartime – being used coercively in industrial relations.

46 NRO, Quarter Sessions, Misc., 368: 'Tribunal Officials and Administration', 1/2: H. Millington's statistical summary, 10 March 1920. The figure is confirmed in *The Report of the Central Tribunal*, p. 16.

47 *Mercury*, 10 March 1916.

48 *Mercury*, 17 March 1916.

49 By 13 February, Central Tribunal had already received some sixteen thousand appeals from attested men in Groups 2–9 alone, suggesting that at least 10 per cent of all Derby attestees might eventually challenge their grouping (TNA MH 47/5, Middlesex Appeals Tribunal Minute Book 1, as dated).

50 *Mercury*, 24 March 1916.

51 *The Times* (editorial, 8 May 1916) noted that some men 'were pressed to attest against their will on the ground that, if they did not, something worse would happen to them'.

52 Below, p. 45.

53 *Mercury*, 25 February, 24 March 1916.

54 Below, pp. 37–39.

55 Northampton Borough Tribunal, for example, though having relatively liberal leanings on other issues, rejected the 'absolute' option entirely. On 1 May 1916, their military representative, A.H. Geldart, presented a letter from Eastern Command which pointed out that absolute exemptions must not be given on occupational grounds: rather, the certificate should be conditional upon the circumstances of that occupation remaining constant. The Tribunal's chairman, Councillor Parker, observed briskly: 'As we do not give absolute exemptions this does not concern us' (*Mercury*, 5 May 1916; *Herald*, 5 May 1916).

56 *Statistics of the Military Effort of the British Empire*, p. 367; Derby's intervention was reported in the *Herald*, 25 February 1916. At a sitting on 8 May 1916, Wellingborough Rural Tribunal devoted 'some considerable time' to reviewing cases in which absolute exemption had been given by them previously, replacing them with temporary or conditional certificates (*Mercury*, 12 May 1916).

57 Edmonds, *Military Operations in France and Belgium, 1916*, I, p. 152; Taylor, *Politics in Wartime*, p. 24.

58 CAB 27/4 (*2nd Cabinet Committee Report on the Coordination of Military and Financial Effort*, April 1916), pp. 15–16.

59 On 'Irish' pressures on conscription policy, see Adams and Poirier, *Conscription Controversy*, p. 168.

60 CAB 37/160, 25 (28 November 1916); *Statistics of the Military Effort of the British Empire*, pp. 83–84.

61 For the medical categorization of recruits, see above, p. vii.

62 LGB Circulars R.107 (as dated), R.114 (20 January 1917), R.122 (1 March 1917).

63 Below, pp. 70–81, *passim*.

64 LGB Circular R.119 (30 January 1917).

65 Below, pp. 112–120, *passim*.

66 *Statistics of the Military Effort of the British Empire*, p. 84.

67 Below, pp. 186–188.

68 5 H.C. 93:1551; *Mercury*, 3 August 1918; see also p. 153 n.5 below.

69 Below, p. 202.

70 LGB Circular R.136 (23 June 1917, revised 8 September 1917).

71 Grieves, 'Recruiting Margin', pp. 396–397.

72 Military Service Act, 1918, 1(i), 2; 5 H.C. 101:71–72.

73 Military Service (No. 2) Act, 1918, 1(i), 2; NATS R.185 (25 April 1918), R.191 (2 May 1918); Adams and Poirier, *Conscription Controversy*, p. 234; Grieves, *Politics of Manpower*, p. 189.

74 In this respect, note the remarks of the clerk to Birmingham Appeals Tribunal following the end of the war: 'the duties of the Tribunals, especially after the passing of the Military Service (No. 2) Act 1918, which brought in men up to 51, have been exceedingly difficult and anxious' (WRO CR1520/62, Clerk's report, p. 2). The chairman of Middlesex Appeals Tribunal expressed almost precisely the same sentiment in his valedictory report (TNA MH 47/5, Minute Book 7: 21 November 1918).

75 Below, pp. 88, 172.

76 The very principle of the 'clean-cut' provisions generated considerable resentment among the Tribunals by rendering irrelevant every circumstance previously considered by them to be sufficient and proper ground for exemption. On such resentment, note Herbert Samuels's comments in the Commons, 24 January 1918 (5 H.C. 101:1223–1224).

77 Below, pp. 85–86.

78 Below, p. 109.

79 Below, pp. 74–75.

80 Below, p. 74.

3

The matter of conscience

Of the hundreds of thousands of men who appeared before the Tribunals, the relatively few who claimed exemption upon the ground of conscience have attracted the most, and the most subjective, attention. Modern empathy with pacifist principles has made almost mandatory the depiction of the conscientious objector as a victim of, and even martyr to, the then-prevailing spirit of militarism. By the same token, posterity has judged the Tribunals' record almost exclusively upon their treatment of such men. Coloured by the early propaganda of the No-Conscription Fellowship and No More War Movement, and by the preconceptions of subsequent commentators, the Tribunals emerge as the pharisaic civilian arm of the Establishment at war:

> Appointed by virtue of their social reliability and unquestioned and unquestioning patriotism, they brought to their work a baffled suspicion of all dissenters, total ignorance of the psychology of religious and political idealism, and a class-bred, bitter hostility to Socialism.[1]

A number of more balanced assessments have acknowledged the difficulties facing the Tribunals, particularly in interpreting the legislation they were intended to implement.[2] Nevertheless, the cliché of their purple-faced antagonism towards pacifism continues to inform a manichaean perspective of tribunalist and recruiting officer as complementary components of the same grinding machine.

That there was a failure on the part of the Tribunals to meet the expectations of many conscientious objectors can hardly be denied. The men (and occasional woman) who sat upon them shared the attitudes of their contemporaries, and, inevitably, personal feelings influenced the decisions they made. Eighteen months into a conflict whose already appalling demands were escalating, they were being asked to judge the sincerity of principles that denied not only the obligation but the very morality of the nation's shared sacrifice. It is hardly to be expected that they would have embraced enthusiastically the ethos urged upon them by Walter Long:

Whatever may be the views of the members of the Tribunal, they must interpret the Act in an impartial and tolerant spirit... Men who apply on this
ground [of conscientious objection] should be able to feel that they are being
judged by a Tribunal that will deal fairly with their cases.[3]

The most trenchant criticism of the Tribunals is that, having been given
the option of granting conscientious objectors unconditional or absolute
exemption from service, they chose not to exercise it. The accusation is
sustainable, but partial. Superficially, the wording of Long's instructions
regarding cases of conscience seems straightforward:

There may be exceptional cases in which the genuine convictions and the
circumstances of the man are such that neither exemption from combatant
service nor a conditional exemption will adequately meet the case. Absolute
exemption can be granted in these cases if the Tribunal are fully satisfied of
the facts.[4]

However, the position was not nearly as unambiguous as the Tribunals'
critics (who promptly interpreted the word 'can' in the above passage
to mean 'should' or 'must') insisted.[5] Neither Long nor his successors at
the Local Government Board ever explained what they meant by 'exceptional circumstances'. The wording seems to allow the interpretation that
an absolutist position – that is, a rejection of any engagement, however
lateral, with the wartime effort – was in itself exceptional, but Long himself
made contradictory statements on the matter. At a conference of Appeals
Tribunal chairmen on 27 March 1916, he stated, apparently unequivocally,
that absolute exemption was available to men on *any* ground of application or appeal. However, less than two weeks later (6 April), he stated in
the Commons that 'total' exemption was available to the conscientious
objector only if he 'was engaged in work of national importance': in other
words, that exemption for conscientious objectors must in every case be
conditional.[6]

Tribunalists who took care to scrutinize the wording of legislation found
little clarification there. In the original Act, the provision of exemptions for
conscientious objectors looked like what it was – an afterthought:

Any certificate of exemption may be absolute, conditional or temporary as
the authority by whom it was granted think best suited to the case, and *also*
in the case of an application on conscientious grounds, may take the form
of an exemption from combatant service only, or may be conditional on the
applicant being engaged in some work which in the opinion of the tribunal
dealing with the case is of national importance.[7]

A point of interpretation arose immediately regarding the above passage,
as to whether the word *also* derogated or supplemented the previous
wording. Long's 'clarification' of 6 April seemed to suggest the former. For

the Tribunals who found this reading amenable, non-combatant service or, at most, exemption carrying a 'work of national importance' condition, were the *only* forms of certificate appropriate to cases of conscience. This view was encouraged implicitly by their instructions' cautionary stipulation: 'The exemption should be the minimum required to meet the conscientious scruples of the applicant.'[8]

On 18 April, inclinations to apply the most unyielding interpretation of legislation were buttressed by a High Court ruling in the case of Rex *v.* Central Tribunal *ex parte* Parton, wherein it was determined that the Tribunals had no authority under the wording of the existing Act to grant anything other than non-combatant certificates to conscientious objectors.[9] Reacting to this, the Military Service (Session 2) Act, 1916, effective from the following month, expanded upon the principal Act to specify that forms of exemption discussed specifically in respect of conscientious objectors were indeed intended to be 'additional to, and not in derogation of' Tribunals' powers to grant absolute, conditional or temporary certificates.[10] However, by the time that this undoubtedly useful clarification had been made, thousands of applications on the grounds of conscience had been processed irrevocably.

Legislation aside, there was also the matter of perception. It has been argued that the original decision to include conscience as a ground for exemption was intended to placate the Simonite wing of the Liberal Party.[11] If so, government's subsequent ambiguity on the matter suggests that it recoiled immediately from the implications of its practical application. Most Tribunals similarly recoiled from the option of utilizing their powers to their full extent. They were aware that they had been passed a poisoned chalice: that, upon a broad interpretation, the legislation was considerably more liberal in its treatment of conscience than the mood of the country warranted. It has been suggested already that 'absolute' exemption in the ostensible sense was not what government had intended to provide: that the possibility – indeed, the likelihood – of individual circumstances changing over time had not adequately been recognized in hurriedly drafted legislation.[12] It might well be argued that a point of conscience, sincerely held, could be immune to the vagaries of time or circumstance, and certainly the No-Conscription Fellowship argued from the start that in such cases absolute exemption was the only proper recourse.[13] Yet to have acknowledged conscience as a ground superior to all others, and, in consequence, to have granted wholesale, unconditional exemptions to men whose self-removal from the war-time nation was not matched by physical removal from their communities, would have been highly provocative. A very few Tribunals ignored this risk in the first few months of the conscription period; most, emphatically, did not. The following discussion will argue that the social context cannot be discounted when assessing tribunalists' responses to pacifist sentiments. Their hostility to expressions of conscience was often apparent; less obvious, but equally prevalent, was their anxiety not to excite local grievances by demonstrably inconsistent or inequitable judgements. If the exemption procedure was a quasi-judicial process, it was one in which the judges, no less than the applicants, stood in the wider court of public opinion.

The broader criticism of the Tribunals – that they maintained an instinctively critical attitude towards conscientious applications – is more difficult to rebut. In an interview given to the *Mercury* only weeks before the end of the war, the Northamptonshire Appeals tribunalist Beatrice Cartwright expressed what was probably the consensus among her colleagues when she admitted that she had little 'forbearance' with conscientious objectors as a species.[14] While her choice of words hints at a slightly more measured attitude than, for example, that of the chairman of Nairn Appeals Tribunal, who appeared to believe that pacifist principles indicated satanist tendencies in their holder,[15] it would be optimistic to assume that her preconceptions could be set aside readily. Even so, Miss Cartwright's opinion may not always have been reflected in her vote. Tribunals have been judged largely upon the statements [or, rather, outbursts] of individual members rather than by the decisions they made collectively. As will be discussed, terms offered to conscientious objectors often belied the tenor of sentiments expressed immediately beforehand – an indication, perhaps, of efforts, however counter-instinctual – to deal 'in an impartial and tolerant spirit'.

Nevertheless, given the absence of firm, unambiguous guidance in the early months of the conscription period, idiosyncratic responses to conscientious applications predominated. Tribunalists who had little, if any, experience of the philosophies they were confronting were expected to formulate questions that would test their sincerity. Unsurprisingly, these tended to concentrate more upon how far a man was prepared to defend his mother or wife from German rapists than upon Aquinian or Grotian theories regarding the just war. It was not until May 1916 that Central Tribunal issued a standard set of ten questions to allow tribunalists to formalize the interrogation of conscience. While the rigid format was not ideally suited to testing the individualistic nature of pacifist principles, it improved markedly upon overtly hostile questions deployed previously by some tribunals in the hope of exciting intemperate responses from men they had no wish to exempt.[16]

Defining 'conscience' was a further problem for the Tribunals – as, indeed, it was for pacifist organizations.[17] In searching men's souls they soon learned that there were almost as many strains of conscience as applications made upon that ground. Some convictions were formed solely by spiritual beliefs; others were grounded entirely in political principles. Between these extremes, an infinitely nuanced range of religious and secular values was rehearsed before the Tribunals. To complicate matters further, applications or appeals were often submitted on multiple grounds, with a conscientious objection appended for what might have seemed to be good measure. Whether those making such applications were being disingenuous or merely reluctant to state conscience as their foremost ground for exemption was difficult – and, again, time-consuming – to determine. Sir Ryland Adkins (who, upon occasion, would prove himself to be no mean baiter of conscientious objectors) anticipated the magnitude and complexity of the coming problem during the committee stages of the military Service Bill: 'A question of conscience is most difficult to decide, and it depends a good deal on the acumen and well-regulated imagination of the members of the tribunal.'[18] As Adkins's own record with cases of conscience reveals, tribunalists' ability to regulate their imaginations often failed entirely when confronted by pacifist sentiment.

If judged quantitatively, conscience was to prove an irrelevance in North-amptonshire as elsewhere. Of 6,801 (original) cases heard by the county's Appeals Tribunal, only 106 were stated on that ground.[19] Predictably, the greatest number (43) arose against the judgements of Northampton Borough Tribunal, which served by far the most populous registration area. Peterborough urban district supplied 16 cases, Kettering 14, Wellingbor-ough and Daventry four each, Brixworth three, with the remainder, singly or in pairs, arising from the proceedings of the county's other Tribunals. The records that would tell us how many conscientious objectors in total made a case at local level are no longer extant, but almost certainly they represented an equally minuscule proportion of the exemption workload. Nevertheless, the attention directed towards these cases by the local press was entirely disproportionate to their statistical impact, and sittings in which several conscientious cases were due to be heard attracted capacity audiences. Again, it will be suggested that this degree of public engagement was at least partly responsible for the apparent inconsistencies that marked the Tribunals' engagement with conscience.

On 2 March 1916, the county's first three applications on the ground were heard at Towcester Tribunal. One man was given exemption by reason of (unspecified) physical disabilities, a second threatened suicide if called up and was referred for a medical examination (during which, unwisely, he informed the doctor that previously he had been imprisoned for arson and threatening behaviour), while the application of the third was dismissed when he failed to provide evidence of any religious affili-ation. In the following week, Northampton Borough Tribunal received their first pacifist lecture with some bemusement: 'Prayer ... is the greatest weapon. It is better than all shells, cannon and rifles' they were told, which drew from Councillor H.E. Gough the wistful observation: 'I wish it was: it would have been over before this.' When the applicant refused to consider non-combatant service, his case was dismissed. At Brixworth Tribunal on 16 March, the chairman, A.P. Geldart, warned a Christadelphian that he was not going to enter into any theological debate and that he must take non-combatant service. The applicant retorted that he would appeal. Dismissing the case, Geldart was almost conciliatory: 'of course, you cannot wonder that the Tribunal does not agree with your views, but we accept them as being honest views'. One week later, Northampton Rural Tribunal listened with apparent patience while a local boot and show worker lectured them on the brotherhood of man and his belief that all disputes could be settled without the taking of life. Offered a non-combatant certificate, he said that he should appeal. At Northampton Borough again on 28 March, four conscientious objectors were subjected to protracted questioning by the military representative, A.H. Geldart (brother of Brixworth Tribunal's chairman). A Voluntary Aid Detachment (VAD) volunteer at a Northampton hospital offered his lifelong vegetarianism as evidence of pacifist convictions and accepted a non-combatant certificate; the application of an absolutist who would consider no work but his present employment was dismissed; an atheist failed to convince the tribunal that his objections to fighting had any moral foundation; finally, a corporation clerk whom Geldart manoeuvred into an admission that he had an instinctive aversion to being killed was offered but refused non-combatant service.[20]

The military representatives' eagerness to challenge every pacifist utterance notwithstanding, these early cases suggest that local Tribunals – influenced either by time pressures, animosity or unease when confronted by this form of application – were dealing peremptorily with conscientious objectors. Most applicants faced outright dismissal or, at best, were offered the minimum exemption (that is, from combatant service), with a swift referral to the County's Appeals Tribunal when this failed to satisfy. In mitigation, many Tribunals appear at this stage to have regarded the non-combatant certificate as the 'correct' exemption. It met – or seemed to them to meet – the requirements of pacifist principles while releasing other men for front-line duty (thereby forestalling threats of appeal by the military representative). The proposition, often expressed with heart-felt sincerity, that to release another man to kill was to bear a moral responsibility for that killing was too novel for most Tribunals in early 1916.[21] Nevertheless, those who held out only the option of non-combatant service were failing, except upon the narrowest interpretation of legislation, to offer the conscientious objector the choices it provided. Their critics denounced this as wilfulness, but, again, confusion played a part. While tribunalists knew that they had the power to maintain a conscientious objector in, or require him to find, 'work of national importance', they were obliged to process cases for almost three months without any guidance on what government considered to constitute such work. The first assistance given by the Board of Trade was its preliminary list of relevant occupations, issued on 14 April 1916 by the Pelham Committee.[22] Following its dissemination, most Tribunals in Northamptonshire adopted the alternative form of exemption to a greater or lesser degree, though some – Peterborough and Daventry were notable in this respect – continued to regard a non-combatant certificate as the most a 'conchie' should expect.[23] Conversely, a few proved notably responsive to their newly clarified options: Northampton Borough in particular appears to have experienced a damascene conversion early in May, not only reversing their former policy but expressing also a willingness to return to and adjust previous decisions.[24]

Northamptonshire's Appeals Tribunal, commencing their business almost two months later than their local sister bodies, swiftly exhibited symptoms of the same blustering indignation towards pacifism that the No-Conscription Fellowship's weekly *Tribunal* news-sheet reported elsewhere in the country. At their inaugural sitting on 23 March 1916, they considered the appeal of Richard Stanley Vyse, Daventry's assistant Borough Surveyor, against the non-combatant certificate given by his town's Tribunal. The earlier decision was upheld, though not before Mr Vyse had been subjected to heated rhetorical questions regarding a German invasion of England and accusations that he was a shirker. To Stopford-Sackville's final demand to know whether he felt he owed the King any loyalty, Vyse retorted that his first, overwhelming allegiance was to the 'King of Kings'.

However, having made this timely and somewhat predictable impression, the Appeals Tribunal hinted at the ambiguity with which they would deal with many cases of conscience. Though dismissing Vyse's appeal, they promptly gave him leave to appeal further to Central Tribunal: one of only fifteen cases (upon any grounds) so permitted from the thousands they would consider.[25] Furthermore, as early as their third sitting (8 April), when no local Tribunal in Northamptonshire had as yet offered conditional exemption to a conscientious objector, they varied the non-combatant certificate of an assistant schoolteacher, Wilfred Tye Watts. Watts had indicated his readiness to do work of national importance, but previously had refused an unpaid position manufacturing anaesthetics ('I cannot live on anaesthetics' he declared, reasonably). The case was adjourned for a month for him to find suitable employment, with the original certificate to stand if he failed. Similarly, on 4 May, the Tribunal allowed conditional exemption to Bernard Harcourt Berrill, who, two weeks earlier, had appealed a non-combatant certificate from Brixworth Tribunal. Given a month to find suitable work, he obtained employment on his uncle's farm – a suspiciously congenial arrangement that the Tribunal chose not to challenge or test. [26]

From their earliest sittings, however, the Tribunal – like many others – insisted that conscientious objectors should accept a degree of personal sacrifice as a *quid pro quo* for obtaining conditional certificates. Men who, as a condition of their exemption, went from urban employment on to the land, or from white-collar work into a factory, were not only undertaking what had been determined to be a useful function for the State but also expiating their refusal to go to war (as, indeed, were men exempted on other grounds, conditional upon their joining the Volunteer Training Corps or Special Constabulary). [27] Where that expiation was considered insufficient or negligible, the Tribunals could be unyielding. Almost immediately following Berrill on the appellants' list of 4 May, the case of John Thomas Gray was heard. Gray also had been allowed a month's adjournment to find work of national importance, and had taken up employment as a miner's helper at the Islip Ironworks. The fact that this was a Ministry of Munitions facility may have inclined the Appeals Tribunal to doubt the sincerity of Gray's conscience, though nothing on record confirms this. What did exercise them was the fact that the change in employment had resulted in his wages rising from 16s. per week (as a butcher/slaughterman) to 25s. They decided that his change in circumstances had involved no measure of hardship or sacrifice, and confirmed the non-combatant certificate previously offered by Thrapston Tribunal. [28] It should be noted that this principle opened up interesting opportunities for enterprising local employers: at least one Wellingborough farmer appears to have followed his Tribunal's proceedings closely and offered significantly underpaid opportunities to conscientious objectors told to find work on the land. [29]

The day after hearing the appeals of Berrill and Gray, the Tribunal considered the cases of twenty conscientious objectors – the largest number to appear before them in a single sitting during the course of the war – all contesting decisions of Northampton Borough Tribunal. Ten appeals against non-combatant certificates were dismissed (one by consent); the remaining appellants accepted certificates conditional upon finding work of national importance, or, in three cases, upon their remaining in present employments. Of the first group, several were absolutists, including two brothers, Christopher Bernard and William Usher Harris, respectively a surgical bootmaker and watchmaker. The former informed the Tribunal that he belonged to an 'invisible church', and that the visible church was a nonentity in his life. In an exchange with Adkins, he declared 'If He had thought it better for me to have your head, He would have put it on my shoulders.' 'He has saved you that misfortune', Adkins replied, to laughter. The other absolutists were questioned at length (though courteously)[30] as to whether they would consider employment other than their present occupations in order to help the country. One, William Wesley Church, a vegetarian who declared that Belgium should have resisted the German invasion passively and who refused several times to consider work other than his present occupation (as chief clerk in Northampton's Public Health Department), was urged nevertheless to consider the option, and given fourteen days to apply to the Friends' Ambulance Unit or similar organization. The Tribunal's treatment of him was considerably less gentle on 19 May, when, after being offered a further two weeks to find suitable work, Church demanded to know whether their decision was unanimous.[31]

If the Appeals Tribunal had acted to date with a little more temperance than their worst exemplars, they seem, superficially, to have conformed to the preconceptions of the system's critics. At least half the appeals made against non-combatant service certificates had been dismissed, while no man had yet received exemption from military service that did not carry also some lateral obligation. However, within the confines of the exemptions they were prepared to offer, the Tribunal were already demonstrating a degree of flexibility that sits uneasily with their reported comments. The three appellants of 5 May given exemptions conditional upon remaining in their current employment worked respectively as a coal porter, a general porter and a labourer. Only the first of these occupations fell within Pelham Committee recommendations. At the same sitting, Albert Tomkins, a school attendance officer, had refused to consider any sort of military service. After being subjected to the usual questions regarding the defence of his mother and sister, he was offered precisely that which he had requested – time to find work with the Friends' Ambulance Unit or similar organization.[32]

More notably, the Tribunal were prepared to take the initiative in setting the terms of their authority in cases of conscience. Christopher Bernard Harris – he of the 'invisible church' and Sir Ryland Adkins's head – was the subject of a further military appeal on 16 June. Following the decision of 5 May, Harris had returned to Northampton Borough Tribunal and asked them to vary his non-combatant service certificate, as he was now amenable to finding work of national importance. Given a fourteen days' adjournment, he obtained a post as an agricultural labourer at Great Billing, and his certificate was duly varied. In the opinion of their military representative (Geldart), Northampton Borough had usurped the authority of the Appeals Tribunal by setting aside the earlier decision. However, far from accepting this – technically correct – plea, the latter declared that it was for them alone to decide whether their authority had been usurped. There had been a change of circumstance: Harris was now in 'a better frame of mind', and the Tribunal therefore had no objection to the new certificate. Attending the same hearing, Herbert Hankinson, clerk at Northampton Borough, attempted to push the principle further even than this. He suggested that, if a conscientious objector had a change of mind and would now accept alternative employment, he had the right to be accommodated even if he had been placed in uniform already. It was a principle that his Tribunal would seek to apply with some consistency thereafter.[33]

Northampton Borough were also to adopt a relatively liberal policy with respect to conscientious objectors who, mistakenly or otherwise, had attested under the Derby Scheme. Upon hearing their first such case on 17 March 1916, Geldart reminded them that legislation did not allow attested men to be considered for exemption on conscientious grounds. Nevertheless, the Tribunal decided to treat such cases no differently from those presented under the Military Service Act.[34] Further, they acknowledged that some men had been tricked into attesting by the suggestion (and often the explicit assertion), made by some recruiting authorities, that unattested men would not be able to appeal against their calling-up if and when conscription was introduced 'Some say it', Parker admitted of the allegation; 'I say it myself', retorted James Gribble.[35] The Tribunal were also capable of soul-searching with regard to individual tribunalists' preconceptions. On one occasion, when Geldart mounted a particularly telling assault upon an attested applicant's integrity ('Is an oath nothing to you? You have taken an oath before Almighty God you will fight for your King'), they divided upon whether to offer a conditional exemption. The acting chairman that day, Councillor Jackson, remonstrated with his colleagues: 'The Tribunal does not come very well out of this. We heard the case, told him to do a certain thing, he did it, and now the vote is equally divided. I voted against dismissal and my casting vote is in the man's favour.' The applicant received two months' exemption.[36]

Such occasions of apparent moderation were relatively rare across the Tribunal system in Northamptonshire (and even Northampton Borough were happy to ignore the vexed question of conscience altogether if additional grounds were stated by an applicant).[37] Statistically, for every man who was treated with consideration, several were processed with what seemed to be a blithe disregard for their convictions. A few obtained exemptions conditional upon nothing more than remaining in their present circumstances; many departed with a certificate that subjected them to military discipline, with often severe consequences.[38] On the evidence of newspaper reports of the first few months' sittings, a man coming before a Tribunal might expect to be met variously with mild (if detached) sympathy, puzzlement, exasperation or outright hostility. What then distinguished the successful applicant from his less fortunate brethren?

Clearly, the convictions of individual tribunalists counted for much, though personal prejudice can hardly be quantified. Even an organization as uncompromisingly hostile to the Tribunals as the No-Conscription Fellowship could acknowledge that some attempted to treat cases of conscience fairly.[39] In Northamptonshire, none achieved the worst excesses reported elsewhere;[40] equally, none was praised for extravagant indulgence of pacifist principles. Upon the middling ground, some Tribunals exhibited greater forbearance than others. Jackson and the irrepressible Gribble at Northampton Borough were more likely to hear a conscientious plea respectfully than Stopford-Sackville and Sir Ryland Adkins at the Appeals Tribunal, though even Gribble (who, upon one occasion, remonstrated with his colleagues for being rude to a conscientious objector) complained of the difficulty of adjudging such cases: 'the Government ... never ought to have allowed a flea a conscience'.[41] Conversely, neither Peterborough nor Daventry tribunalists appear to have offered anything other than non-combatant certificates during the entire conscription period, and openly criticised the Appeals Tribunal whenever their decisions in such cases were adjusted or overturned.[42]

Beyond the relative strength and nature of the prejudices deployed in the Tribunal chamber, responses to each case were shaped by its peculiar nature and presentation. As upon any ground of application, the attitude of the applicant was critically important. If a man was courteous and indicated a willingness to 'do his bit' in any way other than to fight, most Tribunals usually responded favourably. On 19 June 1916, a surreally polite exchange took place between Northampton Borough Tribunal and a conscientious objector with as yet unfocused convictions. Asked if he might consider doing something extraordinary for his country during the emergency, the applicant indicated that he was open to suggestions. Councillor Parker proposed that he join the Volunteer Training Corps (an option likely to satisfy neither party), as he would then release another man for service. Gribble, pursuing a personal preoccupation, suggested that he might also make a contribution to the Allied War Fund. Parker continued gently to urge the young man: 'Think it over and see some of the VTC people, and find out whether you can be of some assistance.' Graciously, the applicant agreed to make enquiries, and the case was adjourned.[43]

Similarly, men who expressed their readiness to find work of national importance often received considerable time latitude in which to do it. The Appeals Tribunal, however their individual members may have expressed themselves, habitually adjourned cases for two to four weeks while a man searched for suitable work, and, where this proved hard to find, offered a further adjournment thereafter (though usually with a stern exhortation to the appellant to try harder).[44] The near-absolutist, who refused to participate in any activity that would further the cause of war, but who was not opposed to finding work that did not traduce his principles, might also be indulged, to a point. Thomas Sydney Smith, a Duston boot and shoe worker appealing against a non-combatant certificate, told the Appeals Tribunal that he would have no objection to working on the land, 'but a strong objection to the abominable wages paid for such work'. Rather than dismiss outright Smith's appeal, they offered a month for him to find work with the YMCA, which he refused to consider until the Tribunal gave him their definitive decision on his claim for absolute exemption. Declining to indulge him further, they confirmed the original certificate.[45]

The true absolutist, whose philosophy allowed none of the compromises demanded by the Tribunals, and who often expressed his principles with defiant self-assurance, had little chance of a sympathetic hearing. Claude Cunnington, manager at Thrapston railway station, made an early and notable impression upon the Appeals Tribunal. Asked what he was prepared to do to help his country, he told them that he thought he was doing best by protesting against the war. The statement infuriated Stopford-Sackville and Lord Annaly: 'You stay at home and get the advantage of the fine fellows who go and get killed' ... 'You benefit by better men than yourself going out and fighting ... You would not have a place to live if everybody behaved as you do'. The appellant's calm demeanour before this barrage further goaded the chairman. 'I think you had better go and preach to the Germans', he told Cunnington, whose reply – 'I should not hesitate to take the opportunity were it given to me' – guaranteed the dismissal of his case.[46]

The precise nature of a conscientious objection also influenced its reception. While neither the Military Service Act nor Long's instructions had attempted to define 'conscience', the Tribunals – and, indeed, many Members of Parliament – almost intuitively regarded some form of spiritual conviction as a defining element of it.[47] Consequently, men who could not demonstrate a long-standing religious affiliation, or who based their claim solely upon political or secular moral principles, found it very difficult to convince Tribunals of the sincerity of their convictions. This did not so much reflect 'a class-bred, bitter hostility to Socialism' as an unwillingness to regard the tenets of socialism – or any other secular philosophy – as moral, rather than political, imperatives.[48] There was also a sliding scale of credibility enjoyed, or suffered, by the various religious sects whose communicants applied to the Tribunals, with those having an unambiguous position towards war enjoying a definite advantage. Members of the Church of England, whose hierarchy was a pillar of the wartime community, were hard pressed to attach any credible spiritual justification to their conscientious applications. Similarly, Roman Catholics might stress their personal convictions yet be hamstrung by their Church's formal support for the war.[49] Christadelphians, who had no formal hierarchical organisation through which their beliefs might be publicized effectively, also posed a problem for the Tribunals in the early months of the conscription period. They claimed to be against all wars except the final one, when their participation would be commanded by Heaven; in the meantime, they would not serve in uniform or take any form of oath, but considered participation in such ancillary activities as the manufacture of uniforms or munitions as morally acceptable. As early as April 1916, Central Tribunal acknowledged the legitimacy of the Christadelphians' refusal to accept military authority, but the message was lost on most Tribunals.[50] Indeed, Middlesex Appeals Tribunal had already taken their own counsel and concluded that Christadelphians, together with Bible students, International Socialists and those merely claiming to be 'a Christian', fell entirely outside the ground of exemption.[51] For several months more, the sect's beliefs were tested far more rigorously before the Tribunals than those, for example, of Quakers, whose uncompromising view on all aspects of warfare was venerable and well-understood, and whose wholesale diversion into the Friends' Ambulance Unit was actively supported by the War Office.[52]

This inconsistency of treatment was apparent from the earliest cases in Northamptonshire. During a protracted examination on 22 March 1916, a group of six Christadelphians failed to satisfy Northampton Borough Tribunal of the sincerity of their convictions and were offered only non-combatant certificates, which they refused to accept. Immediately thereafter, the Tribunal considered the cases of three Quakers, the first two of whom worked respectively in the Friends' Ambulance Unit and a hospital ship. Both were offered exemption for as long as they continued in their present occupation. The third, a teacher at the Town and County School asking for absolute exemption, told the Tribunal that he would not accept his profession being recorded on his certificate as the reason for exemption, as that would 'make his work an acknowledged part of the organization of the nation for war'. Obligingly, the Tribunal gave him exemption conditional upon him remaining in his present occupation, but marked the certificate upon the grounds of conscience only.[53]

Two days later, at a Peterborough sitting of the Appeals Tribunal, three Christadelphian brothers, Stanley John, Howard Alfred and Douglas Maycock, appealed against non-combatant certificates and asked for absolute exemption. The Tribunal noted that the first brother was in a reserved occupation (a lime-keeper in a munitions works); the others, respectively, worked as a linotype operator and an agricultural machinist.

The solicitor representing the brothers (who were not present) pointed out that their sect had been exempted from all military service – combatant or otherwise – during the American Civil War, and that they were not required to serve in the Australian and New Zealand armies in the present conflict. Unable to come to a decision, the Tribunal adjourned the cases to obtain guidance from Central. However, by 8 May only Stanley John Maycock was holding out for a decision on his appeal; his brothers, having been offered the option, had indicated their willingness to work on the land and had been given two weeks to find employment.[54]

Seventh Day Adventists who appeared before the Tribunals also attracted rigorous questioning, though, the sect's objections to war being generally understood, their treatment seems to have been relatively gentle. One 18-year-old Adventist, Frederick George Cooper, was obliged to submit to some teasing regarding his beliefs at the Appeals Tribunal (Wellingborough Town's military representative, Herbert Dulley, observed 'They get Sunday and Saturday as well. I shall have to consider becoming a Seventh Day Adventist myself'), but when he returned following his nineteenth birthday to tell them that he had been unable to obtain employment with the Friends' Ambulance Unit, he was allowed further time to find work that would not disturb his Saturday Sabbath. Another member of the sect, Percy Edgar West, a Kettering window cleaner and carpet beater, went before the Tribunal on 18 August 1916 to appeal the non-combatant certificate he otherwise would have accepted, as the Army could not promise that he would not be soldiering on Saturdays. Again, his case was adjourned for a month to allow him to find a more accommodating employer.[55]

Growing familiarity with the idiosyncrasies of the various nonconformist groups gradually smoothed the processing of such cases. The Christadelphians ceased to be a problem for the Tribunals after August 1916, when a special exemption certificate was devised for them and issued directly by the Pelham Committee.[56] Those few Quakers not already exempted continued to enjoy preference, to the point at which non-Quakers seeking employment in the Friends' Ambulance Unit could be turned away (as was Frederick George Cooper) for want of vacancies in their areas.[57] For those whose objections to warfare were not supported by sufficiently robust spiritual affiliations, a record as a lay preacher, a bible class attendee or, curiously, a teetotaller, often helped to buttress their applications.[58]

Furthermore, the Tribunals' preconceptions regarding what constituted 'genuine' conscience did not prevent them from making occasional concessions regarding political principles. On 26 June 1916, Northampton Borough heard the application of the manager of the ILP Cooperative Boot Society upon both business and conscientious grounds. He was offered three months' exemption with regard to his business activities, conditional upon attending VTC drills, which he declared to be unacceptable. Asked if he would consider work of national importance, he said it would depend entirely upon its nature. He made it clear also that his conscientious objection was grounded entirely in his political convictions. Nevertheless, after consulting briefly in camera, the Tribunal decided to confirm the three months' (unconditional) exemption upon his business application, with the conscientious question to be considered at the end of that period.[59]

The following week, the same Tribunal heard another ILP member – Harold Croft, secretary of the party's Midland Division – on what must have been the most rigorous (and secular) conscientious grounds they would ever hear. He told them that he had longstanding and uncompromising objections to war, which, he believed, corrupted all societies, and said that he would not do alternative work if it were to be a condition of his exemption. Nor would he consider aiding the sick and wounded if they had been so afflicted because of participation in war. For good measure, he declared any man who agreed with the war but did not go off to fight was a shirker. Bemused, the Tribunal chose to ignore his previous statement regarding alternative work and gave him a month to find some. At the end of July he returned to the Tribunal and informed them he had been doing his habitual duties in the intervening time: 'I have stated my case', he concluded. The application was dismissed, and, on 18 August, Croft appeared before the Appeals Tribunal.

Having been raised to a state of near-apoplexy already that day by George Robert Wade, a conscientious objector who did not believe in the monarchy and who refused to play the national anthem on his chapel's organ (Stopford-Sackville considered his opinions 'poisonous'), the Tribunal might understandably have exhibited little patience with Croft's appeal. He was heard at length, however, and only when he had refused to make any sacrifice, concession or other acknowledgement that the nation was at war, and concluded with a declaration of his loyalty to the principles of the Labour Party, did Sir Ryland Adkins chide him with uncharacteristic restraint: 'We all understand the fascination of politics, Mr Croft; some of us feel it ourselves'. The appeal was dismissed, but Croft was given permission to take it to the Central Tribunal.[60] Though their decision was upheld subsequently, Croft's treatment hardly supports one modern commentator's assertion that 'Socialists were virtually doomed to refusal of exemption of any kind'.[61]

The Tribunals might accommodate personal conscience in most of its many forms, but any hint of the organization of pacifist sentiment appeared to contradict or even deny its inward, personal nature and attracted deep hostility, even from tribunalists who were ready to accept the validity of a conscientious objection. The No-Conscription Fellowship had a local office at 11 Derngate, Northampton, where their branch secretary, J.F. Oldham, offered help and advice to men preparing their cases. In line with the Fellowship's policy, Oldham appears to have urged a more absolutist position upon his 'clients' than some might have adopted otherwise. As a result, the Fellowship's voice was often apparent in their testimonies, something that was noticed very quickly (not least because Oldham, perhaps unwisely, had distributed a batch of NCF pamphlets for the Tribunals' instruction). At Northampton Borough on 4 April 1916, Councillor Parker interrupted a preliminary statement by an applicant to observe: 'It's a curious feature that nearly all these conscientious objections seem to be expressed in the same words.' At the same Tribunal on 2 June 1916, during an application by a man who previously had refused to do work of national importance but who now asked for reconsideration, Gribble suggested that many cases of conscience would not have been stated so uncompromisingly had not an 'organization in the town' coached them unnecessarily. Some applicants, he argued, might have received three months' exemption on personal grounds; others would have taken work of national importance which he, for one, would have agreed to in every case, rather than have them go into the Army.[62]

Tribunalists' patience was tested also by the self-defeating obstructionism of some previously exempted conscientious objectors, who regarded the authority of the Tribunals as no less illegitimate than that of the Army and therefore viewed the conditions attached to their certificates as morally invalid. In July 1916, Northampton Borough tightened its surveillance of men placed in work of national importance to counter what it suspected to be widespread avoidance. Work schedules, counter-signed by employers, were to be submitted weekly to ensure that men were actually turning up for the duties they had undertaken. The measures uncovered abuses without, apparently, discouraging them. Considering one applicant's scheduled renewal in November, they asked why he had not been submitting his work schedules. 'It isn't always convenient' he told them. Sometimes he forgot to take his piece of paper to the farm; at other times, the farmer forgot to carry his fountain pen. Sternly (though renewing his certificate), the Tribunal reminded him that their patience wasn't limitless.[63]

Even principled stands upon conscience could degenerate into self-defeating dogmatism. The example of Harold Croft, who seemed almost to invite successive Tribunals to take their best shot at him, was notable but not unique. In December 1916, an 18-year-old conscientious objector, formerly a clerk who had gone to work on the land for his farming father, exhausted the patience both of his solicitor Alsop and of Northampton Borough's tribunalists by steadfastly refusing to sign a medical history sheet to allow him to be examined at barracks. After much fruitless reassurance that his signature committed him to no form of service (during which Alsop resigned the case in exasperation), the Tribunal changed tack and decided to examine the father's accounts to ascertain whether their new arrangement had resulted in any sacrifice to the applicant. Hurriedly, the farmer assured the Tribunal that his son would sign the form, but it was too late: the case was adjourned for a week to allow him to produce his books.[64]

Conversely, a conscience of palpable integrity might entice a notable degree of respect from a Tribunal. Joseph Sault, formerly an Army officer who had resigned his commission on religious principles, returned to Woodford Halse to take up employment as a clerk for the Great Central Railway. Too valuable a resource to escape the recruitment net indefinitely, he was called to the Colours once more in September 1917. The following month, the Appeals Tribunal, having heard a sterling reference regarding Sault's character from one Reverend Bedells of Leicester, adjusted Daventry Tribunal's original, non-combatant certificate: the appellant was offered a three months', open exemption, conditional upon his giving a proportion of his salary to a local hospital and promising not to promote his pacifist principles in the workplace. In January 1918, Daventry, still irritated by the adjustment to their decision, took the opportunity of Sault's renewal application to ask for a review of the terms he had obtained. They claimed that all other railway clerks of the same grade in the district had been called up, and that Sault had been overheard expressing his beliefs. To emphasize their displeasure, they voted to suspend their sittings until Sault was removed entirely from their jurisdiction. W. Murland, their National Service (formerly military) representative, told the Appeals Tribunal that there was considerable unrest regarding Sault in Woodford Halse, where it was generally believed that he had bought himself out of the Army for £1 per week. Murland had also been informed that Sault habitually spoke out against the war, though there was no firm evidence of this (and, indeed, Daventry's clerk had written to the Appeals Tribunal to confirm that they would present nothing to flesh out the rumour). Under the circumstances, he suggested that the Tribunal might require the appellant to find work of national importance outside the area.

In resisting the appeal, Sault claimed that rumours regarding his beliefs had arisen only because he had made unpopular alterations to work rotas at the station and depot. He had observed honourably the Tribunal's proscription, and was guilty only of distributing a pamphlet (a copy of which he provided to the Tribunal) whose content did not contravene the conditions of his exemption. Having heard both testimonies, Adkins admonished Sault, though not harshly. He suggested that he should be more sensitive to the feelings of those whose husbands and sons were at the Front, even if, technically, he had not breached the terms they had laid down. That said, the Tribunal decided to ignore Daventry's ultimatum and extended Sault's exemption upon the same terms as before.

Sault returned to the Tribunal for a further renewal on 5 May 1918. He informed them that his conscience had become too tender for him to continue to hold his exemption under the terms offered. He had done his best not to preach, but if others asked of his Christian principles regarding the war he could not forbear to express them. At this point, the Tribunal had a clear and uncontroversial option: to rescind the existing certificate and issue one for non-combatant service only, thereby removing Sault from the district and soothing Daventry Tribunal's wounded sensibilities. Nevertheless, they continued to urge him to give his word of honour that he should not express his views publicly. Sault refused, giving them little choice but to order Daventry to issue a non-combatant certificate. The appellant was then given leave to appeal to Central.[65]

It is suggested in Chapter 10 below that the Tribunals' priorities and preconceptions, influenced both by growing self-awareness of their powers and responsibilities, and by the developing needs of the military and local economy, shifted conspicuously during the course of the conscription period. Given that the impact of cases of conscience upon both the machinery of war and the resources of the community was minuscule, it might be assumed that attitudes towards such cases remained fairly constant. However, familiarity, war-weariness and the peculiar qualities of conscience appear to have generated their own impetus for change.

The majority of first-time applications and appeals on the grounds of conscience were made in the months following the implementation of the first two Military Service Acts. Consequently, the greatest incidence of outbursts regarding skulkers, cowards and shirkers, the querulous interrogations regarding lusty Germans and ravished English wives and mothers, occurred during this period. Thereafter, the relative rarity of such confrontations seems not to have been due solely to the fact of fewer cases of conscience coming before the Tribunals. As the arguments and philosophies of pacifism became more commonplace, their capacity to outrage seems to have diminished. More than this, the nature of the claim for exemption on conscientious grounds generated its own form of finality. Men whose cases were dismissed outright went into the Army, where they either conformed or went before courts-martial. After mid-1916, the latter cases were reviewed by Central Tribunal, and most were transferred to custody in civilian work camps thereafter.[66] The same choices awaited conscientious objectors who had been offered non-combatant certificates. All of these men were removed permanently from further consideration by the Tribunal system. Those who remained – conscientious objectors who had been offered and had accepted conditional exemption – were obliged, as with those exempted upon other grounds, to reappear before the Tribunals occasionally to renew their certificates or answer a review of their cases.

Yet, unlike cases brought on grounds of hardship, occupation or ill health, the circumstances of 'conscience' rarely changed. A man might dishonour the terms he had been offered by a Tribunal, or it might emerge that his original claims to a conscientious objection had been false; for most, however, the conditions pertaining to their original applications remained constant. In such cases, the Tribunals' function was merely to confirm the appellants' circumstances and renew their certificates. In effect, the vast majority of conscientious objectors who applied for exemption ceased to be an active issue once their original cases had been rejected or certified.

The treatment afforded to Joseph Sault – a recurring appellant – was not unusual, therefore. Anecdotal evidence provided by local newspapers suggests that other conscientious objectors returning to the Tribunals similarly faced little of the animosity they had experienced on their first visits. No one – not even military representatives – had any further interest in putting them into uniform, and government was not slow to put distance between its own legislation and the consequences of applying the same. With striking disingenuity, Lord Derby accused the Tribunals of sending conscientious objectors into the Army when, in his opinion, they should have received absolute exemption from the start.[67] In January 1918, W. Hayes Fisher, President of the Local Government Board, similarly exonerated his predecessor Long: a circular to Tribunals enquired guilelessly whether they were aware that they could in fact offer absolute exemption to conscientious objectors?[68] By this time, any striking reversal of policy would have been practically impossible to effect, but some Tribunals, gifted a degree of latitude by Whitehall's collective hand-washing, moved beyond their processing function and became relatively accommodating of men they had excoriated formerly. A few, indeed, expressed a degree of remorse for having treated men formerly with less than the courtesy to which they had a right.[69]

In September 1918, Rudolph Brambley, exempted on the ground of conscience, went before Northamptonshire's Appeals Tribunal for the seventh time, to renew a conditional certificate first given in June 1916. He confirmed that he was still working as a farm labourer, earning 25s. per week. His certificate was extended once more by three months, but additionally the Tribunal wrote to the farmer – Brambley's cousin – to object to the fact that he was paying his kinsman less than the now-minimum wage.[70] Even more telling of a shift in attitudes was the case of a Hardingstone farmer, Walter Beeson, who had applied to his local tribunal on business and conscience grounds. He was given one month's exemption (final) on business grounds and the conscientious application was dismissed. At appeal in July 1918, Beeson's business exemption was confirmed at one month, but on conscientious grounds he was given an open certificate, conditional upon his helping other farmers on three days each week. Beeson's case was strengthened by a letter, read to the Tribunal, which testified to the strength and sincerity of his convictions. Its author was Sir Ryland Adkins.[71]

As noted, the ground of conscience was not stated frequently in the tribunal chamber. Northamptonshire, furthermore, was a predominantly rural county with a strong tradition of voluntary recruitment, whose cultural conservatism provided a poor breeding ground for relatively sophisticated, and courageous, pacifist principles. Yet, notwithstanding their statistical unimportance, these applications provided the Tribunals with one of their greatest challenges, and many failed to meet it adequately. Peace movements, posterity and, indeed, those who formulated policy with regard to conscientious objectors firmly located the wellspring of the latter's mistreatment in the uncomprehending environment of the tribunal chamber. Of those tribunalists who allowed prejudice to override both courtesy and the proper exercise of legislation, there is little to be said in mitigation. For the remainder, their inescapable association with excesses committed elsewhere has disguised much of the complexity of the issues and imperatives they confronted.

Shaped by their milieu, most shared a distaste for pacifist principles. Many were unable to resist expressing that distaste when confronted by a particularly uncompromising, or starkly expressed, conscientious objection; all rejected the irreducible premise of pacifist organizations that the true absolutist position must be accommodated. Yet they were charged with implementing legislation and consequent instructions, which, however ambiguously, recognized the validity of the sincere anti-militarist stance. As with any other application, they enjoyed (or were burdened by) a degree of latitude in adjudging that sincerity. That some, even when attempting to deal equitably, erred towards severity, is undeniable. Given the lamentable treatment of conscientious objectors once dispatched to the Colours, this has encouraged a general view of tribunalists as *de facto* colluders in the persecution process. Yet the evidence of Northamptonshire Tribunals' proceedings indicates that in a majority of cases there was at least an attempt – or, perhaps, struggle – to deal 'fairly' with conscientious objectors. Most modern opinion would find that effort wanting, particularly when accompanied by outbursts that reflected poorly upon the manners, if not the integrity, of the inquisitors. Again, however, there is little reason to believe that the Tribunals did not reflect the prejudices of a majority within their local communities. Walter Long had asked that legislation should be applied in 'an impartial and tolerant spirit'; if those qualities proved elusive, it is nevertheless unjust to accuse tribunalists *en masse* of seeking to confound the intentions of what one commentator has described as 'remarkably progressive' legislation.[72]

Of the county's local Tribunals, Northampton Borough stand out as relatively enlightened adjudicators of conscientious claims, and, if they refused ever to offer absolute exemption to a 'conchie', it should be recalled that they refused it in all other cases also.[73] More notably, the county's Appeals Tribunal, despite allowing full rein to the invective of Stopford-Sackville, Lord Annaly and the otherwise liberal Adkins, exhibited a degree of flexibility and accommodation of conscience from their initial sittings. Clearly, absolutists received little or no satisfaction at their hands, and the principle that conscience was a quality beyond the State's ability or right to judge was, and remained, anathema to them. However, their treatment of less unequivocally expressed cases of conscience was no harsher than that of appeals presented on other grounds. The Tribunal supported very few dismissed applications, and then only when an appellant refused to consider looking for work of national importance. In no case did they quash a non-combatant certificate and dismiss a case outright.

To put a perspective on that record, of the 577 'conscience' appeals heard by Middlesex Appeals Tribunal during the conscription period, 406 outright dismissals were confirmed. Similarly, Birmingham Appeals Tribunal, hearing 352 conscientious cases, confirmed 116 earlier dismissals and 142 non-combatant certificates, while 'slightly varying' 34 exemptions offered by local Tribunals. In only 60 cases did they make significant adjustments to earlier decisions.[74] It need not be suggested that Northamptonshire Appeals Tribunal's apparent 'leniency' represented an atypical compassion or empathy for the principles of pacifism. Equally (and recalling *The Tribunal*'s valedictory observation on 'the impossibility of judging between conscience and conscience'),[75] one might simply conclude that tribunalists – whatever their personal prejudices – had little incentive to seek new wars on old battlefields.

Contemporary attitudes towards conscience, whether antipathetic or accommodating, were determined by circumstance (whether local or individual) and inclination. More puzzling to the contemporary observer is the ever-present dislocation between the judgements of the more 'lenient' Tribunals and their apparent willingness to indulge in precisely the same sort of verbal invective against conscience that stained the records of their less enlightened sister bodies. The present author would suggest that the factor reconciling this apparent anomaly was public opinion: that is, the relative degree to which tribunalists felt themselves bound to consider the wider impact of their decisions.

Most if not all Tribunals understood that they had an obligation to demonstrate 'fairness'. In adjudging cases stated upon all but one ground, they considered verifiable facts and made their decisions accordingly. The quality of those decisions might be debatable, or their logic flawed; but unless they reflected a particularly discernible inconsistency, or partiality, the results could be sustained by reference to the ever-present 'national emergency'. Conscience was not amenable to such unambiguous tests. Firstly, the ground explicitly denied the validity of the overarching circumstance against which all other cases were measured. Secondly, perceptions, rather than facts, determined the judgements handed down to conscientious objectors. Thirdly, though certainly not least importantly, the visible demonstration of fairness in such cases was problematic, because there was no consensus upon what constituted that quality. Government had determined – if guardedly – that a genuine conscientious objection to war should be recognized. The public mind, particularly during the early conscription period (when the personal impact of compulsion was most dislocating, and resistance to 'special-case' treatment at its strongest), largely rejected that principle. The Tribunals' ability to bridge the resulting gap largely determined the utility of their respective policies on conscience.

Some applied the harshest interpretation of legislation both to satisfy their own predilections and to evince a 'fairness' that was grounded solely in the principle of universal sacrifice. The record of both Peterborough and Daventry Tribunals suggests that any ambivalence they felt regarding their treatment of conscience was resolved in this manner. Conversely, Northampton Borough struggled to reconcile their statutory duty with natural justice. Initially, they, like Peterborough and Daventry, offered only the minimum exemption to conscientious objectors. It is conceivable that, for a time at least, Northampton Borough similarly considered a non-combatant certificate sufficient to square the circle in satisfying both public perceptions of fairness and an applicant's moral objection to war. However, the abrupt manner of this Tribunal's conversion to a notably progressive policy on conscience, and the strong implication of a sense of remorse for its previous decisions, suggests otherwise. Thereafter, they continued to express a degree of ire whenever confronted by a conscientious objection, but this was unswervingly directed against the organization of conscientious resistance to conscription, not its individual expression. Given the degree to which the Tribunal was willing to accommodate conscience, it might be concluded that there was an element of disingenuity in such protestations. Similarly, the pronounced contrast between the stringent comments made by appeals tribunalists during the interrogation of appellants and the relatively lenient conditions they attached to certificates thereafter hints at a ritual enacted for the edification (and pacification) of both the attending public and the Local Government Board.

Without seeking to exonerate or misinterpret the worst excesses of some Tribunals, it is apparent that government had handed them an insuperable dilemma. 'Equity' fell at the first fence, because conscience invited several interpretations of what it was, precisely, leaving tribunalists to search for a balance that might somehow satisfy irreconcilable perspectives. In making decisions to spare last remaining sons or fathers of eight from the front line, or to defy the army's medical boards when palpably unfit men were declared to be prime fighting stock, the Tribunals validated their role in the public eye without testing the anomalies inherent in their brief. In contrast, the examination and judgement of conscience fully exposed them.

Notes

1 Boulton, *Objection Overruled*, p. 124. For similarly uncompromising views, see Graham, *Conscription and Conscience: A History 1916–1919*, pp. 66, 76; Chamberlain, *Fighting for Peace*, pp. 47–58 *passim*; Stephen, 'The Tribunals', pp. 381–382; Moorehead, *Troublesome People: Enemies of War, 1916–1986*, pp. 31–34.

2 Above, p. 8, n.5.

3 LGB Circular R.36 (3 February 1916), p. 6.

4 Ibid.

5 For example, the (anti-conscription) Labour MP Philip Snowden's (1916) booklet *The Military Service Act Fully and Clearly Explained*, p. 12: 'The Instructions to the Tribunals state that in such cases the Tribunal *must* grant a complete and absolute exemption, if they are satisfied of the facts' (present author's emphasis).

6 Conference minutes reproduced in LGB Circular R.76 (26 March 1916); 5 H.C. 81:1460.

7 Military Service Act, 1916, 2(3) (present author's emphasis). On the protracted debate regarding exemptions that might be offered to conscientious objectors (and some Tribunals' resistance to Long's recommendations), see Rae, *Conscience and Politics*, pp. 117–128; Kennedy, *Hound of Conscience*, pp. 99–101.

8 LGB Circular R.36.

9 Reported in *Justice of the Peace*, 13 January 1917.

10 Military Service (Session 2) Act, 1916, section 2: 4 (3).

11 Rae, *Conscience and Politics*, pp. 27–35; Kennedy, *Hound of Conscience*, pp. 82–83; Adams and Poirier, *Conscription Controversy*, p. 140; Bibbings, 'State Reaction to Conscientious Objection', p. 60. Sir John Simon's was the only Cabinet resignation resulting from the decision to introduce the Conscription Bill.

12 Above, pp. 23–24.

13 The point was made in the editorial of the first edition of the *The Tribunal* (8 March 1916).

14 *Mercury*, 6 September 1918. Note, however, the suggestion that female tribunalists held consistently harsher attitudes towards conscientious objectors than did their male colleagues (Graham, *Conscription and Conscience*, p. 65).

15 *The Times*, 4 March 1916; *The Tribunal*, 8 March 1916.

16 LGB Circular R.87.

17 Robbins, 'The British Experience of Conscientious Objection', pp. 696–697.

18 5 H.C. 78:735 (20 January 1916).

19 The figure is arbitrary. The present author has included cases where conscience was presented as the sole or principal ground for exemption, but not those where it was included as one of three, four or even five grounds. If the latter were admitted, a further 19 cases should be classed as ostensibly 'conscientious'.

20 *Mercury*, 3, 10, 17, 24, 31 March 1916; *Herald*, 3, 17, 24 March 1916.

21 Sir Ryland Adkins's comment to Richard Stanley Vyse typified this perception: 'We are bound to respect conscientious objection, but I don't understand how anybody can have a conscientious objection to non-combatant service' (*Mercury*, 24 March 1916). Middlesex Appeals Tribunal considered the matter formally, and concluded: 'A man cannot object to Military Services, but only to Combatant Services. If objection is granted from Military Service, his objection is met' (TNA MH47/144: misc. memoranda).

22 The Pelham committee (under the chairmanship of T.H.W. Pelham, assistant secretary at the Board of Trade) was formed following a Commons debate of 22 March 1916, when the need for a co-ordinating body to advise Tribunals on suitable 'work of national importance' became evident. Its preliminary list (reproduced in Graham, *Conscription and Conscience*, p. 101; Rae, *Conscience and Politics*, apps H, I) recommended various roles in farming, forestry, food supply, shipping, transport, mining, education (curiously) and public utilities including sanitation, emergency services and health.

23 Cf. NRO X180/66, 130–135; X181/710.

24 Above, p. 45. It should be noted that, as early as 28 March, this Tribunal had asked the absolutist whose case they dismissed (above, p. 41) if he would be willing to do something to help the war effort, which implies that they were at least considering a conditional certificate.

25 NRO, X180/22; Quarter-Sessions, misc., 368: Millington's summary of proceedings, 10 March 1920; *Mercury*, 24 March 1916. Central Tribunal confirmed the early decisions (*Mercury*, 21 April 1916). Perhaps significantly, in one of only three other cases of conscience to be referred to Central (Claude Cunnington: NRO, X180/ 243; 10 April 1916: also p. 47), the appellant was similarly reviled with a degree of vehemence largely uncharacteristic of this Tribunal. It may be that, conscious of their injudicious behaviour, they required confirmation that their decision was supportable.

26 NRO, X180/143, 152. Watts subsequently went to Ireland as a teacher, before returning to take up a place in the Friends' Ambulance Unit. By May 1918 he was working as a teacher in Northamptonshire once more; when he applied to have his certificate renewed that month, the Appeals Tribunal agreed on condi-

tion he returned to the FAU once summer term had ended. His exemption was renewed again in August 1918 (NRO X193/9007, 10163; *Mercury*, 3 May 1918).

27 To cite one of many apposite examples, John Miller, a 39-year-old married butcher, was given exemption on business grounds conditional upon also driving a Wellingborough mail cart on four days per week. When he returned to the Appeals Tribunal in September 1918 to renew his certificate, he told them that he was working six days and seven nights each week (NRO, X193/ 9110).

28 NRO, X180/241.

29 *Mercury*, 23 June, 1916. Predictably, a member of Wellingborough Urban Tribunal castigated a conscientious objector for accepting work with this farmer as in doing so he was undermining the pay structure for rural labour.

30 Of the day's encounters, 'Jupiter' noted in the *Independent*: 'I could not help marvelling at the judicial calm and restraint with which the Tribunal listened to their claims.' He went on to excoriate the motives, comments and demeanour of the appellants (editorial, 13 June 1916).

31 NRO X180/328–347; *Mercury*, 12 and 26 May 1916; *Herald*, 12 May 1916.

32 NRO X180/324.

33 *Mercury*, 2, 23 June 1916.

34 This was more than three weeks before Central Tribunal, somewhat condescendingly, ruled that, 'as a matter of grace', applications of conscientious objectors who had attested previously might be heard (Rae, *Conscience and Politics*, p. 96).

35 So too did Lord St Audries (though in reference to agricultural workers, rather than conscientious objectors) on 12 April 1916 (5 H.L. 21:676).

36 *Mercury*, 17 March, 26 May, 2 June 1916. On problems facing conscientious objectors who had previously attested under the Derby Scheme, see Rae, *Conscience and Politics*, pp. 95–96.

37 For example, in the cases of two brothers, market gardeners and nurserymen, who, receiving temporary exemptions on business grounds, were told that the Tribunal had taken no notice of their conscientious claims (*Mercury*, 7 July, 1916).

38 The treatment of conscientious objectors under military and, later, civilian penal conditions has been comprehensively analysed elsewhere. For balanced commentaries, see Kennedy, *The Hound of Conscience*, pp. 134–146, 178–190; Rae, *Conscience and Politics*, pp. 139–190, *passim*. Also Commons' debates, 20–22, 26–29 June, 3–6 July 1916.

39 Rae, *Conscience and Politics*, p. 109.

40 Such as at Lanchester Tribunal, where the chairman's response to a conscientious objection was to tell the applicant to 'get out' (*The Tribunal*, 18 May 1918).

41 *Mercury*, 7 July, 29 September 1916.

42 Cf. the case of Joseph Sault (above, pp. 52–53), and note also that of Frederick George Kennell, whose abiding religious beliefs were confirmed in copious correspondence to the Tribunal (NRO X183/1337, 3 November 1916).

43 *Mercury*, 23 June, 1916.

44 In this respect, note the cases of John Whitmee (NRO, X182/892: 5 October 1916) and Frederick George Cooper (above, p. 49).

45 NRO, X180/260; *Mercury*, 21 April 1916.

46 NRO, X180/243; *Mercury*, 14 April 1916.

47 This despite Bonar Law's insistence in the Commons – as early as 19 January 1916 – that the legislation recognized non-religious convictions (5 H.C. 78: 422, 428). On widespread suspicions regarding non-spiritually based objections, see Kennedy, *Hound of Conscience*, pp. 101–102; Rae, *Conscience and Politics*, pp. 115–117.

48 Boulton, *Objection Overruled*, p. 124 (see also above, p. 36). Kettering Rural Tribunal's reaction to the application of a socialist railway worker was typical in this respect. It was dismissed on the basis that 'although [he] had stated his views, he had not supported them by any religious grounds, and had manifested no willingness to help his country' (*Herald*, 17 March 1916). It appears to have been the absence of these extenuations, rather than the fact of his political views, that encouraged their (majority) decision. Elsewhere, Philip Snowden claimed in the Commons that Accrington Tribunal's military representative (the former Mayor, John Harwood) was playing to his own (Tory) political partialities in attacking the secular conscience applications of his local left-wing opponents. Snowden appears to have underestimated the scope of Harwood's prejudices, however. In another conscience case, the latter told his Tribunal: 'Candidly, I say I don't believe him, nor would I believe any word as regards a conscientious objector' (5 H.C. 81:191; *Accrington Observer and Times*, 6, 13 March 1916).

49 For example, the case (not from Northamptonshire) of Clifford Francis Bird, who appealed to Warwick District Tribunal against a non-combatant certificate. A qualified brass-turner who had refused a high-paid (and protected) job in munitions on moral grounds, he nevertheless failed to convince the Tribunal of the sincerity of his convictions because they were contrary to the officially stated policy of the Catholic Church (WRO CR1520/59, 42; 31 March 1916).

50 LGB Circular R.77, notes of cases decided, 2 (27 April 1916).

51 TNA MH47/144: Misc. Memoranda. At an early stage, the Tribunals were presented with a booklet summarizing Christadelphians' beliefs with respect to war: *EVIDENCE (extending over half-a-century) that The Conscientious Objection to military Service and the Bearing of Arms is a Denominational Characteristic of the Christadelphian Body of Believers* (Mornington Hall Ecclesia, London, February 1916).

52 LGB Circular R.70 (23 March 1916). Note also Walter Long's comment at the conference of Appeals Tribunal chairmen, 26 March 1916 (notes reproduced in LGB circular R.76): 'Everyone … admits that a man who is (e.g.) a sincere member of the Society of Friends is entitled to claim that he has an objection to combatant service.'

53 *Herald*, 24 March 1916; *Mercury*, 24 March 1916.

54 NRO, X180/69, 70, 71; X197: Appeal Tribunal notes of meeting, 24 March, 8 May 1916; LGB circular R.18 (list of reserved occupations, 10 December 1915). In January 1919, Douglas Maycock wrote to Herbert Millington, asking that he might now return to his previous employment as the Tribunals had been disbanded. Millington replied that as, technically, the Appeals Tribunal had *not* in fact been disbanded, he should take up his request with them, though he

provided no guidance on how Maycock might communicate with a body that had not sat since the previous 5 November (NRO X202, misc. correspondence file: conscientious objectors).

55 NRO, X181/759; X182/880; *Mercury*, 4, 18 August 1916, 19 March 1917.

56 Friends' House, London, Temp. MSS 835: T.E. Harvey Papers: Report of the Pelham Committee, p. 5.

57 Similarly, the VAD worker at Northampton hospital, who claimed before the Borough Tribunal that he had offered to serve in the unit in England, France or Italy, but as a non-Quaker had been unable to obtain a place (*Mercury*, 31 March 1916).

58 The teetotal secretary of a Wellingborough Temperance Friendly Society brought as evidence several letters attesting to his long-felt conscientious principles. Unfortunately, he worked as a grocer's manager in a business that also sold strong drink. His application was dismissed (*Mercury*, 25 August 1916).

59 *Mercury*, 30 June 1916.

60 NRO, X182/916; *Mercury*, 7 July, 18 August 1916. Croft was already familiar to readers of the *Independent*, having conducted an ill-tempered correspondence with the paper's 'Jupiter', who, among other matters, objected to Croft's characterization of tribunalists as 'Prussians' (*Independent*, 12 February, 3 June 1916).

61 Moorehead, *Troublesome People*, p. 34.

62 Kennedy, *Hound of Conscience*, pp. 99, 118, 297; *Mercury*, 31 March, 7 April, 7 July 1916.

63 *Mercury*, 7 July, 3 November 1916. Outside Northamptonshire, some Tribunals instituted more formal arrangements for monitoring of the conditions of exemption. Eton Rural Tribunal, for example, required monthly reports from all employers of conscientious objectors to ensure that their work was 'satisfactory' (CBS, DC/10.38/1, *passim*). Similarly, Middlesex Tribunal, after an initial period in which they required merely that conscientious objectors confirm their employment status each quarter, decided to instigate monthly reviews (TNA MH 47/5, Minute Book 1: 21 June 1916).

64 *Mercury*, 8 December 1916.

65 NRO, X193/6815, 7919, 9038 (cases bundled); X197: Appeals Tribunal meeting notes, 21 October, 19 November 1917; *Mercury*, 23 November 1917, 18 January, 3 May 1918.

66 Rae, *Conscience and Politics*, pp. 161–168; Kennedy, *Hound of Conscience*, pp. 167–169.

67 TNA CAB 23/4/246 (I) (a).

68 LGB Circular R.138 (1 January 1918).

69 Note, for example, the rather startling (though alleged) damascene conversion of at least two members of Willesden local Tribunal (*Tribunal*, 2 May 1918).

70 NRO, X195/349, 1045, 1645, 3266, 7321, 8993, 10210 (cases bundled); *Mercury*, 16 June 1916, 6 September 1918. Brambley, a Quaker, had first appeared before the Appeals Tribunal in May 1916, but his case had been adjourned for a month when he informed them that since offering his services to the Friends' Ambulance Unit he had been too unwell to take up his duties with them (*Mercury*, 12 May, 1916).

71 NRO, X195/10145. Note also Adkins's urging, two months later, that his Tribunal should hear an extemporary 'conscience' appeal when no other ground was available to Claude Blencoe (below, p. 176).

72 The suggestion is that of Ceadel, *Pacifism in Britain*, p. 38.

73 Above, p. 34, n.55.

74 TNA MH 47/3: chairman's report, 21 November 1918; Brazier and Sandford, *Birmingham and the Great War*, p. 30. Birmingham City local Tribunal appear to have been more liberal than their appeals body; on August 1 1918 they offered absolute exemption on the grounds of conscience to one J. Douglas Maynard (*Tribunal*, 15 August 1918).

75 Editorial, 8 January 1920.

4

Boot and shoe

It's wonderful how men have gone.[1]

Northamptonshire Tribunals' treatment of, and attitudes towards, the boot and shoe trade are difficult to place in a national perspective. No other manufacturing industry dominated an English region so markedly that was not also afforded comprehensive reserved occupation status. For that reason, the steel, coal, shipbuilding and chemical sectors offer unsatisfactory benchmarks. In terms of what it supplied to the war machine, Lancashire's cotton industry might be considered a reasonably close equivalent, yet the similarities are largely illusory. At the war's commencement, cotton lost a significant number of men to Derby's recruitment of the 'Pals' regiments, but the industry was in a long-term depression – one exacerbated by the imposition of tariffs upon cotton imports into India – and thus could absorb that initial dilution. From 1917, furthermore, imports of raw cotton were significantly curtailed by the diversion of British shipping resources to the transportation of American troops and materials, and most mills were obliged to switch to short-time production. This, and a rota system intended to protect workers' jobs for the future, kept the industry effectively over-staffed until the end of the war (as the subsequent transfer of many Lancashire cotton operatives into aircraft frame production attests). These peculiar local conditions aside, the manufacture of finished cotton, in comparison to that of army boots, was far more amenable to timely female substitution; indeed, from the commencement of the Industrial Revolution, women had enjoyed at least as important a role in the mills as had men, and could readily perform all but the heaviest tasks.[2]

Of the other major footwear centres (London, Leicester, Leeds, Bristol, Stafford and Norwich), none had a remotely comparable share of Army boot production; nor, consequently, did their local economies rely nearly so heavily upon the trade as did Northamptonshire.[3] In an otherwise agricultural landscape, sparsely populated and with few urban centres, the county's dominance in footwear manufacture was a historical oddity. That oddity becomes more marked when we consider that Northampton and its smaller sister towns, together with hundreds of outworkers in the county's villages, took on the supply of boots not only for the British Army but for most of the Allied forces also, and with only partial (and ever declining) protection from the provisions of successive Military Service Acts. Northamptonshire's Tribunals were required, therefore, to exercise a degree of discretion, relating to the consequences for both the local economy and production of vital war materials, which might be said to be unparalleled elsewhere.

Northamptonshire was to boot manufacture during the First World War what Pittsburgh was to steel production three decades later. Having successfully fought off the so-called 'American export invasion' of cheap, popular styles in the 1890s and 1900s, the county's boot and shoe manufacturers had expanded rapidly as mechanized techniques were perfected. The town of Northampton was the nub of this industry: according to the 1911 census, the town's male, working-age population stood at 29,746, of whom 11,005 were classed as shoemakers and a further 1591 as operatives in the associated skin and leather trades.[4] The outbreak of war had a twofold, and contrary, impact upon footwear manufacture. Most obviously, vast new orders were placed hurriedly by the War Office's Army Contracts Department to supply the rapidly expanding New Armies. The majority of these came to Northamptonshire, whose association with the military was venerable (as noted elsewhere, production in at least one district – Raunds – had been entirely devoted to Army orders, particularly for handmade officer's boots, even before the outbreak of war).[5] In January 1915, the *Times* noted that Northampton had become a boom town, 'gayer, more alert and animated than it had been in peacetime', and that new labour-saving machinery had been introduced to reduce the pressure upon manual labour.[6] Conversely, as in other industries, voluntary enlistment significantly diluted the male workforce as rising levels of production strained existing capacity. And, predictably, the War Office saw no contradiction in expressing its dissatisfaction at delays in contract delivery resulting from such manpower losses while continuing to encourage boot and shoe operatives to join the Colours.

This dichotomy ensured an enduring skew to the Tribunals' perspective. Clearly, boots were vital to the war effort, but the certified occupations list of December 1915 protected only the following occupations within the industry (and for the production of military footwear only):

Clicker (skilled cutting by hand of upper sections from hides)
Foreman, all departments
Rough stuff sorter (grading leathers to be used for bottom (soles) stock)
Rough stuff presser (preparing bottom stock for machining)
Machinists

Edge paring (giving final shape to the sole, prepared for finishing)
Edge setting (compressing and burnishing the edge of the sole)
Heeling (attaching the sole to the heel)
Lasting (attaching the assembled shoe or boot upper to the insole)
Loose nailing and billing machine (riveting the bottom of the shoe from the last)
Pulling-over (part-drafting and shaping the sewn upper)
Screwing (attaching the assembled bottom to the insole).[7]

Additionally, the Army Contracts Department of the War Office provided a quota of exemption badges for distribution by boot factory owners, but the system was unpopular both on the factory floor and with management. In May 1916, a major Northampton manufacturer (and Northampton Borough tribunalist), E. Lewis, refused to hand out his factory's allocation of badges on the basis that the system was intrinsically preferential, and, therefore, inequitable. Anecdotal evidence suggests that this was by no means a minority view.[8]

As elsewhere, boot and shoe manufacturers and unions complained volubly of losses to voluntary enlistment prior to the introduction of compulsion, though the scale of this dilution cannot be established precisely. Of 7126 'financial' (that is, paid up) male members of the National Union of Boot and Shoe Operatives Union (NUBSO) in Northampton, 1485 were said to be serving with the Colours by January 1916. From Kettering and Wellingborough in the same month, 424 and 235 men were serving from total union male membership of 2688 and 1037 respectively. From Higham and Rushden district, 722 men had enlisted from a membership of 3794. However, figures for these and other towns' non-union boot and shoe workforce are not extant.[9] At an individual company level, further evidence of losses prior to conscription was provided by employers appealing to the Tribunals. One Northampton factory was said in April 1916 to have lost between two and three hundred men since the war commenced. The owner of another firm, producing fifteen thousand pairs of Army boots per week in March 1916, stated that, of his 48 remaining clickers, only 13 were of military age, and that several women were now employed in this traditionally male-dominated occupation. On 8 April, the owner of the Kettering boot makers G.T. Hawkins and Co., appealing for his son at the Appeals Tribunal, argued his indispensability as one of only two lasting machine operators remaining in a factory that had lost 30 men to date.[10]

Buttressing the statistical argument was a strong, if anecdotally founded, belief that the boot and shoe trade was more than pulling its weight with regard to enlistment. A recurring claim, made both to and by tribunalists throughout the period, was that it had lost a greater proportion of its workforce to the armed forces than other industries, and, in turn, that Northamptonshire had suffered an inordinate share of that loss. In November 1916, James Gribble, exercised perhaps by the statistic he had marvelled at only a month earlier,[11] claimed explicitly: 'the boot trade had sent into the services a higher percentage of men than any other industry'. Six months later, C. Forscutt, a Wellingborough Urban tribunalist and boot factory owner, complained that Northamptonshire's boot and shoe trade was being 'combed out' more severely than elsewhere. In this respect, the allegedly light dilution burden placed upon two other footwear-producing centres, Stafford and Norwich, was mentioned several times (according to Albert Tebbutt, another boot factory-owning tribunalist, a boot and shoe employee in the latter town was a lucky man: 'they are not taking everybody there'). Within the county, each boot and shoe town in turn thought its own contribution the standard against which all others fell short. Finedon solicitors Morgan and George asserted: 'It is well known to the recruiting authorities that Finedon has sent more men in proportion to its population than almost any place in the country, and at the present time there are only about 51 men left in the boot factories in categories A and B1'. Kettering's manufacturers saw themselves in a similarly sacrificial light, though their vision may have been somewhat impaired: NUBSO reported in January 1916 that Kettering was one of only four boot- and shoe-producing districts in the country not to have suffered net losses of manpower during the previous year.[12]

Were these claims sustainable? Certainly, there were great, and, to an extent, peculiar pressures upon the industry. In addition to its now-predominant military commitments, boot and shoe was attempting to preserve at least part of its domestic and overseas trade in the face of foreign competition – a battle for the coming peace that it felt it was losing. American imports in particular had filled the vacuum left by the large-scale switch from domestic to war production. These had more than doubled (to 1.4 million pairs) in the seven months to 31 January 1916, while British exports to America had collapsed from 111,364 to only 25,427 pairs. In October 1916, James Gribble reported to his Tribunal that not only were American factors unable to place a £1 million order for ladies' and children's shoes with Northampton firms for want of capacity, but that the town's shops were now selling American shoes to meet local demand. Figures provided by individual manufacturers to the Tribunals during 1917 indicate that all remaining non-military production had been turned over to export orders so as to prevent their prewar overseas markets from failing entirely.[13]

As the first Military Service Act came into force, the industry's capacity was being tested further. Early in 1916, the predominant part of a new order for six million pairs of boots for the Russian army was placed with Northamptonshire factories. At approximately the same time, a substantial order to supply the Italian armies came to the county.[14] For both projects, local firms were required to draw up new designs for the boots and undertake substantial further modifications to their machinery (part of the Russian order was for a soft ankle boot for Cossack cavalry, while the Italian Army required a lighter, complex mountain boot that Northampton alone, with its significant welting resources, was able to produce in quantity). Even before the Russian order – the first of several – was completed, the British Army placed a further requirement for three million pairs of boots, which the War Office insisted should be met as soon as capacity was freed.[15] In April 1916, one Northampton manufacturer claimed that his firm alone had supplied 900,000 pairs of boots to the Allied armies since the beginning of the war. By July of that year, it would be estimated that English firms had provided some 26 million pairs to the British, French, Russian, Italian, Serbian and Belgian armies, more than a quarter of which had been produced in the town of Northampton alone.[16] With regard to British Army requirements alone, it was calculated that, of a total average weekly value of £400,000 of boots produced nationally since the commencement of the war (to January 1916), Northampton's output was £150,000, and that of the remainder of the county £175,000.[17]

The timing of conscription impacted greatly upon Northamptonshire's boot and shoe industry, therefore, and, from their inception, the county's local Tribunals were sensitive to this. At their first public sitting on 25 February 1916,[18] Northampton Borough Tribunal heard a 'large number' of re-grouping appeals by or on behalf of attested boot and shoe men, of which all but a few were treated favourably. A brief lull in Army production during March and April (at a time when the first tranche of the Russian order had been completed and the second had yet to begin) allowed firms to catch up with their surviving export orders; even so, Northampton Borough, Wellingborough Urban and Daventry Tribunals offered blanket three-month exemptions to all boot trade men at sittings during the latter month.[19] Their military representatives largely acquiesced to this policy (at Wellingborough, Herbert Dulley declared that he did not intend to appeal against any temporary exemptions offered to boot trade men owing to 'the special circumstances' of the Russian order), though it appears that Eastern Command allowed less flexibility outside the urban areas. Wellingborough Rural Tribunal's military representative, Major Stockdale, responding to tribunalist C. Dunckley's suggestion that they should offer blanket exemptions to their own boot and shoe applicants, stated that his orders were to continue to deal with each case on its merits. Almost alone among the Tribunals, Rushden, though having two manufacturers among their number, appear to have been largely unresponsive to the peculiar conditions of the trade (and, indeed, to those of other industries). In April 1916, they dismissed 11 applications for boot operatives made on the grounds of indispensability; some months later, they were singled out for praise by Northamptonshire's recruiting officer, Captain Wright, for having sent more men into the Army than some larger towns.[20]

In May 1916, against the looming implementation of the Military Service (No. 2) Act and its 'capture' of married men, the understanding between the boot and shoe industry and local recruiting authorities was formalized. Charles Mayes, secretary of Branch no. 1 of the Kettering Shoe Operatives Union, informed his fellow tribunalists at County Hall that an arrangement had been concluded whereby Northamptonshire's military representatives would not appeal any exemptions given to married boot operatives while the current phase of the Russian order was in hand (though he took the opportunity to remind them also that the next part of the order – Cossack boots – and the latest British Army requirement were backed up and would commence immediately after the present order was filled). The dispensation did not extend to single men. As yet, dilution pressures upon the industry were not such that larger employers were pressing indispensability cases regardless of age and marital status. Accordingly, the Tribunals were content at this time to see single, higher category boot and shoe men combed out as a *quid pro quo* for the retention of their married co-workers; Northampton Borough Tribunal, for example, asked factory owners to provide schedules of unmarried employees to facilitate their efficient release on a company-by-company basis.[21]

The arrangement was, as indicated, temporary, and its termination brought a further blow to prospects of maintaining production levels. At the beginning of July, a heavily revised list of reserved occupations in the industry was issued by the Local Government Board.[22] All married foremen were to be retained, as were single foremen over the age of 30. All clickers, sole-cutters and lasting and screwing machine operatives were exempted until 25 September 1916, after which the minimum qualifying age limits for exemptions in these occupations would be 41 for single men and 25 for those with families. All other classes of workmen previously reserved remained so until 25 September, but thereafter no married men under 25 would be retained (individually made indispensability applications aside), and reserved status for all non-specified single men would be removed. The only good news for the industry was a subsidiary concession, offered in the same month by Captain Wright, that temporary exemptions given to boot operatives working specifically on the Cossack order would not be challenged by the military representatives.[23]

Wright, who would conclude further industry-specific agreements with the Tribunals in the coming year, readily acknowledged the tension between the War Office's Recruiting Office (who wanted the men) and the Royal Army Clothing Department (who needed the boots). For their part, manufacturers were warning that current orders – Cossack, Italian and British – could not be completed by 25 September, the date at which the new reserved occupations list would come into force (removing, it was estimated, some 2400–2500 men from the trade in Northamptonshire).[24] Several urban Tribunals fully appreciated the potential disruptions this threatened. At the beginning of the month, Councillor Parker at Northampton Borough urged a definitive agreement between the War Office and the Local Government Board's Reserved Occupations Committee to allow war production to proceed unimpeded (and appeared before the latter in person to plead Northampton's case). Twice, on 1 and 18 September, Herbert Hankinson, the Tribunal's clerk, wrote to the Local Government Board to stress the industry's predicament. The Board's reply was uncompromising: no further concessions would be permitted. At precisely the same time, furthermore, the War Office was threatening heavy financial penalties for late delivery of orders they had placed with boot factories – orders, it should be noted, for which they had agreed no fixed price beforehand.[25]

Having by far the greatest concentration of the county's boot and shoe employees within their jurisdiction, it was natural that Northampton Borough Tribunal should have taken a lead in attempting to reconcile the conflicting demands of government departments. In that same month, they constituted a special sub-committee (of Gribble and the three boot factory-owning tribunalists) to examine the current manpower/production situation and make recommendations. Their first conclusion was that which Parker had been pressing upon the Local Government Board for several weeks: an arrangement covering the industry as a whole was a mandatory first step if manufacturers were to maintain sufficient resources to meet hastily placed War Office orders.[26]

Pressures were increasing upon both the industry and the Tribunals, however. In October, new War Office instructions to the military representatives required that they should appeal any exemptions offered to men below 30 years of age, regardless of circumstances. This had the potential to disrupt existing boot contracts even more severely than the revised reserved occupations list, and local opinion in Northamptonshire was unequivocally hostile. On 20 October, the *Mercury* fulminated against the 'malignancy' of the measure in an editorial: 'Where the War Office Fails':

> By the MSA [Military Service Act]... the Tribunals were set up to stand between the people and the military authorities ... This is a violation of the spirit, if not the letter, of the Military Service Act. It is a crooked method of attaining an end which should be approached straightforwardly.[27]

Northampton Borough Tribunal, equally outraged, despatched a resolution (drafted by Gribble) to the War Office and Local Government Board:

> That this Tribunal, whilst desiring to help the Government in every possible way to secure for the Army all men who can be spared from civil occupation, strongly protests against the invidious position in which members are placed as the result of recent instructions to the military representatives … The Tribunal would suggest that if the Government desire that all men of the ages mentioned must join the forces they should seek to amend the Act, and not by regulation force Tribunals into the unsatisfactory position of hearing cases and at the same time taking away their powers to give effect to their judgement.[28]

Amidst the growing political furore generated by the crisis of the French Armies in November, and with the first calls for compulsory National Service being made in Parliament, the 'suggestion' went unheeded. It is difficult to determine what further, unofficial representations (if any) were made to the Tribunals prior to 1 December, at which date the Local Government Board urged them not to offer exemptions on business or employment grounds to men below the age of 26.[29] A full week earlier, however, the first formal recommendations by Northampton Borough's boot and shoe sub-committee appeared to recognize the inevitability of a more stringent release policy. Having canvassed the town's manufacturers to assess remaining manpower levels, Gribble reported that, in federated factories, there were now a total of 1755 married and 460 single able-bodied men of military age (688 of the latter in all factories, federated and non-federated).[30] With the agreement of the Manufacturers' Association and NUBSO, the sub-committee proposed that all single men up to age 30 and married men up to age 25 should be released by 31 December. A second release, of single men aged 30–35 and married men aged 26–30, would follow by 31 March 1917. The proposal was submitted formally to Eastern Command, who promptly rejected it.

On 1 December, the sub-committee submitted a second proposal. The boot factories would now agree to release 750 men after 31 December (of those in classes A and B1, unmarried men up to age 31 and married men below age 26), and a further 750 after 17 February 1917 (all remaining single men of military age and married men up to age 30). To encourage a spirit of accommodation on the part of the military authorities, it was intimated by Councillor Parker – in the presence of newspaper reporters – that, if this new proposal were to be rejected, firms might choose to exercise their right to appeal each case individually, thus slowing the release process considerably.[31]

By the following week's sitting, Eastern Command had yet to respond to Northampton Borough's latest proposal. Consequently, Parker suggested to his fellow tribunalists that they should proceed to give blanket exemptions as planned, thereby setting 'an example of prompt action'. More aggressively, Gribble, anticipating official rejection of their proposal, urged that cases be considered on an individual basis, though he withdrew a motion to this effect when several manufacturers who were present stated that they would prefer the arrangement as outlined. As for men falling outside the remit of the second proposal, the Tribunal agreed to offer two months' exemption to C1 men, three months' to C2 and C3 men, and six months to the remainder. Northamptonshire's other urban Tribunals made their own arrangements with similar despatch. In the same week, Wellingborough agreed what appears to have been a partial version of Northampton's (second) proposal with Captain Wright, who accepted exemptions for certain men until the end of the month, and stated that he had been authorized to make a further bargain until 31 March 'in certain circumstances'. However, he emphasized also that almost all married and single men of military age would have to be released in the near future. Wellingborough Rural Tribunal accepted their local Advisory Committee's advice that married men over 30 should be exempted until 31 December, but that applications by younger married and all single men should be dismissed. At Daventry, 13 boot operatives received short exemptions and the town's manufacturers were urged to prepare lists so that the Tribunal could follow Northampton's example.[32]

On 19 and 20 December, Northampton Borough processed more than six hundred cases from Northampton's largest boot and shoe factories, on the basis of the 'second proposal'.[33] As had been requested beforehand, employers brought with them details of prewar and current output, with numbers and categories of men of military age remaining in their factories. Individual applications made for highly skilled, 'indispensable' men were adjourned, while all other Category A and B1 men, considered by schedule (that is, on a company-by-company basis, rather than individually), were given final exemptions to either 31 December or 17 February. At other local Tribunals, most of the industry's applications were similarly considered by schedule. Even Kettering Rural Tribunal processed 55 boot and shoe cases in a single sitting on 9 January, at which the indefatigable Captain Wright outlined a new arrangement he had agreed with Eastern Command and the Manufacturers' Association. He proposed that all remaining class A men, married or single, up to age 31 should go the Colours immediately, while older 'A' men and those in lower categories should be released after 31 March. The arrangement would cover all but mechanics. Of the latter, married men would go after 31 March, while single men's existing applications would be considered dismissed but their removal to the Colours would be postponed until adequate substitutes were found. Personal appeals were unaffected by the arrangement.[34]

Captain Wright's efforts were made redundant by events elsewhere, however. Weeks earlier, Cabinet had committed to placing a further 940,000 men in uniform to meet the Army's anticipated needs for 1917.[35] On 18 December, even as Northampton Borough began the implementation of their second proposal, the War Office stated that all Category A and B1 boot and shoe operatives below the age of 31 could – and should – be spared by the industry. Receiving word of this at their 2 January 1917 sitting, the Tribunal suspended consideration of all industry cases and sent a deputation to Whitehall to clarify their understanding of government's intentions.[36] The detail of what they heard was not reported, but its tenor could not have been encouraging. On 15 January, the Local Government Board issued Circular R.115, containing revised regulations specifically regarding the boot and shoe trade – a belated answer, in effect, to the 'second proposal'. Its preamble stated unequivocally that no A or B1 man need be retained in the production of Army boots, and that foremen so classed below the age of 31 (if single) or 27 (married) were no longer to be considered as falling within a certified occupation. For all other boot and shoe workmen in these classes and age groups, no one was to be considered as being in certified employment after 1 February 1917, though by concession each employer would be allowed to retain up to 5 per cent of his military-aged workforce until the end of that month. The instructions concluded:

> Consequent upon this reconsideration of the position of the trade by the Reserved Occupations Committee, any local arrangements are brought to an end, and exemptions are immediately to be brought into correspondence with the list of certified occupations. This is of the greatest importance since complaints have been received that the boot trade is receiving different treatment in different areas.

The unyielding provisions of R.115 and its companion circular R.114 (which emphasized that no man in Category A or B1 under the age of 31 should be exempted from military service beyond the end of January 1917), were the clearest indication to date that the Tribunals, despite constant reassurance by the Local Government Board as to their powers of discretion, were considered to be balancing their judgements too far in favour of the boot and shoe industry.[37] While that appreciation was not everywhere as strong as at the War Office, the new instructions explicitly invalidated the 'arrangements' which Captain Wright and other local military representatives had painstakingly concluded with Tribunals and the industry. They also placed an onus upon the Tribunals to justify future decisions that kept any higher category boot and shoe operatives out of the Army.

The implications of the new instructions were appreciated immediately by Northampton's bootmakers, who deployed their most effective weapon

– their representatives on the Tribunals. On 19 January, as Northampton Borough continued to implement their second proposal unilaterally, A.E. Tebbutt warned his fellow tribunalists that half of the town's factories would close if they applied the letter of the new instructions. The following week, A.E. Marlow, president of the Northamptonshire Boot and Shoe Manufacturers' Association, appeared before the same Tribunal to claim that some two to three thousand women and girls employed in closing-rooms (who were dependent upon the machinists' output) would be thrown out of work for the sake of the Army getting three to four hundred men a little earlier.[38] The same point was not lost on some sections of government, and internal divisions increased markedly. Even as the War Office demanded the release of all A and B1 men, their Army Contracts Department were placing an urgent order for 1.25 million pairs of boots, to be delivered by 31 March. The latter, and the Ministry of Munitions, wrote separately to boot manufacturers, urging them to retain their skilled workers notwithstanding the new instructions, and went so far as to provide a draft letter to be sent to the recruiting officer, specifically to argue the case for men decertified by the Reserved Occupations Committee. Tebbutt and his fellow factory owner Councillor Lewis promptly presented their own copies of this document at Northampton Borough's next sitting to buttress the production argument.

This departmental schism in government passed responsibility for managing 'policy' straight back to the Tribunals, as the *Mercury*, in an editorial of 19 January, noted at length:

> Is there any need to point the moral? The failure of Government Departments to agree about their requirements adds to the power and authority of the Tribunals. They are under obligation to decide on the cases brought before them after consideration of all the facts – the need for soldiers, the need for equipment, the essential services for the civilian population, and exceptional personal conditions. In brief, they have to decide between the claims of the Army and of industry.[39]

To date, 23 factories in Northampton had been dealt with under Borough Tribunal's 'second proposal': 2340 men had been processed, of whom 1277 were in classes A and B1. Of the latter, 408 had been offered certificates to 17 February, 409 to 28 February (in each case with finality attached) and 337 'indispensables' to 31 March (open). Given the confusion of directives currently emanating from Whitehall, Gribble suggested at the Tribunal's 16 January sitting that the finality imposed upon the shorter certificates should be withdrawn as a precautionary measure, and that longer exemptions should be offered to those whom the manufacturers could claim to be indispensable. This was agreed, as was the need for a further review of the industry's remaining manpower.[40]

Meanwhile, the county's military representatives were mobilized by the War Office to ensure that the provisions of R.115 were put into effect. On 2 February, Geldart informed Northampton Borough that Eastern Command were insisting that *all* A and B1 men of military age should be released by the end of February. Accordingly, he would be obliged to appeal any exemptions for men in these categories, regardless of exceptional circumstances. James Gribble, furious at this revelation, suggested that the Tribunal should have exempted 'the lot', as the military seemed willing to appeal whatever decisions they made. Councillor Parker pressed Geldart regarding the mooted War Office concession that 5 per cent of 'special' men might be retained temporarily, but the military representative remained adamant: his latest instructions allowed for no exceptions other than that regarding older foremen. At Kettering Urban Tribunal, three days later, their own military representative, J.A. Gotch, warned that he was obliged to appeal all the boot and shoe exemptions – excepting those for mechanics – previously agreed under the arrangement with Captain Wright (that is, B1 men under the age of 31 whose certificates had been extended from 31 December 1916 to the following 31 March).[41]

Taking the lead once more, Northampton Borough Tribunal reacted strongly to the Recruiting Department's obduracy. At their next sitting, in addition to re-opening the 408 exemptions to 17 February, they reviewed and withdrew finality from a further 527 (28 February) certificates. Geldart, as his instructions directed, lodged appeals against every one of them. In turn, the Tribunal placed a forthright justification of their decisions (individually signed by Councillor Parker) on each appeals form R.43 certified that day:

Prior to the hearing of the applications, a visit of inspection was made by the members of the Tribunal to several of the factories of the town, to see for themselves the various machines in working [*sic*].

Having regard to the present output of the factory, both for army and export trade, the Tribunal are satisfied that it is necessary, to maintain the minimum requirements for army and export work, that the men referred to in the schedules annexed, should be retained for the periods mentioned. The Tribunal are also satisfied that the men to whom open exemption to 31st March next has been granted, are, for the time being all engaged on absolutely essential operations.

Furthermore they are convinced that it is imperative that the men referred to should be retained until substitutes can be trained – a process that will take time – otherwise a very considerable number of female operatives (who are dependent upon the skilled labour) will be thrown out of paid employment.[42]

To date, Northamptonshire's Appeals Tribunal had not been troubled unduly by the boot and shoe trade. Arrangements concluded independently by local Tribunals had slowed the release of men and forestalled any mass appeals by employers. Boot operatives had appealed on their own behalf to County Hall on personal or domestic grounds, and a number of smaller manufacturers had attempted to retain individual employees whose departure would have prevented the completion of existing orders. However, any survey of the Tribunal's business for 1916 alone would not have concluded that the trade was in any sense a predominant one in the county.[43] The impact of R.115 was to redress any such misunderstanding. On 17 January, appeals tribunalists, having received their copy of the circular, and anticipating an imminent glut of industry appeals, voted to invite A.E. Marlow to join the Tribunal. At their sitting of 2 February (at which they heard and explicitly rejected Geldart's characterization of R.115 as a necessary means of getting the most men into the Army in the least possible time), it was agreed that their new colleague, with NUBSO tribunalists Charles Mayes and Samuel Thompson, should form a sub-committee to formulate a boot and shoe policy while the remainder visited boot factories to familiarize themselves with processes and issues.[44]

It soon became apparent that Geldart – or rather, the Recruiting Department – had made a tactical error in challenging Northampton Borough's decision to re-open the February certificates. Submitted too late to be heard before the exemptions' earliest expiry dates (the Appeals Tribunal gave warning on 2 February that their workload would not allow any boot and shoe appeals to be heard until the end of the month), the military representative's appeals had the effect of keeping certificate-expired men out of the Army until their cases could be heard. Belatedly, he realised this and attempted to withdraw them, but the Appeals Tribunal reminded him that one party to an appeal could not withdraw it without the other's consent. Predictably, not a single employer obliged him.[45]

This first large tranche of boot and shoe appeals clashed with an equally substantial submission from agricultural workers, whose release was being sought as part of the same recruitment drive that had generated circular R.115.[46] The latter were already scheduled to be heard at sittings on 9 and 12 February. Postponement of the boot and shoe cases was unavoidable, therefore, but the implication that the Tribunal were refusing to be hurried by the military's sense of urgency sent a useful signal to the new administration at Whitehall, where some banging of heads appears to have taken place. At the Tribunal's 23 February sitting, Captain Cook read out a letter from the War Office, indicating that its sub-departments were approaching a degree of consensus, if only on principle. Helpfully, it noted what was already palpably apparent to every Tribunal in Northamptonshire: that 'men were urgently required for the Army, but it was equally necessary that the Army should be adequately equipped'.[47] The letter did not, however, offer any guidance upon how these antagonistic objectives might be achieved.

The following day, Owen Parker, President of the Incorporated Associations of Boot and Shoe Manufacturers of Great Britain and Ireland (and also, from 30 April 1917, an appeals tribunalist), wrote to S.G. Stopford-Sackville, warning of the effects of any further mass removal of A and B1 men upon boot production, and predicting that the Tribunal would be busy for months with appeals from up to 250 local manufacturers. To forestall this, he offered to form a committee comprising a number of local boot factory owners, who would identify some 400 top-category men, predominantly over 35 years of age, who should be regarded as absolutely indispensable to the industry. The proposal was accepted.[48]

On 1 March, the Appeals Tribunal heard their first scheduled boot and shoe cases from firms in Northampton. Captain Cook reminded them that the March exemptions had been appealed as per instructions, but added that he and Geldart were now authorized to consider a reasonable compromise. The first batch of cases comprised 25 employees of Arnold Brothers and Co., represented by solicitor H.W. Williams.[49] The latter told the Tribunal that he could not consent to dismissal of the 28 February certificates previously appealed by Geldart (ten men, all over 31 years of age), as the company was busy with a new Italian Army order and their removal would reduce production to only 2700 pairs per week.[50] Geldart conceded that he would not appeal any new certificates to 31 March, provided that finality was imposed thereupon. The Tribunal's decision in all cases was 15 April, final.

Following Arnold Brothers, cases stated by a further 13 companies were considered – a total of 334 appeals (all made by Geldart).[51] By consent, the 28 February appeals were dismissed, but so too were Geldart's efforts to challenge all but a handful of the new certificates. Captain Cook, unhappy with the 15 April exemptions, requested leave to appeal to Central Tribunal. When asked the point of legality upon which he intended to proceed, he admitted haplessly that there was none: he had been instructed to challenge any certificate expiring beyond 31 March. The application was refused, and, in concluding, the Appeals Tribunal made a point of declaring their 'full confidence' in Northampton Borough's recent strategy.[52]

Having been placed on the back foot in allowing its Army Contracts Department a dissenting voice, the War Office offered no further guidance in the following weeks. In that partial vacuum, the county's Boot and Shoe Manufacturers' Association, with the agreement of NUBSO, drew up an offer regarding the release of men that their representative, J.C. Wilson, presented to local Tribunals during May. The Association's 'indispensables' committee, chaired by Owen Parker, had been through operatives' lists supplied by its members, and recommended that men in lower medical categories, together with foremen and mechanics, should be given open certificates conditional upon their remaining in their present occupations. Of other employees, those over 35 years of age should have a further, temporary period of exemption, while two-thirds of younger men (both single and married) should be released immediately. It was stressed that the proposal was irreducible, in that any incremental dilution would result in 'complete disorganization' of boot production in the county.[53]

In the intervening weeks, local military representatives had received no new instructions from the War Office, and predictabably, their response to this initiative was uniformly negative. At Wellingborough Urban Tribunal on 4 May, Herbert Dulley heard Wilson's outline of the proposal but warned that he was obliged still to appeal any certificates offered to Category B1 men. Nevertheless, the Tribunal, responsive to the Association's offer, dealt with almost all of the town's outstanding boot and shoe applications that afternoon, giving conditional exemption to 69 men below class B1 and certificates to the end of June to several hundred others. Dulley entered appeals against all B1 exemptions. At Wellingborough Urban Tribunal in the following week, Lieutenant Newton, deputizing for Major Stockdale, listened to Wilson's offer and then declared blandly that he did not know what his position should be. The Tribunal proceeded on the basis of the Association's proposal.[54]

Given the confusion as to whether, or how far, the War Office had retreated from its previously unyielding enforcement of R.115, several appeals tribunalists travelled to London on 18 June to meet with representatives of the Ministry's Recruiting and Army Contracts Departments, and of the Local Government Board. The guidance they received was no more useful than upon previous occasions. It was emphasized once more that the Tribunals had 'complete discretion', but also that all A and B1 men under the ages of 41 (single men) or 35 (married) had to be released unless their indispensability could be demonstrated. It was stated, furthermore, that, although government contracts undertaken by the industry had to be filled as a matter of urgency, all remaining non-indispensable men in the target categories should be released within the next few weeks.

Returning to Northampton, the tribunalists drafted a statement that conceded the official directions almost to the letter:

> Nothing will be allowed to interfere with the full discretion of the Tribunal in individual cases, but in the absence of special reasons the Tribunal consider that the time has come when unmarried men under 41, and married men under 35, who have been passed A or B1, should go into the Army unless occupying positions indispensable to the carrying on of necessary business.
>
> With regard to married men between 35 and 41, Class A or B1 who are not so indispensable, it seems reasonable that they should go in the next few

weeks, perhaps in stages corresponding to age. Men claimed as indispensable will be subject to particular investigation, and obviously those firms mainly employed in Government work are entitled to special consideration as compared with those chiefly engaged in private trade.

At their next sitting (22 June), the Appeals Tribunal agreed to reconstitute their boot and shoe sub-committee (with their newest colleague, Owen Parker), to consider claims on the grounds of indispensability, and asked whether the employers' representatives present would abide by their recommendations. J.C. Wilson confirmed that Northamptonshire manufacturers were amenable 'so far as consistent with not crippling any individual factory', and solicitors representing non-federated firms agreed to follow his lead. It was decided that appeals respecting those men the employers were prepared to release should be dismissed by consent, while some fifteen hundred further military appeals were adjourned for four days, pending the sub-committee's report.[55]

This extremely tight schedule was met, but the committee's findings exposed the limits of consensus. Sir Ryland Adkins, chairing the 26 June sitting with more than a hundred boot and shoe employers present, expressed considerable surprise that the latter were now providing lists implying that up to half of their remaining A and B1 were indispensable. Previously, the proportion had been stated at closer to a third, and it was on this basis that the Tribunal had approached various government departments to secure an agreement. Adkins considered that the change of heart reflected badly upon the industry, and, more pertinently, that the War Office would be neither pleased nor responsive. The manufacturers were invited to retire, consider their position and submit new, more realistic lists. The Tribunal, in turn, proposed to offer six months' certificates to the truly indispensable men, thus allowing both employers and unions to allocate their resources ahead of future orders.

Responding to Adkins, Wilson defended the manufacturers' position. They had never intended, he claimed, that the two-thirds proportion of released men should include men over 35, nor any foreman or mechanic. Had they known the Tribunal assumed otherwise, they would have increased the minimum estimate of men necessary to be retained in coming to their (March) calculation. Notwithstanding this, Adkins remained adamant that the manufacturers were setting unrealistic targets, though he offered the possibility that 'really special' cases might be considered individually outside of the agreed one-third blanket exemption, while Owen Parker (who, as midwife to the manufacturers' initiative, must have been considerably embarrassed by its outcome) warned Wilson that, if the War Office rejected the arrangement, many indispensable men might go to the Colours in any case.[56]

The employers had little choice but to accept the arrangement, and they revised their lists accordingly. In the following three weeks, the Tribunal dealt with cases from more than two hundred Northamptonshire factories, applying their one-third 'indispensable' proportion on the basis of recommendations from the sub-committee (who, in the meantime, attempted to compile a list of skilled clickers of above military age to replace the released men).[57] Almost without exception, those exempted received six months' certificates, while men to be released were offered short-term exemptions to a maximum of one month, the military being instructed not to take them until fourteen days following the expiration thereof. A few manufacturers pleaded exceptional circumstances, notwithstanding the Tribunal's determination to proceed consistently. Messrs S. Collier Ltd asked to be treated 'more liberally' as they had appealed for no man under the age of 35, and had lost more than a hundred employees to date. The plea brought extended exemptions for just two men: a sorter and a consolidated lasting machine operator. Daventry Tribunal reported that its own sub-committee's examination of the workforce of Messrs Rodhouse and Sons Ltd had found that only one of their remaining workforce – a clicker, Harry Adams – could be spared, as every machine in the boot-making process was operated in each case by a sole operative, one of whom was the owner himself. In the case of Rodhouse, the Appeals Tribunal concurred: Adams was offered one month's exemption, while three of his colleagues received six months' (open) certificates.[58]

In total, almost six hundred cases were heard on 6 and 20 July 1917.[59] The speed and efficiency with which the Tribunal's arrangement with the War Office was put into effect during these days (albeit some six months after the circulation of R.115) may have led the former to believe that their boot and shoe problem had been solved – an impression reinforced, perhaps, by the gentle reception afforded to James Gribble by the National Service Department on 4 July, during a visit to discuss further combing out in the industry.[60] If so, disillusionment came promptly. Even as the Appeals Tribunal cleared its backlog of industry cases, new instructions from the Recruiting Department brought clashes elsewhere. At Northampton Borough on 20 July, Geldart, when pressed by Parker to confirm that he would not automatically appeal all cases in certain classes, admitted that he had now been ordered to challenge exemptions given to any C1 man not in work of national importance. Again, it was Gribble who led the Tribunal's response to this latest example of bad faith. If that were to be the case, he suggested, they might as well send every applicant straight across the road to County Hall. For once, his colleagues concurred unreservedly: in the session that followed, a large number of boot and shoe employees, including B1 men, were given exemptions of one to four months. All certificates were appealed by Geldart.

At Daventry the same day, Councillor Edgar asked his Tribunal's military representative, W. Murland, what the point of their sitting might be if the latter was going to appeal every decision they made. Abashed, Murland insisted he was only following orders, though he reminded them also that, to date, the boot and shoe industry had been unique in that all employees under Grade B1 had enjoyed exemption. The chairman sympathized with Murland's dilemma, but observed that his Tribunal were being treated like 'absolute nonentities', and that, speaking for himself, he should resign if it continued. Wellingborough Rural tribunalists regarded themselves as similarly superfluous; at their sitting a day earlier, they had peremptorily dismissed all employer applications, referring them instead to the Appeals Tribunal for consideration. The reaction of (the usually rigorous) Rushden Tribunal was even more dramatic: informed by their military representative that he would appeal exemptions given to any class A or B1 men in whatever circumstances (as directed by the recruiting officer), they promptly declared themselves to be on strike.[61] The Appeals Tribunal were equally determined to draw a line in the sand against the Army Council's new instructions. On 3 August, they gave exemptions until 26 December to almost all boot and shoe workers appealed that day (among whom were several class A men) on the grounds of indispensability, notwithstanding Captain Cook's plaintive observation that some were not even engaged upon Army contract work.[62]

Having seen the implementation of much of what R.115 was intended to achieve, the Army Council appears to have been testing new waters with this initiative. The vigorous response of the Tribunals resulted in a swift and somewhat craven withdrawal. The recruiting officer hurriedly instructed local military representatives that they were not obliged to appeal exemptions where they themselves concurred with the Tribunals' decisions. On that basis, Rushden graciously agreed to recommence their sittings.[63] Elsewhere, having been released from their straitjacket, military representatives ended the blanket appeals of boot and shoe exemptions and resorted instead to piecemeal challenges whenever individual applications were made on behalf of A and B1 men (a notable exception being the military appeal against exemptions offered by Kettering Urban Tribunal to 20 high-graded operatives employed by the Cooperative Clothing Company, all of which the Appeals Tribunal brusquely dismissed).[64] The atmosphere thereafter was further calmed by a three-week suspension of many Tribunals' business for the summer holidays, and by the developing distraction of Mayor Stanley's ordeal at Daventry.[65]

Only weeks later, however, the military's attention turned once more to the remaining boot and shoe workforce. At the Appeals Tribunal on

7 September, H.W. Williams, representing several firms, suggested that 23 military appeals to be heard that day should be dismissed, pending the military representative's anticipated response to any renewed certificates offered to A and B1 men. Geldart, present at the sitting, agreed to this, following which both he and Williams made conciliatory statements about the other's difficulties. Nevertheless, Eastern Command was already putting pressure upon its representatives to be unyielding. At the next major consideration of boot and shoe cases at Northampton Borough (110 applications on 17 September), Geldart warned that he must appeal any exemptions offered to A and B1 men as per his instructions, rather than consider the relative indispensability of each.

The Tribunal retired to discuss their response *in camera*, following which they issued a resolution suspending consideration of all boot and shoe cases:

> That so long as the military representative has instructions to appeal in the cases of all men in the boot and shoe trade in the Categories A and B1, irrespective of the merits of each case, it is useless for the Tribunal to consider and give decisions in such cases ... That the Tribunal therefore adjourns consideration of all boot and shoe cases in order to ascertain whether the War Office and the Local Government Board confirm such instructions.[66]

The following day, Councillor Parker travelled to London to meet with representatives of these departments, and reported back to his Tribunal at their next sitting. What he had been told explicitly contradicted the recent instructions to the military representatives. Each boot and shoe case, apparently, was to be considered on its merits, and Geldart was entitled to appeal only those decisions he thought incorrect. With some apparent satisfaction, Parker noted that he and his colleagues were able finally to take the course they had long urged upon the Local Government Board.[67] On 4 October, they made recommendations to the Appeals Tribunal regarding a batch of 458 renewed applications from 14 firms. The latter accepted these *nem con*: all men below B1 and C1 were given certificates to 26 December (open), while cases involving classes A, B1 and C1 men were considered upon their individual merits.[68]

However, at the moment at which Northamptonshire Tribunals managed to wrest the initiative from the War Office's Recruiting Department, their role as surrogate manpower policy-makers effectively ended. The Board's forthright response to Parker's approach (so different from that given to the Appeals Tribunalists in the previous June) signalled government's wider determination to implement a co-ordinated manpower strategy. With responsibility for policy lying solely with the newly constituted National Service Ministry under Sir Auckland Geddes, the maintenance of viable resources in strategically important sectors was to constitute a priority rather than an afterthought.

Geddes's first task was to assess those resources. At the end of the month he wrote to all Appeals Tribunals, requiring that employers in non-protected industries should submit new applications for men whose exemptions were due for renewal.[69] At Northamptonshire County Hall on 27 November, H.W. Williams, again representing several boot and shoe manufacturers, agreed to their making such applications immediately. Additionally, he suggested that the duties of men applied for should be identified at departmental level, so that each company's entire workforce – male and female – could be scrutinized in relation to its output. In the meantime, all boot and shoe appellants considered at that sitting (92 cases from 38 firms) were given exemptions – the majority to 31 December – so that the position of the employers as a whole could be considered at that time.[70]

The figures provided by manufacturers in early December are no longer extant, but almost certainly they made for salutary reading. In absolute terms, workload had fallen off during the previous month as several Army contracts concluded.[71] Conversely, dilution of the workforce appears to have reached a critical level, with any remaining A or B1 men being, almost by definition, indispensable to production. Already, the Tribunal had received some indication of manpower losses from the tenor of individual applications made by employers. On 5 November, Crockett and Jones, appealing for a single employee, stated that over six hundred of their men had been called up. Three weeks later, W.E. and J. Pebody, who had lodged appeals for four men, claimed to have lost 100 of their 120–strong prewar workforce to the Army (though substitutes and women had partially made up the shortfall). The problem was not merely one of emptied workbenches. Increasingly, the incremental loss of highly skilled men from the industry – particularly machinists – had a disproportionate impact upon the value of those remaining. Mountain and Daniels Co. Ltd, for example, appealing for two class A men (both machinists), claimed that their work supplied that of 58 others.[72]

The new survey provided an industry-wide perspective, and the Appeals Tribunal were unequivocally sensitive to its revelations. Between 12 and 21 December, 354 appeals from many of Northamptonshire's major boot and shoe manufacturers were processed. The shortest exemption offered or confirmed was to 30 April 1918, with most men obtaining a further three months thereafter. Only three operatives' appeals were rejected.[73] Many of those receiving certificates were rated fit for general service; of 25 men from Lewis and Co, for example, five were (new) Grade II men, the remainder Grade I: all received exemptions to 31 July 1918. Similarly, of

25 men successfully appealed for by Manfield and Co, all except one were Grade I. In almost every case, exemption came with the obligation to join the VTC.[74]

All remaining boot and shoe appeals were to have been heard on 14 January 1918 (the Appeals Tribunal's first post-Christmas sitting took place on 8 January), but a further postponement was agreed to allow representatives of Northampton Borough and Appeals Tribunals to meet to discuss a co-ordinated policy for the future. The precise nature of those discussions, and their agreed outcome, was not committed to record; however, the subsequent history of the boot and shoe trade's dealings with the Tribunals suggests that a broad consensus prevailed throughout the county. This was further assisted by government's new willingness to allow them the expert view of local conditions. In February, Sir Ryland Adkins went to London for discussions with Sir Ioan Gwilym Gibbon at the Local Government Board. Upon his return, he reported that Gibbon's only qualification regarding the Tribunal's recommendations – and that no more than implied – had been to express a hope that future exemptions offered to men in classes A, B1 and C1 should continue to carry the VTC requirement. A month later, A.E. Marlow presented the sub-committee's recommendations, which were accepted by the Tribunal in their entirety. All men aged 33 and over, of whatever medical grade, would be exempted until 31 July, to bring them in line with certificates offered in the previous November. Cases involving Grades I and II men below that age were to be heard on their individual merits.[75] On 10 April, the Appeals Tribunal processed their outstanding boot and shoe cases accordingly. Several hundred men from 33 firms were considered: 20 were given open or final exemptions of one to three months, the remainder to 31 July (all open, but carrying a requirement to drill with the VTC).[76] No leave to appeal was made by Captain Cook.

Almost every boot and shoe worker of military age in Grades I, II and III had now been placed into a synchronized schedule of exemption. All except those appealed for individually as indispensable men could expect their certificates to expire and be reconsidered at the same time, allowing a county wide reassessment of resources against the needs of production, rather than the piecemeal struggle against dilution that had characterized the Tribunals' work to date. There was, however, to be one further obstacle – or, rather, challenge – to the efficient disposal of remaining manpower resources within the industry: the 'clean-cut' provision of 20 April 1918, cancelling exemptions held by all men below the age of 23.[77]

The (albeit short-term) reversion to a priority recruitment policy overturned the fragile consensus of the previous months at Tribunal sittings. In Northamptonshire, National Service representatives were ordered to demand the removal of any conditional exemptions previously given to boot and shoe men (to be replaced with fixed-term certificates). At Wellingborough Urban Tribunal on 28 May, men were lined up in the hallway outside the Town Council chamber and processed one by one, having their conditional certificates cancelled and replaced by new exemptions for up to six months. Two weeks later, Herbert Hankinson told his own Tribunal that he had received a Certification Order (No. 53) from the National Service Ministry which removed all certificates from Grade I men in certain sections of the boot and shoe trade. Councillor Parker expressed his opinion that their position had been rendered 'impossible', and predicted severe dislocation of the industry.[78]

Rumours of the proposed de-certification spread rapidly in the urban areas. It was noted that clause 6 of the Certification Order proposed that older men in lower grades might also, in certain circumstances, be de-certified. On 25 June, approximately nine hundred boot and shoe workers in Northampton downed tools and marched to the Trade Hall in Overstone Road, where a resolution was passed condemning any form of industrial conscription. Eventually, the men dispersed, having agreed to reassemble that evening. In the meantime, the Northampton Arbitration Board convened hurriedly, noted the widespread unrest and passed its own resolution, to be dispatched to the War Office and the Ministries of National Service and Labour, warning of 'considerable unrest' locally, and noting for the record that Northampton Town alone had lost 62 per cent of its prewar boot and shoe workforce to the Army.[79] It also urged that representatives of the union and industry should be consulted before any de-certification took place, and that the regional director of recruiting should defer the calling-up of men until a delegation had visited Whitehall. Mollified by the resolution, the boot and shoe workers agreed at their evening meeting to return to work the next morning.[80]

In fact, government was already retreating from its 'manpower crisis' perspective of the previous weeks. While the boot and shoe trade had been defending its corner tenaciously, large-scale quota-releases of men from previously protected vital war industries – including munitions – had been under way. However, on 19 July, the War Cabinet concluded that the strain on industry was becoming unsustainable, and instructed Geddes to adjudicate demands for further enlistments.[81]

Ironically, the most significant effect of the 'clean-cut' upon the boot and shoe industry was to make clear just how deeply manpower cuts had proceeded to date. Contradicting Parker's prediction of severe dislocation, one (unnamed) local manufacturer suggested that the proclamation would have only a limited effect upon the trade, as there were no more than two hundred Grade I operatives remaining in the county.[82] NUBSO figures appear to support this: no significant rise in enlistments occurred at a time

when other important industries were losing men heavily.[83] It seems that
the Tribunals played their part in this achievement. Geddes complained
in Cabinet that the struggle to increase recruiting had been undertaken
in an atmosphere of 'almost open resistance to the administration of the
Military Service Acts'.[84] This was hardly hyperbole: when next considering
their boot and shoe cases, Northamptonshire's Tribunals were to express
themselves unequivocally against any further combing-out.

The majority of the many certificates offered in December 1917 and April
1918 were due for renewal at the end of July. At the same time, new applications were made in respect of older men brought into military age by the
latest Military Service Act. In all, original or renewed exemption forms for
561 men were submitted by the county's manufacturers during mid-July.
All new applications made to local Tribunals were dismissed and passed
on to the Appeals Tribunal without being considered individually.[85] With
deliberate tardiness, the latter scheduled the appeals to be heard no sooner
than 20 September.[86] The chairman that day, Sir Ryland Adkins, began by
noting new National Service Ministry regulations, due to come into force
five days later, which substantially restored the certified occupations list of
January 1918 and placed the onus upon National Service representatives
to show why a man falling within the list should not have exemption as
of right. He proposed that the Tribunal should proceed as if the regulations were already in force, and that, unless Captain Cook showed good
reason otherwise, all men should be given a further six months' exemption,
with the VTC requirement to apply to those falling within Grades I and
II. The 561 listed cases were then considered by schedule, and only three
operatives' appeals were dismissed (the cause is not stated, but non-attendance at VTC drills was the most likely transgression). Approximately two
dozen more received exemptions until the end of December 1918, while the
remainder were offered certificates until 20 March 1919.[87] Succinctly, the
Appeals Tribunal had declared the remaining military-aged workforce of
the county's boot and shoe trade off-limits to the Recruiting Department.
Captain Cook made no objection.

The record of the Tribunals' dealings with the boot and shoe trade effectively ended here. It was one that most clearly revealed the extent of local
pressures upon their deliberations, but it also reflected a wider, more
nuanced appreciation: that the lack of a manpower policy could not be
allowed to impede this particular element of vital war production. There can
be little doubt that the presence upon the Tribunals of so many members
of the industry, whether from management or the unions, weighted the
national versus local debate in favour of the latter, or at least provided
a powerful counter-pressure to that exerted by the military representa-

tives. Northampton Borough Tribunal in particular, which supervised by far the most substantial reviews of the industry's capacity to absorb further dilution, repeatedly used their discretion to act as a brake upon the recruiting officer's efforts. Similarly, the Appeals Tribunal, though proceeding with the 'bigger picture' more clearly in mind, also interpreted its instructions in a manner that attempted to ameliorate the worst effects of successive calls upon manpower. To that extent, it might be assumed that localist preoccupations, with regard to this industry at least, nuanced the Tribunals' decisions.

Yet were these just local concerns? Pressure from the War Office regarding the enlistment of men was constant. Equally and contrarily, however, pressure from its Army Contracts Department regarding the timely fulfilment of contracts, and threats of significant financial penalties for default, gave to the Tribunals a powerful incentive to see the needs of the country and of the local economy as synonymous. Men could be had from every industry, boots from just one; the reconciling mechanism, apparently, was substitution, strongly urged by government upon the boot and shoe industry as elsewhere. Yet substitution had a very limited relevance to such a highly skilled process as boot manufacturing. Replacement workers had to come from within – that is, from a pool of equally skilled, older men – but this was a resource whose scarcity the manufacturers would stress to the Tribunals at every opportunity. The only viable alternative – to train substitutes from scratch – required existing workers to be employed side-by-side with their successors, a lengthy process that was as unsatisfactory to the manufacturers as it was to the military representatives.

Despite these demonstrable facts, the boot and shoe trade remained an attractive hunting ground for Eastern Command. Like the agricultural sector, it employed an unusually high percentage of men whom the Army Medical Board categorized as A and B1 men. Therein, however, lay another obstacle to substitution. Several key occupations in the production process, and 'rough stuff' work in particular, could be undertaken only by fit males whose work, as has be seen, supported that of many female operatives further down the production line. Clearly, there was no resistance *per se* to the employment of women in boot factories. The 1911 census had indicated that almost six thousand Northamptonshire females were employed in the industry and its associated trades, and, even before the advent of conscription, the unions and boot and shoe management had agreed the necessity of widespread female substitution (provided that the jobs of those enlisting should be preserved for their eventual return). Women clickers – a species almost unknown before the commencement of the war – were appearing in some numbers prior to 1916.[88]

However, there were limits to what women could do effectively. Though

NUBSO reports predictably overstated the physical inadequacies of female labour, its introduction into what, traditionally, had been considered 'men's' departments appears to have impacted unfavourably upon productivity. A broad range of tasks – pullover-machine work, bed-lasting, upper channel-closing, sole-moulding, welt-sewing, heel-attaching, heel-paring, edge-setting, padding black work, consolidated-lasting, pounding-up, slip solid block-lasting, screwing, rough-rounding, heel-compressing, edge-trimming and auto-setting – required a degree of strength that could not be assumed of the average female physique.[89] Statistical evidence suggests, furthermore, that local women themselves did not regard the work as attractive, notwithstanding the relatively high wages offered by the industry. In absolute terms, the number of unionized females employed in Northampton factories rose from 3481 in January 1916 to 4208 in mid-1918, but during the same period 2069 of the town's unionized male boot and shoe workers went to the Colours. For Kettering and Wellingborough respectively, female employment in the boot factories rose by 469 and 202 during the period, while corresponding male losses were 907 and 413.[90] Clearly, substitution did not come close to compensating for the loss of men to the Army.

For Tribunals considering boot and shoe cases, the balance between serving the Army and the local community was not, therefore, the simple either/or equation that was often applicable elsewhere. The industry could not be allowed to sink or swim, and no tribunalist questioned the necessity of maintaining a level of production far surpassing that of the prewar years. Yet it would be simplistic to assume from this that boot and shoe workers were shown atypical 'leniency' by the Tribunals. The principle of fairness – of an equality of sacrifice – was seen as being as applicable to them as to others, and, certainly, no complaints were reported of the industry escaping the VTC obligation (indeed, most of Second Battalion comprised boot and shoe men), or of being a haven for 'shirking' young men – as were, for example, the munitions and agricultural industries and the Wolverton rail engineering works.[91] Upon numerous occasions, a manufacturer would plead the indispensability of a young, single man to his operations, only to be told that it was simply inequitable for him to remain out of the Army. Indeed, claims of indispensability were scrutinized very carefully throughout the life of the Tribunals, and in that respect the expertise of boot and shoe tribunalists might be considered disadvantageous to the applicant. It is notable that upon the one occasion when the manufacturers – sensing perhaps that they enjoyed a brief initiative – chose collectively to exaggerate the number of their 'indispensables', they were brought up sharply by the Appeals Tribunal and lectured sternly by their own Association President, Owen Parker.[92]

The British and Allied armies suffered no 'boot-crisis' during the war. The former alone ordered and received 45,351,488 pairs between 4 August 1914 and 31 January 1919, a large proportion of which were made in Northamptonshire.[93] Consequently, it might be assumed either that the industry exaggerated its difficulties in order to slow dilution of the workforce or that, broadly, the Tribunals managed to balance the needs of production against those of the Army. However, boot and shoe cases presented a unique challenge. No other industry came close to representing a yardstick by which local feeling in Northamptonshire measured its contribution (or loss) to the war effort, and no other sector of the local economy relied so heavily upon the Tribunals to ameliorate the vagaries of governmental manpower 'policy'. As will be observed in the next chapter, the only other industry to be considered in any collective sense in Northamptonshire – agriculture – had its case stated forcibly by representatives from the Board of Agriculture, who attended sittings specifically to counter the efforts of the War Office and its military representatives. It might be argued that those boot and shoe manufacturers and trades unionists who sat upon the Tribunals fulfilled the same role for their own industry. That they ensured their concerns were fully aired cannot be doubted; nevertheless, the large-scale releases of men they oversaw in November 1916 and again in July 1917 make any accusation of favouritism difficult to sustain. Indeed, the President of NUBSO, T.F. Richards, commenting in February 1917 on the implementation of R.115, observed that some employers had read the circular 'very rigidly and determinedly and permit of no laxity'.[94] Many within the industry, whether in management or in labour representation, had lost sons to the war (including Richards himself); it is hardly likely that their concern to save others that misfortune was predicated upon anything other than their intimate understanding of the needs of production.[95]

Notes

1 James Gribble, commenting upon the claim that, by October 1916, only 2700 men remained in the boot and shoe trade in Northampton (*Mercury*, 13 October 1916).

2 Hurwitz, *State Intervention in Great Britain*, pp. 196–198, 202–204; Fowler, 'The Impact of the First World War upon the Lancashire Cotton Industry and Its Workers', p. 86; 'British Textile Workers in the Lancashire Cotton and Yorkshire Wool Industries', p. 7. In 1906, some 60.6 per cent of cotton mill employees were female (Boot and Maindonald, 'New Estimates of Age- and Sex-specific Earnings … in the British Cotton Industry, 1833–1906', p. 383).

3 Above, pp. 67–68.

4 Church, 'The Effect of the American Export Invasion on the British Boot and

Shoe Industry, 1885–1914', pp. 223–254, *passim*; Griffin, *The Northampton Boot and Shoe Industry and its Significance for Social Change*, p. 162. A.E. Marlow Ltd, whose owner features prominently in this chapter, was said to be Europe's largest producer of 'American' styles (Church, 'American Export Invasion', p. 252).

5 Above, p. 18.

6 *The Times*, 15 January 1915.

7 LGB Circular R.4 (19 November 1915), List D; Harding, *The Boot and Shoe Industry*, pp. 50, 55–56, 117, 155–156, 166, 174.

8 *Mercury*, 14 April, 19 May 1916. Lewis and his fellow employers regarded the reserved occupations list as being a better method of retaining vital men within the industry, and believed that badged men (who were not affected by the revision of reserved occupations lists) created resentment in the workplace. A subsequent request from the Ministry of Munitions, that firms refusing to distribute badges be named, drew from Lewis's Tribunal the brusque response that they were not prepared to 'enter into an enquiry of that description' (ibid., 26 May 1916). Note also the negative comments regarding badging made by Sir Ryland Adkins in the Commons (5 H.C. 77:318: 21 December 1915).

9 NUBSO Monthly Reports, 1916: Registry of members 1916, pp. 50–67, 228–232, 243–250; Branch Reports, January 1916, p. 113. The Kettering branch figures included union membership for Walgrave, Burton Latimer and Rothwell; Wellingborough's for Earls Barton. Higham and Rushden district included the unionized workforces of Irthlingborough, Finedon, Wollaston, Bozeat, Irchester, Ringstead, Raunds and Stanwick.

10 *Independent*, 15 July 1916; *Mercury*, 31 March, 14 April, 28 April 1916. In March 1917, the Hawkins factory was one of two visited by members of the Appeals Tribunal attempting to learn more of the boot-making process and its indispensable elements (*Mercury*, 2 March 1917).

11 Above, p. 89, n.1.

12 *Mercury*, 13 October, 15 December 1916, 15 June, 24 November 1917; *Herald*, 15 December 1916; NRO Quarter Sessions, Misc., 368: Boot and Shoe Trade, 16; NUBSO Monthly Reports, Editorial, January 1916. Contradicting these perceptions, extant figures indicate that Leicester's boot and shoe workforce, not being so predominantly devoted to military orders, suffered a greater degree of 'combing-out' of unionized men than did Northampton between April 1916 and mid-1917 (NUBSO Monthly Reports, *passim*).

13 *Mercury*, 13 October 1916; NRO, X198/2037–2882 (broken sequence); NUSBO Monthly Reports, May 1916, p. 299, October 1916, p. 591.

14 The NUBSO monthly report for January 1916 (p. 3) stated that the Northampton County Board had negotiated a price for the nailing of the Italian Army Boot, an order for half a million pairs of which was already in place by December 1915 (p. 120). Of 345 English firms involved in the Russian order by May 1916, 208 were located in the county (ibid., May 1916, pp. 293 -297).

15 *Mercury*, 26 March, 26 May 1916, 3 March 1917. The War Office's Army Contracts Department also placed an order for a new style of mounted service boot at the end of 1916 (ibid., 29 December 1916).

16 *The Times*, 26 July 1916. This percentage, based solely on *The Times*'s data, may be a significant understatement, given the figures provided by individual Northamptonshire factories.
17 *Independent*, 22 January 1916.
18 That is, as a Military Service, rather than Derby, Tribunal.
19 NUBSO Monthly Branch Reports, March 1916, pp. 196, 198, April 1916, pp. 241, 243; *Mercury*, 4 April, 28 April, 5 May 1916.
20 *Mercury*, 5 May, 28 July 1916. Rushden Tribunal's boot and shoe manufacturer was Fred Knight, JP (NRO Quarter Sessions, Misc. 368, Boot and Shoe Trade, 17: Rushden).
21 *Mercury*, 26 May, 9 June 1916.
22 LGB Circular R.94 (7 July 1916).
23 *Herald*, 28 July 1916.
24 The calculation, made by Councillor Parker, was reported as 2500–2600 by NUBSO (Monthly Report, September 1916, p. 566).
25 *Mercury*, 1, 29 September 1916. On the Army Contract Office's preference for imposing retrospective contract prices upon the boots it ordered, cf. the *Independent*, editorial, 2 September 1916.
26 The War Office's habit of submitting boot orders almost at whim was noted by Gribble when presenting the sub-committee's first proposal on 24 November 1916 (*Mercury*, same day's edition). Similarly, the *Independent* (editorial, 22 January 1916) cited an order for mosquito-proof boots for soldiers fighting in tropical climates, placed on a Saturday with delivery demanded for the following Tuesday (the firm involved dispatched the completed order on Monday afternoon).
27 *Mercury*, as dated.
28 Text given in full in the *Mercury*, 20 October 1916.
29 LGB Circular R.106, as dated.
30 That is, federated to the Northamptonshire Boot and Shoe Manufacturers Association.
31 *Mercury*, 24 November, 1 December 1916; *Independent*, 2 December 1917. The *Independent* praised the Tribunal's second proposal as 'another commendable case of Northampton leading the way'.
32 *Mercury*, 8, 15 December 1916.
33 Ibid., 22 December 1916.
34 Ibid., 12 January 1917.
35 Above, p. 27.
36 *The Times*, 3 January 1917.
37 LGB Circular R.114 was issued on 19 January 1917.
38 *Mercury*, 19 January 1917; *Northampton Chronicle*, 26 January 1917. The closing-room is where the various sections of the shoe upper are stitched together, and, where appropriate, eyeleted. From the beginning of mechanization in footwear factories, this department employed the greatest concentration of female labour (Harding, *The Boot and Shoe Industry*, pp. 82, 89–90).
39 *Mercury*, 19 January 1917.
40 *Mercury*, 19 January, 2 February 1917.

41 *Mercury*, 9, 16 February 1917; NRO X197, Appeals Tribunal meeting notes, 5 February 1917.

42 Sample wording from NRO X198/2037. The statement was adjusted marginally to reflect the circumstances of each firm.

43 To date, the largest single group of boot and shoe employees to appear before the Tribunal comprised 13 Raunds men whose (one month) exemptions had been subject to military appeal. The appeals were dismissed (NRO X180/505–517).

44 NRO Quarter Sessions, Misc., 368: Tribunal Officials and Admin. 1/3; X197, Appeals Tribunal meeting notes, 2 February 1917.

45 NRO X197, Appeals Tribunal meeting notes, 2, 16 February 1917. These appeals were dismissed by consent on 1 March. In the Commons a few weeks later, Sir Ryland Adkins cited Geldart's error of judgement when urging the War Office to instruct its military representatives not to appeal short exemptions (5 H.C. 91:1973 (21 March 1917)).

46 Below, pp. 114–115.

47 NRO X197, Appeals Tribunal meeting notes, as dated.

48 NRO Quarter-Sessions, misc., 368, file 'Military: Women's War work/Boot and Shoe Trade, 1–11'.

49 NRO X198/2037–2061.

50 Arnold Brothers operated a number of welting machines; the argument regarding the laying-off of female labour for want of male machinists was particularly relevant to the welting process.

51 NRO X198/2062–2493.

52 NRO X197: Appeals Tribunal meeting notes, as dated; *Mercury*, 2 March 1917.

53 Both the Rushden and Kettering branches of the NUBSO referred to the offer as 'generous' (NUBSO Monthly Branch Reports, May 1917, pp. 263–264).

54 *Mercury*, 4, 11 May 1917.

55 NRO X197, Appeals Tribunal meeting notes, 22 June 1917; *Mercury*, 22 June 1917; Tribunal statement reproduced in the *Independent*, 23 June 1917.

56 NRO X197, Appeals Tribunal meeting notes, 26 June 1917; *Mercury*, 29 June 1917; *Herald*, 29 June 1917. The *Independent* (23 June 1917) calculated that a total of only 1420 A and B1 men under 41 (if single) or 35 (married) remained in the trade in Northamptonshire.

57 On 20 July, the Appeals Tribunal divided and sat simultaneously at Northampton and Peterborough to hear boot and shoe cases; to achieve a quorum at the latter venue, two of the Tribunal's 'reserve list' members, Jabez Bird and Hugh de Burgh Wilmot (both Peterborough residents), sat for the first time (NRO Quarter-Sessions, Misc., 368: Tribunal Officials and Admin. 1/3; X197, Appeals Tribunal meeting notes, 20 July 1917).

58 NRO X189/6575–6578 (25 July 1917).

59 NRO X197, Appeals Tribunal meeting notes, as dated; *Mercury*, 20 July 1917.

60 NUBSO Monthly Report, July 1917, p. 337.

61 *Mercury*, 27 July 1917.

62 NRO X197, Appeals Tribunal Notes, as dated.

63 The Tribunal went on strike once more a fortnight later, when five of the seven

boot and shoe employees whose cases they had originally disputed with the military representative went before the Appeals Tribunal and had their certificates varied (*Mercury*, 31 August 1917).

64 NRO X197, Appeals Tribunal Notes, 31 August 1917. Pointedly, the Tribunal expressed 'their full confidence' in Kettering's decision.

65 Below, pp. 173–175.

66 Full text in the *Mercury*, 21 September 1917.

67 *Mercury*, 28 September 1917.

68 NRO X198/2037–2882, 3045–3089, 3628–3906, 4226–4387, 4497–4550, 4563–4567 (broken sequence).

69 Reporting the communication, the *Mercury* (30 November 1917) mistakenly identified its author as Sir Eric Geddes (First Lord of the Admiralty and Sir Auckland's brother).

70 *Mercury*, 30 November 1917; NRO X198/7223–7313 (broken sequence).

71 NUBSO, Monthly Branch Report, Northampton, December 1917, p. 634.

72 NRO X197, Appeals Tribunal Notes, 3 August, 5 November, 26 November 1917.

73 NRO X198/7500–7510, 7528–7533, 7535–7555, 7589–7625, 7690–7716, 7718–7738, 7740–7763, 7824–7850.

74 NRO X198/7690–7716, 7718–7730.

75 NRO X197: Appeals Tribunal meeting notes, 22 February, 19 March 1918.

76 Ibid., 10 April 1918; *Mercury*, 12 April 1918.

77 This followed NATS instruction 72 (9 April 1918) which allowed the withdrawal of certificates previously given on occupational grounds). On the same day, NATS Circular R.49 raised the age limits for exemptions offered to boot repair workers, but not – as yet – to those in boot manufacturing.

78 *Mercury*, 31 May, 14 June 1918.

79 In the Commons, Sir Walter Essex put the proportion for the industry as a whole at 50 per cent (NUBSO Monthly Reports, July 1918, p. 415).

80 *Mercury*, 28 June 1918.

81 Grieves, *The Politics of Manpower*, p. 197.

82 *The Times*, 12 April 1918.

83 For example, 3506 men belonging to Northampton Branches 1 and 2 were serving in March 1918. By August, the figure had risen only marginally, to 3587. The corresponding figures for Kettering were 1296 and 1346, for Wellingborough 629 and 665, and for Higham and Rushden district 2187 and 2223 (NUBSO monthly Reports, March, August 1918). Note also that, of several hundred men whose exemptions were extended by the Appeals Tribunal on 10 April 1918, only six were below the age of 31, and, of these, two received a mere one month's extension (NRO X197, Appeals Tribunal meeting notes, as dated).

84 TNA WO32/9954: War Cabinet minutes, 19 July 1918.

85 All of these forms were certified as having been received by the Appeals Tribunal's secretary on 23 July.

86 The delay may have been caused in part by the influenza epidemic that was sweeping the country during the summer months. NUBSO monthly branch reports for June–August 1918 make frequent reference to its impact upon the industry.

87 NRO X205/10213–10874.
88 At Enderby in Leicestershire, for example, 12 females were working as clickers in a single shoe factory as early as March 1916 (NUBSO Monthly Report, March, 1916, p. 207).
89 NUBSO Monthly Branch Reports, March 1917, p. 194. Note also the opinion of the correspondent from Northampton Branch no. 1 (ibid., p. 191): 'although girls and women are being substituted in their places it will be impossible for them to do anything like the quantity'.
90 NUBSO Monthly Reports, 1916, pp. 64–7, 216–232, 246–8; 1918, pp. 74–75, 80–86, 268–288, 307–310.
91 *Mercury*, 21 October 1917, 3 May 1918; also below, p. 172.
92 Above, p. 79.
93 *Statistics of the Military Effort of the British Empire*, p. 548.
94 NUBSO Monthly Reports, February 1917, p. 129.
95 NUBSO reports throughout the conscription period carry obituary notices of union members and/or their sons who had fallen in action. Richards's own son was reported missing on 6 April 1917.

5

Agriculture

I am bound to say that the military representatives whom I have met – charming men as they are, nine out of ten of them being solicitors in khaki – seem to know even less about agriculture than do the War Office.[1]

By the outbreak of the First World War, the nation grew enough grain to provide for the population for just 125 days in a year, or, as one commentator put it, 'from Friday night to Monday morning'. The production deficit was caused in part by a long-term depression in agriculture that had resulted in a 48 per cent reduction in the area devoted to cereal production in England and Wales since 1874. In that year, arable land had fed some 26 million Britons; by 1914 it was able to feed only 16 millions. Corresponding figures for Northamptonshire were 286,000 tilled acres in 1872, declining to 188,622 acres in 1912. There had been a corresponding rise in the area of pasture during the same period, but the only entirely home-produced animal comestible was milk. Analysis of a wide range of basic foodstuffs indicates that only 42 per cent of the calories necessary to sustain the home population were grown, manufactured or bred domestically.[2]

Broadly, the period of Asquith's administration (to December 1916) saw the continuance of a prewar *laissez-faire* attitude towards agriculture, reflecting the political temperament of government, optimism that the war would be of short duration and uncertainty as to how formal direction might be imposed upon an extremely individualistic industry. During this period, policy consisted largely of encouraging farmers to grow more (principally through the medium of county-level War Agricultural Committees, established in October 1915), and of ensuring the import stream, by intervention where necessary. With the advent of Lloyd George's administration, the emphasis switched markedly to increasing domestic production: by encouraging the cultivation of allotments and compulsorily improving farming techniques during 1917 (including the seizure and reletting of badly farmed land), and, in the following year, by implementing plans for the large-scale conversion or reconversion of pasture to arable land (known as the 'plough policy').[3] Ostensibly, the process reflected (and required) a growing appreciation of the importance of keeping the farming population on the land; again, however, what government considered important was not necessarily reflected by any consistent effort to retain the male agricultural population. Prior to the formulation of a comprehensive manpower policy in late 1917, the official attitude towards dilution of the agricultural workforce was influenced, as elsewhere, by the Army's short-term needs and by fluctuating domestic circumstances.

There has been considerable scholarly debate regarding the scale of agricultural losses to recruitment prior to the introduction of conscription. Traditionally, the poorly paid and insecure nature of unskilled farming work made it vulnerable both to the recruiting sergeant's efforts and to the attraction of higher-paid industrial work, but applying a measure to the trend is difficult.[4] As the 'industry' was organized at a family level, and much of the agricultural workforce was non-unionized, statistical mechanisms, even where based upon the regularly employed workforce, are lacking in comparison to the manufacturing and retail trades. Contemporarily calculated figures, utilizing the Board of Trade's quarterly ('Z8') reports, encouraged an early consensus that some 210,000–245,000 men of military age departed the land for the Army in the first two years of the war, representing approximately 28–33 per cent of the peacetime male labour force. A strongly revisionist work by P.E. Dewey, published in the 1980s, suggested that these estimates, based upon a flawed model (utilizing data from a relatively small number of atypically large farms), significantly overstated the true figure, and offered instead a much lower estimate, of some 22 per cent. More recently, a figure at the lower end of the original estimates has been argued.[5] No work, however, is able to cite any more substantial evidence than that provided by the Z8 reports, which leaves the debate somewhat in the air at present.

Other statistical evidence is equally ambiguous. Domestic production of cereals, livestock and ancillary foodstuffs diminished only marginally during 1915, which might indicate variously that lower estimates for manpower losses are indeed more accurate, that the farming family managed on the whole to absorb the loss of casual or seasonal labour, or that improved or improvised techniques ameliorated the same loss. Conversely, the fact that Home Army men were utilized as early as that year to assist with the hay harvest and autumn cultivation indicates that significant labour shortages were already being experienced in some areas. And while local opinion in the industry was vociferous in identifying the loss of labour to the Army as an increasingly serious obstacle to maintaining or increasing production, equally local, non-agricultural opinion was convinced that many farmers' sons were shirking their duty by choosing *en masse* to remain on the land.[6]

Herein lies one of the problems of reaching broad conclusions regarding the effect of enlistment upon agriculture: all opinion, and experience, was local. Each farmer brought his own story to the Tribunals when applying for exemption for his employee, his son or, occasionally, himself. He might make observations regarding conditions in his locality, or mention (usually by way of complaint) the latest requirements of the Board of Agriculture and the War Agricultural Committees; but these were essentially anecdotal comments supported – or contradicted – by evidence that only rarely distinguished data at a local level. It will become apparent, therefore, that the impact of personal perception was no less than that of official instructions and statistics in informing tribunalists' opinions as to how much more agricultural manpower a district could afford to lose.

The condition of British agriculture was important. Even those who mistrusted farmers' claims for the indispensability of their sons knew that the process of dilution could be permitted to go only so far. No tribunalist asked if the country needed farmers, or suggested at any time during the period of military conscription that the industry enjoyed a surplus of labour.[7] In the autumn of 1916 and again in summer 1917, a widespread belief in Whitehall and elsewhere that agriculture was approaching a production crisis resulted in near total, if temporary, freezes upon recruitment from the land. At other times, agricultural applicants to the Tribunals were obliged to justify their exemptions in much the same manner as those from other sectors of the economy, though the underlying issue of food supply almost always weighted, to a degree, the decisions handed down. However, the essential nature of an occupation did not necessarily deem a man within it equally essential. Military representatives had the right to challenge a certificate on the grounds that someone other than the applicant – an older man, woman or other substitute – could perform his vital role just as effectively.[8] This question of indispensability, raised so often during the Tribunals' deliberations, was nowhere more strenuously applied than in agricultural cases. Farming required an extraordinary level of commitment, nurtured by an intimate identification with the working environment that was absent from most other occupations. Consequently, the issue of agricultural substitution often asked an incremental question that the Tribunals found difficult to adjudge: who could work a man's farm as effectively as himself and his family?

Linked inseparably to the measure of indispensability was the availability of substitutes. Government, even while neglecting to establish consistent plans for the removal or retention of manpower, requested, cajoled and, eventually, took steps to organize sources of alternative labour for the land on a scale unprecedented elsewhere. The search for substitutes began in the farmhouse itself and continued to the neighbouring farm, to schools, barracks, prisoner-of-war and internment camps, gentlewomen's homes and even, apparently, the asylum.[9] Statistical evidence gathered soon after the end of the War suggested that these measures, together with the fruits of the 'plough policy', effectively defeated the submarine threat to the food supply. However, examination of the impact of initiatives, ad hoc arrangements and, eventually, policy indicates that the results of official intervention often fell significantly short of their intended effect.

At the commencement of the conscription period, there was as yet no food 'policy' in an actively interventionist sense, but this did not reflect indifference on government's part to the potential problems of over-dilution in agriculture. In 1915, even before the advent of the Derby Scheme, recruiting authorities had been directed not to enlist certain classes of worker from the land unless men of non-military age or women were available in the same district to fill their roles, and not to take any more agricultural engine-drivers, blacksmiths or thatchers under almost any circumstances.[10] The first Reserved Occupations list, circulated to local Tribunals after the introduction of the Derby Scheme, fully recognized agriculture's special status. It identified 23 categories of skilled farm workers who, having attested their willingness to serve, were be placed in the Army Reserve but not taken for service until such time as Central Tribunal decided that their retention in civilian life was no longer necessary. These were: agricultural engine attendant, driver and mechanic, bailiff, beastman, byreman, cattle- or cowman, dairyman, carter, foreman, horse-keeper, horseman, milker, milkman, ploughman, shepherd, stallion man, steward, stock-keeper, stockman, thatcher, wagoner and yardman.[11] Clearly, one man might discharge several of these functions (and on smaller farms almost certainly did), but the comprehensive nature of the list indicates that there were few aspects of non-labouring farm work that the government did not regard as being essential.

With the implementation of limited conscription in January 1916, the previous December's Reserved (re-categorized now as 'Certified') Occupations list was incorporated within the new Act. It has been noted already that some Tribunals offered absolute exemptions during their early sittings with greater frequency than the government had intended.[12] The list of certified agricultural employments, which seemed to suggest that the entirety of the farming profession was off-limits to the recruiting officer, encouraged this tendency to the point at which local advisory committees and even some military representatives urged sympathetic treatment of agricultural cases coming before them. At the first sitting of Thrapston Tribunal on 23 February 1916, absolute exemptions were offered to five applicants, sons or employees of farmers with substantial holdings (though lesser certificates were offered to men working farms of less than 100 acres), none of which was challenged by the military representative, J. Edmonds.

At Hardingstone on 1 March, a widow applied for her only remaining son, who tended 80 cattle, 130 sheep and 12 horses. The Tribunal's military representative, R.G. Scriven, promptly recommended absolute exemption. The following day, at Northampton Rural, a farmer applying on his own behalf claimed that two-thirds of his men had gone to the Colours already and that he employed women in their place. The visiting regional military representative, Colonel Bairstow, less sympathetic to local concerns than his subordinates at Thrapston and Hardingstone, suggested a certificate be offered for a mere six months. The Tribunal listened respectfully and then decided for absolute exemption.[13] There is no reason to suppose that these decisions were atypically lenient. At Dundee Rural Tribunal during two sittings in March, only one agricultural worker from 170 cases heard was refused exemption. At the first sitting of Kirkby Stephen Tribunal in Westmorland, the 'great bulk' of applications from farmers received long exemptions. In Warwick district, a spate of early military appeals was devoted to reversing absolute exemptions offered by local Tribunals to their own farmers. Finally, Bletchley Urban Tribunal in Buckinghamshire had an early 'policy' of giving six-month exemptions to men solely upon being satisfied that they worked on the land (and, on one occasion, obliged an elderly spinster who asked for absolute exemption for her stockman, without considering what other labour she employed).[14]

Misperceptions regarding what legislation had intended for agriculture occurred countrywide, therefore, and 'lenient' decisions abounded. In particular, an early (and marked) tendency of farmers' sons to claim and obtain exemption on the grounds of indispensability was identified as one of the principal weaknesses of the Tribunals' relationship with agriculture.[15] The official reaction came in April, with a revised list of protected occupations that de-certified single farm bailiffs, foremen, grieves and stewards under 30 years of age, and single beastmen, cattlemen, byremen, teamsters, wagoners, hinds and servants under 25.[16] It was determined, furthermore, that no unmarried man of military age would be regarded as being in a certified agricultural occupation had he not been so employed prior to 15 August 1915 (a discouragement to farmers' sons discovering a hitherto unsuspected affinity for the soil).

Even before the new instructions were issued, Northamptonshire's Appeals Tribunal had begun to apply the legislation more literally than most of the county's local bodies. The very first appeal at their inaugural sitting of 21 March 1916 was made by an agricultural worker on a 300–acre farm, Jack Thornton, whose employer claimed that no replacement was available. The case was dismissed briskly; it was observed that no evidence had been presented to suggest that a substitute had been sought. Their third appellant was Arthur William Goode, a market gardener whose employer (his father) also claimed that a substitute was unavailable. The Tribunal agreed with Goode's local Tribunal, Peterborough, who had decided that a woman could do the work as well as he, but they allowed him two months' exemption to give his father time to find an adequate replacement. Peterborough had also denied exemption to the next appellant, Ernest Arthur Harris, a general farm labourer, on the basis that it was not in the national interest that he should be exempt. Again, the Appeals Tribunal agreed with the original decision but offered Harris a two months' certificate to carry his employer through the calving season.[17] Decisions of Tribunals less rigorous than Peterborough were similarly corrected that day. Joseph Charles Brittin, a milker, milk seller and agricultural engine manager, was the subject of a military appeal regarding the absolute exemption given to him by Thrapston Tribunal. While not deliberating the point of Brittin's indispensability, they adjusted the certificate to two months.[18]

As in non-agricultural cases, the imposition of temporary certificates where indispensability had been claimed was intended both to emphasize the conditionality of exemptions on occupational grounds and to test the willingness of employers to seek out substitutes. At this first sitting, the question of whether such substitutes were available did not arise. Two weeks later, however, the Board of Agriculture made its first intervention with regard to the issue during the cases of two farming brothers, Percy and Charles Jackson, who had been refused exemption at Potterspury on the grounds that their land was contiguous and could be worked by older members of their family. During their appeals, Captain Cook suggested that one of them might remain out of the Army, and the Tribunal agreed with the brothers' solicitor's suggestion that Charles might have a short period of exemption to allow Percy to take on his land. They were given certificates for one and five months respectively.

While the Tribunal were deliberating these cases, Douglas Thring, their newly appointed agricultural representative, commenced his defence of his department's interests by claiming that Percy Jackson, as head of a food production business, was necessarily certified, and therefore should have been offered an absolute certificate. Sir Ryland Adkins disagreed: such was the case only if his indispensability could be demonstrated, and that was a matter for the Tribunal to decide. 'As regards indispensability', retorted Thring, 'the question arises whether he can be replaced. It is exceedingly difficult to replace any man at the present moment either by a man or a woman. Farmers are not taking farms because they cannot get labour.'[19]

In establishing his preliminary negotiating position, Thring perhaps overstated the latter problem (on the same day, the Tribunal dismissed an appeal by George Campbell Douglas, a Chipping Warden farmer, on the grounds that he had recently leased 93 of his 113 acres for the sole purpose of evading military service),[20] but other were looming. To allow the large-scale release of young single men envisaged by the revised Certified Occupations List, adequate mechanisms for equally large-scale substitution were required. The Army was in the process of formalizing loans of Home Army personnel to farmers, but the 1916 arrangements were restrictive. Furloughs were authorized to a maximum of only four weeks, so, while soldiers might be of use at harvest time, their contribution to stock rearing and cultivation would be minimal. Their utilization on farms, furthermore, remained at the discretion of the military, and applications for soldiers had to be made through the Labour Exchanges, which farmers, usually living several miles from urban areas, were reluctant to visit. The rate of pay established for military substitutes – 25s. per week, to be paid to the Army, not the men themselves – was higher than the going rate for farm labour, and farmers were also expected to pay soldiers on 'wet days' (traditionally, farm labourers forfeited pay on days not worked). Until July 1916, furthermore, Home Army men released for agricultural work were required to return to barracks each evening, making their employment in outlying districts impractical.[21]

Non-military substitution also presented distinct problems for agriculture. Farming was hard work, and a certain level of physical fitness was required of the effective replacement. As will be seen, the Home Army, largely comprising men categorized as unsuitable for service overseas, was often unable to provide the necessary quality of substitute, while the available civilian labour pool consisted predominantly of men above military age or those whom the Army had rejected outright. In August 1916, the War Office reminded officers commanding recruiting districts that the availability of many lower-category men not presently required for service gave them 'a bargaining power with employers which can be used to the advantage of the Army'.[22] That might have been the case with regard to some urban industries, but Category C men made very imperfect agricultural substitutes, particularly given the declining rate of food production that had already seized the Board of Agriculture's attention and which, presumably, would require even greater physical exertions to reverse.

Regarding the use of female labour, the Board of Trade's (somewhat ambiguous) calculation indicated that there were some 130,000 female agricultural workers in England and Wales in 1914, the vast majority being farmers' relatives or seasonal employees.[23] Efforts during the early part of the war to encourage greater female participation in agriculture achieved little. The first, obvious recourse was to village women, but it was reported that many were reluctant to volunteer. Again, the work was hard and poorly paid, and the hours unsociable. In Northamptonshire, it was a common complaint that farms – particularly those sited near to urban areas – could not compete with the booming demand for labour in the boot and shoe trade and munitions factories (one reason, possibly, why Hardingstone and Northampton rural Tribunals, serving registration areas immediately surrounding the county's largest conurbation, heard agricultural cases sympathetically).[24] It is also the case that many farmers' attitudes towards female labour were, to say the least, traditionalist.[25] Breeding farms were thought by many to offer unsuitable or potentially corrupting sights for ladies, while early morning starts were suggested by at least one appellant to be conducive to moral laxity. It was also claimed upon several occasions before Northamptonshire Tribunals that women were temperamentally averse to milking cows.[26] Without the willing collaboration of individual farmers, achieving a greater female presence in agriculture was problematic. In May 1916, a small training facility for women was established at the County Experimental Farm at Moulton, but this could process only six applicants at any time owing to limited accommodation, and it relied entirely upon volunteers coming forward individually to take up training. It was not until the following year, when government took a firm initiative and women found safety in numbers and organization, that significant female substitution became a practical option.[27] In the meantime, female agricultural labour remained predominantly family-sourced, comprising women who were often contributing already to food production and therefore unlikely to supplement existing resources.

Consequently, the initial period of conscription witnessed the greatest sustained pressure upon the agricultural labour supply without, as yet, any adequate system of substitution to ameliorate manpower losses. How did the Tribunals respond to this dilemma? As in other matters, empathy was an important factor. An amenable Tribunal such as Hardingstone would apply the letter of the Certified Occupations list and sidestep the issue of indispensability entirely. In mid-April, they offered absolute exemption to an engine driver who threshed for thirty farms, and a conditional certificate to a steam plough driver – both occupations that the government had identified as becoming more vital to the industry as men left the land. However, they were hardly less generous where a farm worker's status was ambiguous. In May, they listened as R.G. Scriven read out an Eastern Command directive that men should be given absolute exemption only if they were either medically unfit or their circumstances were immutable. Immediately thereafter, they offered an absolute certificate to an able-bodied man farming 257 acres, and, for good measure, a certificate to 30 September to one of his labourers. Scriven concurred with both decisions, and declined to enter appeals in two further cases where farm labourers received 30 September certificates after he had recommended exemptions to 30 June.[28]

Subtly different was the policy of Northampton Rural Tribunal, whose (predominantly generous) decisions in agricultural cases were usually justified by some mention of the crisis in food production. On 4 May 1916, their farming chairman, A. Britten, interrupted a formal observation on the crisis in agricultural manpower to declare that he, personally, had found it impossible to find a farm hand. His Tribunal then offered long exemptions to two wagoners. Later in the month, they commented once more on farmers' difficulties before offering three months to the brother of a starred farmer to allow him to get in the harvest, and six months to a farmer's son who operated a threshing machine. Only one agricultural application was dismissed during the day's sitting: that of a farm labourer whose employer had managed to hire seven women and a girl (the latter, remarkably, could drive a steam plough), and had been overheard announcing his intention to take on thirty more during the forthcoming pea-picking season.[29]

In contrast to these relatively sympathetic policies, Brixworth Tribunal, assisted by an energetic military representative, Adam Cross (the antipode of Hardingstone's Scriven), showed an early disinclination to indulge farmers. On 6 April, they heard a long preamble from the local advisory committee, expressing the hope that the Tribunal's decisions would recognize the difficulties farmers were experiencing. A report was presented also from a delegation of Market Harborough farmers who had travelled to London to ask Lord Selborne to use his authority to keep foremen, wagoners and shepherds on the land (and had been assured by him that official instructions to that effect would be issued).[30] The Tribunal then promptly refused the option of recommending home service for a man in the Yeomanry who farmed 300 acres for himself and his widowed mother. The fact that the applicant was already in uniform might have swayed their decision (and certainly raised a question as to their jurisdiction), but the outcome of a similar case some two weeks later suggests a somewhat pedantic reluctance to test their discretion. In the latter, a farmer made an application for his cowman, Oliver Archer, 33, who was training already in khaki. Archer's employer did not apply to have him brought out of the Army; rather, he requested that he be kept from foreign service until October to help get in the harvest. At the time, the Army itself was willing to allow the resilient Archer to go to back to the farm from Northampton barracks every night, and also from each Saturday lunchtime until Monday morning. Once more, however, Brixworth dismissed the application (a decision that was overturned by the Appeals Tribunal on 11 May). Only when faced with irrefutable proof of over-dilution in the local agricultural workforce did the Tribunal acknowledge that a problem existed. On 16 May, a farmer applying for two labourers told the Tribunal he had been obliged to give up one of his two farms for lack of men (though it had been in good productive order), and had ceased livestock-breeding, when formerly he had raised 40 calves each year. Even Cross admitted that he had never heard of a farm being abandoned for want of men, and concurred with the Tribunal's decision to offer 30 September certificates to each man.[31]

Between the Hardingstone and Brixworth extremes, most of Northamptonshire's Tribunals acknowledged the problem of addressing two conflicting imperatives but made few efforts to resolve it. Equally reluctant to dismiss agricultural applications outright or put their names to open-ended certificates of exemption, they largely employed a 'strategy' that was rather a handwashing exercise. Many smallholders were told to make arrangements with neighbours to take over cultivation of their plots, while farmers with more substantial acreages were required to find substitutes within a specified (usually, a short) period, but given no practical advice or assistance on how to do so. The Appeals Tribunal, lacking any more useful guidance from government, was similarly unhelpful. Thus, on 13 April, the case of John William Berrill, a smallholder appealing Wellingborough Rural's dismissal of his application, was disputed between the Army and Board of Agriculture and thereafter discarded for want of a satisfactory policy. The military representative of Berrill's local Tribunal argued that the average labour on farms in his district was one man for every 70 acres (Berrill farmed 16, of which 11 were arable, with a further 60 acres ploughing elsewhere), and that someone else could work the holdings. Thring resisted this: the issue, he proposed, was not size but principle. As Berrill's sole occupation was farming, he was a farmer under the act and it was in the national interest that he remain on the land. The Appeals Tribunal gave Berrill a 17 days' certificate (which, with the two-month grace period, exempted him to 1 July), and told him to make arrangements with neighbouring smallholders to farm his land.[32] The decision was no different from that meted out to many businessmen and sole proprietors in other occupations during these months; nevertheless, it failed entirely to address the special circumstances of agriculture that even government had acknowledged explicitly.

By the end of May, however, energetic lobbying by the Board of Agriculture had brought a discernible shift in the manner in which some agricultural cases were treated. Discussions with the Deputy Assistant Adjutant of Recruiting resulted in an informal agreement that blacksmiths, wheelwrights and engine and steam plough operators of whatever medical category should be retained on the land. On the last day of the month, Thring, defending the appeals of two threshing machine attendants, attempted to extend the principle. He claimed that the omission of their occupation from the agreement must have been an oversight, as bread could not reach the table without the threshing process. The Appeals Tribunal concurred, offered six months' exemption in each case, and indicated that one certificate would be renewed at the end of that time if the other man went into the Army.[33]

The agreement was welcomed, though its implementation was uneven. Prematurely, Northamptonshire's agricultural Advisory Committee summoned several ostensibly qualifying workers and told them that they would be exempt from military service for the present. Rightly, Oxendon Rural Tribunal took strong exception to this as an abrogation of their authority, but their own agricultural and military representatives seem to have collaborated in assisting such extemporary initiatives. The latter, Sir James Heath (who, upon at least one other occasion, stood shoulder to shoulder with the agricultural representative in seeking to keep men on the land), admitted that he had received corroborating instructions from the War Office, and had thereafter advised his opposite number to 'take a bold line … with regard to men absolutely vital'.[34]

This – modest – accommodation between the War Office and Board of Agriculture coincided with the introduction of the Military Service (Session 2) Act 1916. Instructions relating thereto were circulated to the Tribunals on 1 June. They repeated Lord Selborne's recent (and apparently unequivocal) declaration in the House that 'the Government hold that the maintenance of the highest possible output of home-grown food supplies remains a national object of the most essential nature'. They also revealed that the two departments of State were working to produce agreed scales establishing the minimum labour necessary to protect food production. Finally, a first, tentative effort was made to clarify the position of the small-holder. If he contributed 'materially' to the food supply, and if lack of an available substitute meant that his land would otherwise fall out of cultivation, it was considered preferable that he be retained in civilian life. What constituted a 'material' contribution was not defined.[35]

As welcome as these clarifications might have been to the Tribunals, there was nothing in the instructions that allowed intent to be translated, as yet, into policy when adjudging individual cases. The impact of the new Act upon married agricultural workers, furthermore, promised to more than offset any relief afforded by as yet vague promises of minimum labour scales and more favourable treatment of smallholders. Some Tribunals appear to have been sensitive to this, and, having been given hopes of yardsticks by which the value of a farm worker might be measured, attempted to anticipate them or establish their own. As the new Act came into force, a conference between representatives of the Board of Agriculture and military representatives agreed provisionally that two hundred sheep needed at least one man to tend them. Reported by Douglas Thring

on 5 June, this conclusion-in-progress encouraged Northamptonshire's
Appeals Tribunal to send John Pickering, a single, 19-year-old shepherd
with charge of a thousand sheep, back to the land until September to assist
with shearing. Two days later, Sir Ryland Adkins invited Fred Perkins, a
'well-known' Kingsthorpe nurseryman, to give his opinion of what acreage
a man could handle without overworking himself. If digging rather than
ploughing, Perkins thought an acre-and-a-half reasonable. 'We are much
obliged to you, Mr Perkins', Adkins told him; 'we wanted some expert
advice, cheap.'[36]

However, if the Tribunals began to pay closer attention to acreages and
ratios, they were obliged also to enforce the spirit and letter of the new Act.
At their sitting of 16 June, the Appeals Tribunal began to impose finality
upon certificates. The following day, Hardingstone, blithely attempting to
continue their policy of offering open-ended certificates in agricultural
cases, were pulled up by the usually amenable R.G. Scriven, who informed
them that he would now be obliged to appeal conditional certificates offered
to single men (a month later, however, responding to such an exemption,
given to a single 22-year-old who milked 12 cows, bred stock and supported
his invalid mother, Scriven told his Tribunal only that he would 'consider'
an appeal). Elsewhere, and as witnessed in other sectors of the economy,
the position of unmarried agricultural applicants suffered relative to those
brought into the net of conscription by the new Act. In the shorter term,
this trend was no less pronounced among those Tribunals who, previously,
had exhibited a marked reluctance to meeting the army's demands for men
from the land. On 28 June, Northampton Rural reviewed a 30 September
certificate previously offered to a single tenant farmer and, untypically,
imposed finality upon it. Following this, they gave almost a dozen open-
ended certificates to married farmers and agricultural employees, conditional only upon their remaining in their present employments.[37]

During July, the military's willingness to release Home Army men for
agricultural work was first tested on a large scale. Soldiers made available
for the land were supplied with tents and permitted to be detached from
barracks, subject to recall at short notice. The results were not encouraging: 33,089 applications were made by farmers to labour exchanges in
England and Wales, in response to which 14,227 soldiers were supplied.[38]
In Derbyshire, an irate military representative complained to his rural
Tribunal that not a single soldier had been made available to any farmer
he knew personally, though many had applied.[39] Figures for Northamptonshire alone are not extant, but the near-dearth of anecdotal evidence
regarding this potential source of labour suggests that Eastern Command's
reputation for retaining men in barracks may have been deserved.[40] Most
farmers complaining of the lack of available adequate substitutes during

these months referred to the problem of hiring or retaining civilian males, or, more frequently, women; the matter of soldiers was hardly raised, much less discussed as a viable resource. The only recorded references to the use of soldiers on Northamptonshire farms made during summer 1916 were those by W.H. Dunkley, a Wappenham farmer appealing for his last cowman, who complained to the Appeals Tribunal that recently he had obtained two convalescents (both had been wounded in the back) whose weakness made them 'useless'; and a vague protest by an unidentified farmer to Potterspury Rural Tribunal, that the Army were taking all the men off the land and sending him semi-fit soldiers instead.[41]

If arrangements for military substitution were unsatisfactory as yet, the use of female labour remained even more sporadic and disorganized. The Northampton farmer with ambitions to create a regiment of female pea-pickers was atypical.[42] More prevalent were complaints that the munitions and boot factories were snapping up all the available women, or that females were not suitable for the work a particular farm required of its employees. On 28 June, the father of John Wallis Spokes, an unmarried milker, told the Appeals Tribunal that he could not match the wages paid by the nearby munitions works, while in the cases of William and Harry Waters, brothers and cattlemen on a Middleton Cheney farm, even Beatrice Cartwright was moved to admit that the chances of their employer finding female substitutes were minimal, as the same munitions works stood practically upon his land. George Pickering, a Canons Ashby farmer appealing for himself and his son, told the Tribunal that he had tried but been unable to hire a single women; his only other help was a tramp who had tired of farm work and had announced that he was moving on.[43]

It was (and is) difficult to determine how many of these claims were genuine, or rather reflected farmers' reluctance to employ women. The Board of Agriculture was not insensitive to the latter problem, but early efforts to counter it were at best optimistic. In April 1916, the Board issued a circular detailing examples of the successful employment of women in farm work, which concluded: 'These instances are sufficient to show that women are capable of performing satisfactorily many forms of agricultural work, and that farmers will be well advised to enlist their help to replace the male labour they have lost.'[44] A significant element of its intended audience thought otherwise. At a rare Kettering sitting of the Appeals Tribunal in April 1916, Sir Richard Winfrey was reduced to incredulity by the logic of the employer of Arthur Tee, a shepherd, ploughman and horse-keeper: 'You must remember this is a shepherd. You never heard of a lady shepherdess except Little Bo-Peep, and somebody else cut the sheep's tails when she was asleep.' The chairman could only observe helplessly: 'the prejudice of the farming community is beyond me altogether.'[45] Other comments made before the Tribunals, if less absurd, illustrated an abiding aversion to female labour. Appealing for his unmarried son, William Walters was asked by Sir Charles Knightley if he had attempted to find women to milk his cows. 'No ... they may be a lot of help, but they won't do for me ... they want too much looking after.' At Hardingstone, a farmer applying for an unmarried teamsman told the Tribunal that he had employed three women previously, but that they had been dismissed: 'We could not stand them any longer.' At Towcester, another farmer expressed the opinion that women previously hired by him had not stayed long 'because they had to go such a long way to spend their money'.[46]

Farmers who chose to present more considered arguments consistently stressed the inadequacies of female labour. As noted, complaints that women refused to milk were common, though these were not always accepted uncritically by the Tribunals, and, upon one occasion at least, failed entirely to convince. In the latter case, an Aston-le-Walls dairyman told his local Tribunal that four women in his employment would not milk, but when he went to appeal he was challenged by a local, Beatrice Cartwright (her childhood home was Edgecote House, little more than a mile from Aston), who said that she had heard otherwise, and threatened to speak to the women involved to gauge their opinions first-hand.[47] The milking claim in general, though popular, seems to have been unsustainable. Writing after the war, Lord Ernle declared confidently that dairying had proved one of the outstanding areas of success of female farm labouring, and that women tended to be more empathetic stock-handlers than men.[48]

One claim made by farmers was more supportable, however, at least during 1916. In the absence of formalized arrangements to train women for farm work, it was the already hard-pressed employer who would be obliged to act as tutor, supervisor and assistant to any women (or, indeed, any other unskilled hand) he might take on, thereby reducing his own productivity. Under the circumstances, farmers – particularly smallholders – were reported to be trying 'to keep going' with what remaining male labour they had, or to be pooling their dwindling workforce. A threshing machine driver, applying to Northampton Rural Tribunal for his son, told them that they now did the threshing for 30 farms, while at Hardingstone, an 86-year-old farmer, also seeking to retain his son, claimed that the only other men on the farm were 75 and 70 years old. Even Douglas Thring, a farmer himself (and keen advocate of female substitution), admitted that he had been obliged to work overtime the previous winter and would probably do the same the next for want of labour. Perhaps the most eloquent example of undermanning was alleged by farming brothers appealing in August for the removal of finality from the certificate of their sole remaining employee,

George Henry Preedy. Preedy, who supported six young children and a widowed mother, had lifted every load of hay on the brothers' 750–acre farm that summer. He had also been obliged to trap and kill three thousand rabbits in three months, as all the poachers upon whom they usually relied had been taken to the Colours (the carcasses were taken up to Birmingham and sold at market, where they had proved very popular). Without discussion, the Appeals Tribunal withdrew finality from his certificate.[49]

There is ample anecdotal evidence, therefore, that manpower dilution in the industry, if geographically inconsistent, had become an urgent issue by mid-1916. Furthermore, unseasonably wet and cold weather threatened what official statistics later confirmed: that the harvest of grains, potatoes and peas would be notably poorer that year than at the commencement of the war.[50] The threat stirred the government into providing much needed (though non-binding) guidance on agricultural labour requirements. In late June, the Tribunals were provided with the manpower scales agreed by the Board of Agriculture and Army Council as being necessary for the preservation of food production (known as the 'Bath Agreement'). These were: one skilled man or able-bodied lad for each of the following: every team of plough horses; every 20 cows in milk (even where the assistance of boys or women was available); every 50 head of yard or stall stock (ditto); every 200 sheep (excluding lambs) grazing on enclosed land; and every 800 sheep roaming on mountain or hill pasture.[51] The scales did not fully address the issue of arable acreages; nor was there any mechanism for returning men to the farms where labour was already significantly below the scale (according to a *Mercury* editorial of 26 January 1917–when agriculture had enjoyed the benefits of a freeze upon enlistment for several months – there were many such holdings). Nevertheless, they proved a first yardstick against which the Tribunals might measure their decisions meaningfully.

Having wrested agreement to the labour scales from the War Office, the Board of Agriculture immediately attempted to apply them arbitrarily, and encouraged the War Agricultural Committees to issue badges – without first consulting the Tribunals – to agricultural employees on holdings where manpower was in clear deficit. In one such case (that of George Pickering, whose employment of a tramp has been discussed above), Sir Ryland Adkins complained strongly to Douglas Thring of the Board's usurpation of his Tribunal's authority. Minutes later, however, having offered only two months' exemption to Percy Brown Jackson, who worked 59 acres of 'four-horse' land and a further 7 acres laid out to market garden produce, the Tribunal guilelessly informed Thring that they would not object to his bringing the case to the attention of the Board. This tacit collusion was not unprecedented. In the same week, Wellingborough Rural Tribunal dismissed – on their military representative's urging – the application of a farmer's son milking 15–20 cows, but then recommended that he appeal the decision, and intimated that the Board might well take up his case, should he apply thereto.[52]

The Board's struggle against the War Office was further assisted by early news of unusually poor cereal harvests in North America and Argentina, the nation's traditional recourses when domestic production faltered.[53] Lord Crawford (Selborne's successor as President of the Board) complained to the Director of Recruiting, Auckland Geddes, that, with regards to production, the problem facing farmers was not just the loss of manpower in absolute terms but the uncertainty regarding future planning that it engendered. Geddes took the point; in September, he agreed to halt recruitment from the land pending a comprehensive survey of the remaining agricultural workforce.[54] On 5 October, the Board of Agriculture issued instructions outlining a new agreement with the War Office: to protect food production, no man remaining in the agricultural sector was to be called up until 1 January 1917 (for those involved entirely in milk production, the date was extended to 1 April 1917). The following day, the Local Government Board issued instructions, drawn up by the newly constituted Man-Power Distribution Board, which confirmed the agreement. It was not unqualified good news for the industry, however. The instructions stressed the urgent need of the army for younger, Category A men, and these would still be taken if viable substitutes could be provided. To that end, the Board of Agriculture committed itself to co-operating with recruiting officers in identifying and releasing for general service those who, previously, had been refused exemption by Tribunals but as a result of the Board's intercession had not been sent to the Colours thereafter. Such men would now return to the Tribunals for re-consideration for service. To assist the process of substitution, the army appointed substitution officers for each district, who would visit farms, identify men fit for service and arrange for substitutes to be found. Furthermore, the instructions gave a thinly veiled warning that such respite as the agreement might afford was not likely to be followed by further concessions:

> The President of the Board accordingly thinks it his duty to urge in the clearest possible manner that farmers should strain every nerve to prepare for changes which may become necessary during January and April 1917.[55]

In the meantime, Home Army officers were ordered to prepare lists of older farm workers and soldiers from agricultural occupations who could be transferred to the Reserve to form a pool of substitutes. To facilitate the War Office's census of agricultural labour, the police were to distribute canvassing forms to all farmers with holdings of more than 5 acres. The top copy was to be returned to the War Office, with a duplicate, ominously, to be passed directly to the local recruiting officer.[56]

The response of Northamptonshire's Tribunals to the 1916 recruitment freeze was uneven. Surprisingly, Northampton Rural, having largely treated agricultural cases favourably to date, reacted circumspectly. At a sitting on 11 October, they debated their agricultural representative's recommendation that nine farming cases before them be postponed until the instructions (of whose content they were at least partially aware) arrived, but decided to consider each on its merits at that sitting. However, meeting strong resistance to this from one applicant's solicitor, they relented and gave conditional exemptions to the end of the year to all nine men. Two weeks later, having perused the instructions and reassured themselves as to the scope of the concession, they ignored several interruptions by their military representative and two recommendations from the Advisory Committee, to offer 31 March 1917 exemptions to several men, including three not involved in milk production.[57]

More measured was the response of the Appeals Tribunal, which attempted to apply the instructions literally. The three technically incorrect exemptions offered by Northampton Rural were reduced to 1 January upon appeal; similarly, they shortened a 1 April 1917 certificate offered by Thrapston Tribunal to Benjamin Smith, an unmarried blacksmith, notwithstanding his responsibility for shoeing almost two hundred horses locally. However, they also resisted military appeals where the shorter agreed exemption period had been given, even in the cases of unmarried younger men. John Michael Peden, single, 22 years old, was allowed to stay on his father's land until 31 December (the certificate was to be final 'unless the Government said something further in the meantime about agricultural workers'), and several other 31 December certificates appealed by military representatives were adjusted, pointedly, to 1 January. Furthermore, despite the terms of the 'freeze', cases continued to be debated on their merits. When Captain Cook admitted that Ralph Burton, a Thrapston farm manager, was truly indispensable to the running of his father's property and agreed that a 31 December certificate was appropriate, Thring urged: 'In that case, give him 1 April. Farmers [have] to know where they stand in the matter of labour.' The Tribunal concurred.[58]

Elsewhere, regardless of a bare appearance of departmental consensus, agricultural and military representatives attempted to test every word of the arrangement in fighting their respective masters' corners. At Rushden, the Board of Agriculture's representative, Eady Robinson, told the Tribunal that domestic wheat production had fallen by 25 per cent, and that not a single man more should be taken from the land. For the Army's part, Colonel Bairstow, attending a sitting of Towcester Tribunal, promised to appeal any exemption offered to men not entirely engaged in milk production, while Adam Cross at Brixworth told his own tribunalists that it required a 'very strong case' to convince him that any man under 25 should remain on the land.[59]

Towcester Tribunal appear to have taken Colonel Bairstow's threats to heart, and were said in November to be tightening their interpretation of the agreement. In contrast, Brixworth, arriving belatedly at the conclusion that they had sent enough agricultural workers into the Army, decided to apply the freeze conscientiously (responding to Cross's forthright opinion against their doing so, one of their tribunalists, J. Brambley was almost contrite about their past record: 'in many cases that came before them the men were needed more on the land than in the Army'). Wellingborough Rural, though continuing to offer conditional certificates where appropriate, took care also to resist applications for or from younger men, or from those for whom a viable substitute could be found.[60] Elsewhere, there were few aberrant decisions handed down by Tribunals, who appear to have been awaiting developments following the end of the 'freeze' and the results of the War Office's promised census.[61]

Fundamental political and military developments overshadowed both events, however, bringing mixed prospects for agriculture. The Allied military crisis of late 1916, and the corresponding need for fresh recruits, threw into doubt any long-term protection for the younger agricultural workforce, whatever the result of the War Office's census. Conversely, Asquith's departure on 5 December ushered in an administration that was far more willing to contemplate direct intervention to protect the food supply. Innovations came quickly. On 20 December, Rowland Prothero, the new President of the Board of Agriculture, announced a policy to improve domestic production by means of arable land reclamation, powers to improve farming techniques and management compulsorily, and the decentralization of agricultural administration.[62] Known subsequently as the 'plough policy', it was given teeth by the creation, on 1 January 1917, of the Food Production Department, charged with the supervision of new, county-level bodies – the War Agricultural Executive Committees. Ten days later, the Committees were given powers to enforce cultivation orders, inspect land, and, where resistance or incompetence was evident, to take over farms and install alternative management.[63]

The new policy also provided clarification regarding the position of smaller-scale food producers. For a number of reasons, the treatment to date of market gardeners and allotment holders by the Tribunals had been less consistent than that afforded to larger-scale producers. Though the original definition of 'farmers' in the first Military Service Act had included both market gardeners and fruit growers, men who worked less extensive holdings – no matter how intensively cultivated – were vulnerable to

challenges from military representatives that their activities did not constitute a full-time occupation, and, therefore, that they did not fall within the
Certified List. There was also the matter of non-essential produce. Many
market gardeners, then as now, habitually met the demand for more expensive foodstuffs and flowers. Grapes and peaches were named by at least
one Tribunal as being 'luxury' items, and surplus berry fruits were often
earmarked for the manufacture of jam, another non-essential food. Nor
did cultivation of any type of flower or non-edible plant fall within legislation's definition of 'agriculture'. Again, such activities, even where supplementary, could be seized upon as undermining the full-time qualification
in determining whether a man fell within the list of certified occupations.

Market gardeners could – and did – emphasise that, acre for acre,
they produced three times as much food as farmers did, but the reception of that argument depended upon the Tribunal who heard it. Predictably, Hardingstone chose not to apply any size test to market gardening
businesses, and, usually, offered exemptions no less generous than those
they gave to men working larger-scale farming concerns. Conversely, at
the Appeals Tribunal on 5 October 1916, Captain Cook was able to obtain
a variation to (though no finality upon) a certificate previously given to a
smallholder, George Hornsey, on the basis that he worked only one and a
half acres (though precisely that amount of land had previously been stated
to be the optimum for one man, digging).[64] Fortunately for Hornsey, the
Army Council's 'freeze' on agricultural enlistment, announced the same
day, explicitly included market gardeners; but ambiguities regarding the
degree to which they fell within successive concessions and more formal
arrangements persisted for a further nine months, until the general freeze
on agricultural recruitment in summer 1917 brought further clarification
regarding their role.[65]

As regards the cultivation of allotments, this was necessarily a part-time
activity that fed the family first and only incidentally produced a surplus;
such work was useful, but could hardly, in itself, constitute a ground for
exemption under either the Military Service Act or informal concession.
However, as part of the raft of legislation that inaugurated the work of
the Food Production Department, local authorities were given powers
to enter into and occupy vacant land for conversion to allotments.[66] The
subsequent take-up of these council plots was very high: the number of
allotments worked in England and Wales rose from some 570,000 at the
outbreak of war to 1.4 million by June 1918. Accordingly, from early 1917
the Tribunals began to take into consideration a man's working of an allotment as one (though only one) of a number of circumstances that might,
collectively, merit an exemption certificate.[67] In fact, enthusiasm for allotment work swiftly outpaced both legislation and, apparently, Scripture.

Complaints were made to local police forces in Northamptonshire that men were breaking regulations regarding Sunday work, a habit that grew significantly after the Archbishop of Canterbury suggested publicly that men cultivating their allotments on Sundays were doing God's and the King's work. By March 1917, Northampton Allotment Society had between three and four hundred members, several of whom had been reported for their desecration of the Sabbath. Northampton Borough Tribunal, though having no higher jurisdiction, expressed their tacit approval: 'We assume that in the present circumstances the anti-Sunday labour rule will not be pressed.' Two months later, a further four hundred allotments had been laid out on ground broken up on Miss Mary Bouverie's 3000–acre Delapre Park estate, and, in June, the Appeals Tribunal decided to assist the process by withdrawing the VTC condition on existing certificates where the appellant also worked a plot in his spare time, a policy that continued until the end of hostilities.[68]

These and other manifestations of the new government's 'hands-on' wardenship of food production did not, however, lessen external pressures on the agricultural workforce. On 6 January, Prothero, explaining his new policy to a meeting at the Bedford Corn Exchange, had stated confidently: 'What [the War Office] has promised me is this: that until the census returns are fully in and are carefully analysed, they will make no further call for men.' However, as noted elsewhere, the new War Cabinet had already accepted the War Office's urgent demand for 100,000 men for the Army in January 1917. It was determined that agriculture's 'share' of this should be 30,000, half of whom would consist of men previously refused exemptions by the Tribunals.[69] With the Cabinet's agreement, Prothero secured the Army's agreement to release further Home Army personnel to cover this dilution: 15,000 were allocated for the cultivation season, and 10,000 more (4000 from Infantry Works battalions and 6000 men in lower medical categories) were to be placed into Army Class W Reserve for the remainder of the war – military necessities allowing – to 'fire-fight' short-term manpower crises in food production. Prothero also persuaded Lloyd George to direct the War Office to take men due from agriculture over a period of two to three months, rather than immediately (as had been planned).[70]

The purgative effect of these new manpower demands, and the exigencies of the 'plough policy', encouraged a more structured initiative to bring women into agriculture in significant numbers. Prothero indicated that he wished to recruit a total of 100,000 village women and 40,000 urban volunteers to counter the effects of dilution; accordingly, in January, a Women's Branch of the Board of Agriculture was formed, and, two months later, designated a sub-section of the Food Production Department. At the same time, an appeal was launched nationwide for women to join a Land Army, to be mobilized and sent wherever agricultural manpower needs were most pressing. Initially, 45,000 women responded (though only 5000 of these were accepted), and, if the organization was only ever to provide a fraction of the female labour supplied by village women, its creation nevertheless signalled the first concerted official commitment to non-military substitution.[71]

The impact of these measures would necessarily be felt only in the long term, and pressures upon existing manpower levels were felt immediately, notwithstanding the Army's declared optimism in its substitution arrangements. On 13 January, Captain Farrer, substitution officer at Northampton Barracks, addressed a Farmers' Union meeting at the Grand Hotel to explain how substitution would work. Men unfit for service abroad were being brought back to depots; full details of their former employments were being gathered, and, where feasible, former agricultural workers would be sent back to their own parishes or farms. Farrer stressed, however, that men would be replaced only on a one-for-one basis, that he could do nothing to enhance existing manpower levels, and that soldiers rated B2 or above would not be brought into the scheme. There were complaints from the floor that to replace A or B1 men with C3 substitutes was pointless, and Alderman Thornton proposed a resolution, instantly seconded, that agricultural manpower in Northamptonshire was at 'an irreduceable [*sic*] level'. The *Mercury* journalist who reported the meeting concluded: 'I am afraid the farmers who attended … were not greatly impressed.'[72]

Locally, there was a growing sense (expressed both in the press and before several Tribunals) that in this latest combing-out of agriculture the War Office had reneged upon its agreement to abide by the labour scales. In fact, the scales had never been binding, but the point was lost upon men whose farms already lacked the agreed level of labour needed to sustain them, who were being subjected to unprecedented pressure to increase their arable acreage, and whose produce prices were being frozen by statute. Nor was there the slightest faith expressed in the much-advertised substitution system: many farmers claimed that adequate men were not being released by barracks, and some tribunalists agreed. At Hardingstone, W.D. Sturgess observed of several agricultural cases: 'They never will be substituted … the substitutes can't be found' (in response to similar complaints from Eton Rural Tribunal, South Buckinghamshire's substitution officer informed them on 17 January that the scheme had been 'curtailed' at present, and that 'serving soldiers will not be demobilised for the purpose').[73] Even military representatives acknowledged the arrangement's shortcomings. At the Appeals Tribunal on 21 February 1917, Daventry's W. Murland, attending to challenge an appeal by Charles M. Froome, an unmarried, 24-year-old farmer, conceded that he couldn't be spared unless substituted. Adkins asked precisely what he meant by substitution. 'Ask me something easy', Murland retorted.[74]

This widespread lack of faith in the scheme ended somewhere short of Whitehall. Pressed by Lloyd George to slow the rate at which he took his thirty thousand recruits from the land, Lord Derby replied tersely that there was in fact evidence of a surplus of labour in several counties, due in no small part to the effectiveness of Army substitution.[75] Yet, despite claims by Eastern Command that 'hundreds' of men were at the depots by March 1917 and wanted only applications to get them out on to the land, take-up remained sporadic and the quality of substitutes was poor. Stories of convalescent or inexperienced C3 soldiers who were fit for no strenuous work were heard often at the Tribunals – sometimes from the tribunalists themselves. W.D. Sturgess's pessimistic opinion, noted above, had been nurtured by his own experience: in the previous January he had applied to barracks and had been sent a horsekeeper to assist on his farm. The man had been shot in both legs at the Front and in convalescence had received a week's experience of tending horses. In March, W. Woods, chairing his own Tribunal, Wellingborough Urban, told them that he had been sent four soldiers who had never been out of London in their lives (one of them had asked Woods if he wanted his sheep brought in at nights). Even when the system was better established, farmers applying for soldiers complained variously of having been sent a Bermondsey leather-dresser (the personal claim of the agricultural representative, T.C. Woods), lunatics and men who 'didn't know the difference between a cabbage and a gooseberry bush'.[76]

Notwithstanding its obvious flaws, the substitution scheme was pushed strongly by recruiting officers in the short term, though there remained considerable uncertainty regarding precisely what had been agreed between the War Office and Board of Agriculture. According to Kettering Rural Tribunal's military representative, C.R. Knollys, substitution officers could recommend and provide a man from a military depot to replace a farm worker. The farmer would then have two weeks to satisfy himself that the substitute was satisfactory; if not, he might then complain to the local military and agricultural representatives. Should no agreement result at this stage, the military representative had the right to appeal against any further exemption for the farm worker on the basis that a suitable substitute had been made available. However, at the Appeals Tribunal's sitting of 12 February, Douglas Thring disputed this interpretation. His own reading of the agreement suggested that if consensus on a substitute could not be reached, the ultimate arbiter appeared to be Colonel Fawcett, the officer commanding the Northamptonshire military district, against whose decision no appeal was possible. Adkins and Thompson objected that, if this were the case, the jurisdiction of the Tribunals was entirely under-mined. After discussing the matter *in camera*, they responded decisively: a number of open certificates were issued to agricultural workers, condi-tional upon suitable substitutes being found who were satisfactory to their employers, or, failing that, to the Tribunal. There is no evidence that the military were allowed a final say thereafter in any individual substitution issue in Northamptonshire.[77]

In the weeks that followed, further agricultural appeals were processed on the basis that the men would go into the Army only if and when suitable substitutes were found. On 20 February, Thring convinced the Tribunal that conditional certificates should not be time-limited once the condition had been stated, in order to allow farmers to plan ahead with what they had. To a degree, the resulting concession assumed a greater willingness among agricultural employers to seek substitutes than was the case. Many had indeed secured men from the depots who proved to be unsuitable; many more had heard their stories and decided not to test the system. Military representatives and substitution officers complained repeatedly to the Tribunals that Home Army men were available in Northampton-shire depots, but that farmers were not applying for them. Yet, in a sense, the arrangement between the Board of Agriculture and War Office had bypassed the Tribunals: it was the latters' duty to recognize the substitu-tion system, and (in the opinion of the Appeals Tribunal at least) to adjudi-cate, but not to implement or otherwise administer it.

The matter of jurisdiction was complicated further by new instructions. Firstly, on 20 March, a revised list of certified occupations in agricul-ture was issued. Unmarried farm bailiffs, foremen, grieves, stewards and seedmen below the age of 31 were de-certified, as were unmarried stockmen, horsemen, wagoners, shepherds, ploughmen, nursery and market garden foremen, thatchers, teamsters and carters below the age of 26 (unless, in all cases, indispensability could be demonstrated, or, upon medical examina-tion, a man fell within category C).[78] All those whose existing certificates were invalidated by the new list required to make fresh applications to the Tribunals within two weeks.

In a separate initiative, the Food Production Department and the War Office entered into a new arrangement whose complexity confounded those who were obliged to implement it. It related both to agricultural workers with continuing exemption certificates and to those whose certifi-cates, having been cancelled, were not now renewed. In either case, where an agricultural representative considered that a man's enlistment would unduly deplete labour on his farm, a cumbersome ballet ensued to find a lower category substitute (from a neighbouring farm or military depot) or

National Service volunteer (usually female), with the military or agricultural representatives, and, in turn, the Agricultural Executive Committees and Area Commanders, able to object or consent at various stages of the process. Where the men concerned had existing exemption certificates, the question of how far an arrangement trespassed upon the authority of the Tribunals provided another layer of abstruseness to confound the process.[79]

Predictably, attempts to implement the agreement revealed several understandings of what it actually comprised. On 11 May, Thring's successor at the Appeals Tribunal, Towcester tribunalist and farmer T.C. Woods, asked plaintively if the Tribunal might give their opinion on the instructions they – and he – had received.[80] He had spoken to the local recruiting officer, Lieutenant Dorrington, whose own opinion was that he had no authority (or obligation) to leave agricultural workers on the land beyond the end of their exemption periods. Furthermore, it seemed the 'hundreds' of potential substitutes at the military depots had now been returned to their habitual postings (the day before, 18,000 'ploughmen', temporarily transferred to Army Reserve W, had been withdrawn from depots across England and Wales and had rejoined their units).[81] Might the Tribunal, Woods asked, suggest a solution? Stopford-Sackville argued that, when the Tribunal had made a decision, it ought not to be overturned: the system was a farce otherwise. He also agreed with the new agricultural representative that 'it was almost impossible to keep up with the various authorities' instructions anyway'. Drily, the *Mercury*, reporting the exchange, entitled the piece 'Another Solomon needed'.[82]

In fact, the new instructions, relying entirely upon a supply of substitutes that had (temporarily at least) disappeared, were effectively stillborn, notwithstanding the degree to which individual Tribunals applied the wit or patience to interpret them. Some military representatives, seemingly as confused by the process as their tribunalists, appear to have had little faith that substitutes might be found. On 18 May, Captain Cook half-heartedly insisted that a soldier would be available to replace David Robinson, a single, 24-year-old cowman whose exemption, previously, he had requested be reviewed but conceded, almost in the same breath, that the substitution system was currently being revived, 'he hoped with success'. Minutes later, having been tested further by his tribunalists as to the likelihood of finding substitutes, Cook washed his hands of the matter, stating that, as Northamptonshire had already contributed fully to its quota of the thirty thousand new recruits from agriculture, he would not seek to take more men from the land at present.[83]

If the Appeals Tribunal found the new instructions perplexing and unrealistic, some rural Tribunals chose either to sidestep the issue of substitution entirely or merely to note 'subject to substitution' when offering (usually long) exemptions to farm workers. Misapprehensions abounded as to what constituted 'policy'. At Oxendon Rural on 9 May, the agricultural representative, W.E. Attenborough, stated baldly that he was going to press for exemption for all land workers except 18-year-olds, as the target increase of 75,000 acres of arable land in the county could not be worked without labour. One of the tribunalists, Barwell Ewins, asked helplessly 'Then we must ignore our instructions regarding men under 25?' At Brixworth, in June, a Tribunal that prided themselves upon the rigour of their interrogations arbitrarily gave six-month certificates to a number of agricultural workers despite Adam Cross's strong protest. In the same month, Northampton Rural briskly disregarded their military representative's claim that he could find a substitute for an 18-year-old, category A under-wagoner, and gave the young man an (open) certificate to 30 September.

Inevitably, the arcane processes of the new substitution arrangement greatly increased the workloads of military and agricultural representatives, and their returns were relatively meagre. Promises that adequate substitutes could be found were repeatedly exposed by the reality of inadequate distribution and/or quality of the Home Army's manpower resources. In turn, farmers had little incentive to apply for substitutes as long as Tribunals – fully aware of the arrangement's weaknesses – showed themselves willing to listen favourably to applications for existing employees. This relative lack of success, and the War Cabinet's agreement on targets for the 1918 tillage, brought a decisive shift in the balance of power between the Army and Board of Agriculture – though not without further, contradictory initiatives. On 23 June, a new list of certified occupations tightened age-limited exemptions for certain classes of farm workers; three days later, however, Captain Cook announced to the Appeals Tribunal that he had received a War Office telegram, stating that no man (of whatever medical category) certified by the Executive committees as having been on the land since 31 March was to be called to the Colours.[84] A memorandum from the Board to the committees confirmed this development in more detail.[85] No one engaged in agriculture would go into the army unless the committees themselves decided that it was no longer in the national interest that he should remain on the land (though even in such a case, the man had the right to apply to the Tribunal and be exempted until a satisfactory substitute could be found). All others would receive protection vouchers (or war agricultural certificates) directly from the committees rather than through the Tribunal system; these, effectively, would 'badge' the men. Agricultural workers eligible under the scheme but not yet certified should be told to apply as soon as possible. Further, the War Cabinet directed that all Home Army soldiers presently working on the land should remain there, rather than be withdrawn at the end of their furlough periods, and committed to providing an additional fifty thousand serving men. As part of this initiative, the role of the market gardener was further defined. Now, even fruit growers whose produce was partly allocated to jam production might be eligible for vouchers if they were not engaged substantially in growing 'luxury' fruits.[86]

These measures effectively ended large-scale manpower dilution in the industry during 1917. Indeed, in absolute terms, the agricultural labour force in England and Wales grew slightly between July and December.[87] With the Board of Agriculture effectively deciding whether the nation could afford to lose more land-workers, the Tribunals were able to relinquish a responsibility that had been at least partly circumscribed by previous 'arrangements'. For the moment they continued to process existing applications, principally by issuing temporary certificates to keep agricultural workers on the land while they applied to the Committees for their vouchers. Thereafter, there was a pronounced hiatus in agricultural business before the Tribunals. A very few Category A 'men', newly fallen within provisions of the Military Service Act as they reached their eighteenth birthdays, were obliged to apply for exemptions for want of a voucher; otherwise, the very few cases comprised reviews of existing exemptions demanded by military representatives, usually on the basis that a man was not fully employed in farm work or had recently swapped employments within agriculture. None of these challenges appears to have been successful. Nor did a belated attempt by the Army Council to test the extent of what might constitute an 'acceptable' proportion of land laid out to luxury fruit production incline any Tribunal in Northamptonshire to send a single market gardener into the Army during this period. Some military representatives, in the county and elsewhere, misunderstood their instructions and attempted to file appeals with the Tribunals when the committees issued vouchers to Category A men, but this was a forlorn strategy: it was the committees alone who – for the moment at least – determined the fate of agricultural workers.[88]

Though Prothero and his government had flagged major changes to the strategy and conduct of food policy from early 1917, inertia, poor planning-management and unforeseen military commitments had prevented their implementation for almost half a year. Now, however, security of manpower resources and, from August 1917, guaranteed minimum prices for grains provided a foundation upon which the intended 'plough policy' could be built. Consequently, the harvest of 1918 was to produce an increase of more than six million tons of grain, potatoes, beans and peas over that of two years earlier; in Northamptonshire, farmers managed to increase their total tilled acreage by between one-fifth and one-third during 1917–1918.[89]

The process was assisted by a marked improvement in the supply of substitute labour. As noted, earlier large-scale arrangements for soldier substitution had been markedly mistrusted, and, consequently, under-utilized by farmers. However, the retention of significant numbers of serving men on the land after mid-1917 allowed more effective training of the many who, despite their claims when applying for agricultural furloughs, had little or no prior experience of farming. As late as August 1917, a firm of nurserymen applying to Northampton Rural Tribunal for five of their employees stated that they had 12 soldiers working for them, but could lose ten of them 'comfortably'. Thereafter, however, the few complaints regarding soldiers made to the Tribunals tended to refer to the shortage, rather than quality, of men supplied by the Army Depots. By early 1918, the system of substitution had achieved a notable, if belated degree of effectiveness: the employment experience of all Home Army men had been placed upon a card index, allowing more focused targeting of men to where their talents might best serve.[90]

The incidence of female labour on farms also increased during this period, though precise figures are elusive. Throughout the war, the vast proportion of women on the land were villagers, and very cursorily represented in the Z8 statistics (owing largely to farmers' reluctance to report their presence, notwithstanding an Army concession that women should not count in measuring a farm's 'manpower' for the purposes of the labour scales). The Women's Land Army contribution continued to be negligible, rising from approximately five thousand participants at its inception to only 6672 by November 1917 and a maximum of 16,000 prior to the Armistice.[91] However, the most notable breakthrough in the utilization of female labour resulted not from the training of women but from the changing attitudes of farmers. Contemporary commentators acknowledge that opinions modified considerably from 1917 as prejudice was supplanted by personal experience.[92] Again, though there is little explicit evidence of this in Northamptonshire, incidents of complaints regarding women workers on farms fall off dramatically in case notes and Tribunal reports. This weakening of traditional preconceptions facilitated a greater role for female labour in the following year, when dilution pressures upon the male agricultural workforce increased once more. However, the improvement can easily be overstated; women's penetration of agriculture as a whole during the war was relatively slight compared to their growing industrial emancipation.[93]

One other source of substitute labour, uncommon before early 1918 but prevalent thereafter, was the pool of German prisoners of war with agricultural experience. Information on how many Northamptonshire farmers had the opportunity or inclination to access this resource is ambiguous. There was a POW camp at Eastcote, some six miles from Northampton; on one occasion, Brixworth Tribunal recorded their 'emphatic opinion' against the use of prisoners in ironstone quarries while approving their employment in coal mines (which hints at the availability of prisoners, locally). A single reference to the use of Hungarian internees on the land in Northampton-shire suggests also that the non-combatant enemy was being utilized, if not extensively. Some weeks before the end of the war, Beatrice Cartwright expressed her distaste at the prospect of Land Army women working upon farms where enemy combatants were employed, indicating that she had some knowledge of the practice (though she admitted it had by that time been abandoned in most parts of the country). Firm evidence regarding the participation of German POWs in the county's war effort is sparse. A Towcester engineer stated in October 1918 that his firm employed a number of them on lathes, and six months earlier an *Independent* article revealed that 40 Germans had been assigned to agricultural work in the Oundle area. However, the same newspaper observed as late as June 1918 that only 15 POWs had been provided to farms in the county on an overnight basis (lack of suitable accommodation had been the principal cause of their low utilization).[94] From the paucity of further evidence, it may be assumed that the use of prisoners of war in Northamptonshire's agriculture sector had only a minor impact upon local manpower issues.

The 1917 freeze upon agricultural employment, the most sustained phase of protection for the sector during the conscription period, came to an end – though not abruptly – with renewed manpower pressures in the after-math of the Passchendaele offensive. As 12 months earlier, the industry's proposed share of the reinforcement of the army's combat strength was fixed at thirty thousand Grade I (formerly Category A and B1) men, a figure agreed between the Board of Agriculture and the Ministry of National Service. These were, however, to be released gradually, over the coming six months. In the event, very little happened in the short term; the govern-ment's gradual re-ordering of manpower priorities ensured that the power to withdraw exemptions given on occupational grounds (as enshrined in the Military Service Act 1918) was not, as yet, exercised.

However, the panic generated by the German *Michael* offensive in late March firmly, if briefly, reasserted the BEF's first call upon men. From agriculture, the requirement for 30,000 men was reaffirmed hurriedly: the 'clean-cut' proclamation of 20 April removed exemptions and war agricul-tural certificates from Grade I agricultural workers below the age of 23, a measure that was anticipated to release almost 16,000 men.[95] The remainder were to be taken from age groups up to 31. It was stated, furthermore, that this was to be only a first call upon men, and subsequent comb-outs should be expected. Highly skilled or 'key' men, identified as such by the executive committees, could reapply for exemption before 15 May, a provision which brought the Tribunals decisively back into the agricultural question.

The Food Production Department reacted strongly to this fundamental threat to its plough policy, and, by 8 May, had obtained from the War Office a concession that the call for thirty thousand men would be the last (future military exigencies permitting). Additionally, the Ministry of National Service issued instructions five days later that the Tribunals might, at their discretion, ignore the 'clean-cut' provisions in the case of applications made by agricultural machine mechanics, drivers and operators.[96]

On 17 May and again five days later, Northamptonshire's Appeals Tribunal devoted their entire sitting to (116) agricultural cases. As a preamble to the former day's business, they warned younger appellants that it would be useless to bring cases on occupational grounds unless they had first been certified by the executive committee. In that respect, the solicitor H.W. Williams, representing several men, reminded the Tribunal that the Committee had turned down 60 per cent of applications they had heard to date. During that sitting, men under 23 with certificates received a range of exemptions based upon their individual circumstances. The majority of certificates had finality attached, though hardship cases or men with several brothers serving already received open exemptions but were warned that they should not expect them to remain so. Men above the clean-cut age received exemptions of three to four months (the majority open). On 22 May, 71 cases from Brixworth, Brackley, Thrapston, Towcester and Daventry were processed. Again, most received exemptions, their status – open or final – determined by the age and skills of the appellant.[97]

These sittings were the final large-scale consideration of agricultural cases by the Tribunals. In retrospect (and as with the boot and shoe trade), it is clear that the clean-cut did less to meet the Army's need for men than to reveal the true extent of prior dilution of skilled labour. Lord Ernle, apparently referring to Northamptonshire, stated that, of the county's recruitment quota of five hundred men, only 422 were found, and these included 89 wagoners, carters and horsemen, 20 skilled ploughmen, 19 shepherds and 60 cowmen. Across the country as a whole, only 23,000 men were secured for the Army from agriculture.[98] Within weeks of the hearings, furthermore, the sense of crisis had faded, and the imperatives of the 'plough policy' reasserted themselves. From 11 June, the power to issue certificates on occupational grounds to certain classes of agricultural workers was removed from the Tribunals (though those who applied on other grounds, such as personal circumstance, would continue as before to be heard). Thereafter, such men would apply directly to the executive committees for protection vouchers.[99]

There was an immediate and marked reduction in agricultural

applications or appeals to the Tribunals. The few cases processed in the following weeks were those either of land workers citing personal circumstances or applications for renewals of certificates granted during the 'clean-cut' (men holding the latter fell outside the protection voucher system for the moment).[100] Decisions made in these cases indicate that the Tribunals, having reluctantly applied the clean-cut provisions, were by now almost wholly amenable to applications from the local farming community. No local Tribunal in Northamptonshire imposed finality upon a certificate issued during the summer of 1918, and even the Appeals Tribunal (who had warned young men that they could not expect to remain in civilian life indefinitely) treated personal circumstance case with marked leniency. In July, Herbert T. Harrington, an 18-year-old, Grade 2 agricultural machinery apprentice and sole support of his widowed mother, was offered a six-month open certificate, a technically incorrect decision by Crick Tribunal,. This, and their subsequent decision, that Thomas R. Ashby, a Grade 1 market gardener, should not be called up before 2 September (his application on the ground of personal circumstance had been rejected), was briskly upheld on appeal, despite Captain Cook's objections.[101]

From the Tribunals' perspective, the agricultural question disappeared entirely after 24 September 1918, when the Ministry of National Service issued new instructions that all workers falling within a revised list of agricultural occupations should apply to their local executive committee for a protection voucher. The list was long and comprehensive, commencing with agricultural machine managers and concluding with rabbit, mole and rat catchers.[102] In a parting gesture that same day, Hardingstone Tribunal, adjudging the application of a 43-year-old gardener's labourer who helped to tend 8 acres of vegetables and 120 poles of allotment, offered a six months' certificate, conditional upon the applicant agreeing to assist other farmers. Before he could withdraw, one of the tribunalists offered him a job, which he promptly accepted.[103] Thereafter, the Tribunal, who, more than any other in Northamptonshire, had striven to be the farmer's friend, rested upon their record.

The 'plough policy' and associated initiatives increased the tilled acreage in England by some 20 per cent in the two years to 1918. As noted, Northamptonshire witnessed an increase in the range of 20–30 per cent, which, while not quite matching the achievement of neighbouring Leicestershire (a spectacular 50–plus per cent), reflected creditably upon a county whose topography favoured grazing.[104] At no point did the food supply to the British people fail, though a limited system of rationing was introduced during winter 1917 to ensure that the working classes and socially vulnerable were not exposed to shortages created by distribution difficulties.[105]

Agriculture can therefore be regarded as one of the unequivocal success stories of the Home Front. Nevertheless, its achievements were often built in spite, rather than because, of interventions from Whitehall. Being composed of individual, owner-occupied concerns, the industry did not enjoy the level of internal organization of, for example, the boot and shoe trade, and could present no united 'face' when resisting pressures upon manpower. However, farmers enjoyed powerful political support in Whitehall, and the sympathetic attitude of many rural Tribunals to their plight was buttressed by very effective lobbying on the part of the Board of Agriculture. From mid-1916, growing perceptions of the potential for significant food shortages had the effect of halting and even partially reversing the manpower losses suffered during the voluntary phase of recruitment, but the process was neither uniform nor consistent. As with its wider search for a manpower policy, government recognized that something should be 'done' about agricultural production long before the viable measures to protect the industry were conceived, much less implemented. It was therefore due in great part to independent arrangements agreed between the Board of Agriculture and War Office, rather than to formal policy, that the recruitment freezes of 1916 and 1917 eased pressure upon Northamptonshire farmers.

The principle of substitution, as has been seen, was nowhere more strongly pressed than upon agriculture, and its widespread failure prior to 1918 – particularly with respect to the employment of soldiers – is perhaps the most emphatic testament to the disingenuity of Army claims that remaining higher-category men could be removed from the land without compromising production. Indeed, so marked was the inadequacy of the Home Army's arrangements that military representatives at the Tribunals often shared the disillusionment of applicants regarding substitution, and their unwillingness to defend the 'system' contributed in no small part to its temporary abandonment in May 1917.

Given the role of the Board of Agriculture with regard to farmers and other land workers, the Tribunals' role, in both moderating and facilitating rates of dilution, was intermittent. Indeed, for several months in each year of the conscription period, the exemption process regarding agricultural workers was removed almost entirely from their hands. At other times, however, the Tribunals were subjected to two almost equally strong, and contradictory, pressures to consider the agricultural workforce on a wider than case-by-case basis. From the latter part of 1916, they received constant reminders from the Board of Agriculture, and, subsequently, the Food Production Department, that arable farming output had to be maintained or increased; yet equally persistent were War Office demands that an industry utilising a high proportion of an unhealthy nation's fittest men should release more of them. Some Tribunals, naturally sensitive to the place of the farmer in their communities, consistently applied their own understanding of the balance between these imperatives to the disadvantage of the recruiting officer. Others, whether more mindful of the 'national emergency' or amenable to local perceptions that farmers' sons were avoiding service in much the same manner as young, single munitions workers, showed little discernible sympathy for the unique circumstances of the agricultural life until the impact of over-dilution in their localities became marked. Attempts by the Board of Agriculture and War Office to apply their increasingly complicated arrangements to share out the dwindling stock of higher-category men encouraged confusion, over- or under-reaction on the part of individual Tribunals, and, gradually, a consensus that agricultural workers should be taken only when adequate substitutes were available. In a sense, the Tribunals threw back upon the Army the onus of showing that its much-mooted military substitution system worked. It was a consensus that predated government resolve by several months – encouraged, in great part, by an appreciation of the scale of efforts necessary to implement the plough policy in a county where, traditionally, arable farming had not been predominant.

Notes

1 Lord St Audries, 12 April 1916 (5 H.L. 21:680).

2 Middleton, *Food Production in War*, p. 90; Sheail, 'Land Improvement and Reclamation', pp. 110–111; Ministry of Agriculture, Fisheries and Food, *A Century of Agricultural Statistics, 1866–1966*, p. 13; Beaver, *The Land in Britain*, p. 391; Harris, Hartop and Buckley, *Northamptonshire: Its Land and People*, pp. 82–84; Ernle, 'The Food Campaign of 1916–1918', p. 6; Dewey, *British Agriculture in the First World War*, p. 16, table 2.7.

3 Sheail, 'The Role of the War Agricultural and Executive Committees', pp. 144–145.

4 Mansfield, *English Farmworkers and Local Patriotism, 1900–1930*, pp. 80–82, 89–90.

5 Dewey, 'Military Recruiting and the British Labour Force During the First World War', p. 205; Mansfield, *English Farmworkers*, p. 111. In an earlier work ('Agricultural Labour Supply in England and Wales during the First World War', p. 104), Dewey suggested that the loss of 'conventional' (that is, non-seasonal) agricultural labour in England and Wales by 1916 was as low as 9 per cent.

6 Montgomery, *Maintenance of the Agricultural Labour Supply*, p. 22; Mansfield, *English Farmworkers*, pp. 111–112.

7 Cf. *Mercury*, 26 May, 20 October 1916.

8 LGB Circular R.3, Section v (i): 'The local recruiting officer may apply ... to the Tribunal ... upon any of the following questions ... (c) (iii): Whether it is no longer necessary in the national interest to retain him in civil employment.'

9   In March 1918, an Irishmen described as an 'agricultural instructor of lunatics' appeared before Northampton Borough Tribunal (*Mercury*, 8 March 1918).

10 Montgomery, *Agricultural Labour Supply*, p. 3.

11 LGB Circular R.4 (15 December 1915).

12 Above, p. 24.

13 *Herald*, 25 February 1916; *Mercury*, 3 March 1916.

14 *The Times*, 11 March 1916; *Herald*, 25 February 1916; WRO CR1520/62/3, 11, 17, 21; CBS DC/14/39/1, Tribunal minute book, pp. 8. 14. Note also Viscount Midleton's fulminations against two Tribunals 'north of the Tweed' that had offered long exemptions to all but a handful of agricultural applicants during their first sittings (5 H.L. 21:267: 2 March 1916).

15 *The Times*, 24 February 1916.

16 MAF Circular A187L: 26 April 1916 (effective from 1 May 1916).

17 NRO X180/1, 3, 4.

18 NRO X180/7.

19 NRO X180/51, 52; *Mercury*, 7 April 1916.

20 NRO X180/43.

21 Montgomery, *Agricultural Labour Supply*, pp. 22, 24; Dewey, 'Agricultural Labour Supply', p. 104.

22 TNA WO 27/5652/A.G. 2 (14 August 1916).

23 Dewey, *British Agriculture*, p. 51. No explanation was ever offered by government as to how this figure reconciled to the (widely dissimilar) statistics from the 1911 census.

24 *Mercury*, 30 June, 21 July 1916.

25 Cf. Lloyd George's recollection (*War Memoirs*, III, p. 1299): 'the idea that women could do the ordinary work of a farm called forth bucolic guffaws'.

26 *Mercury*, 21 July, 6 October 1916. See also below, p. 108.

27 Montgomery, *Agricultural Labour Supply*, pp. 51–2; Ernle, 'Women's Land Army', p. 52; *Mercury*, 5 May 1916.

28 *Mercury*, 7 April, 12 May 1916.

29 *Mercury*, 5, 19 May 1916.

30 Reporting the meeting, *The Times* (15 March 1916) noted Selborne's sympathetic attitude and condemnation of the 'zealous' attitude of military representatives attempting to remove important men from agriculture.

31 NRO X180/348; *Mercury*, 7 April, 12, 19 May, 1916. The farmer in the Yeomanry appears to have fallen within the remit of the Military Service Act as he had opted for home service only.

32 NRO X180/272; *Mercury*, 21 April 1916.

33 NRO X180/435, 436.

34 *Mercury*, 2 June 1916. On 31 October that year, Heath told his tribunal that they had been lenient with regard to agricultural applications, but that he did not think that they had 'overdone it' (ibid., 3 November 1916).

35 LGB Circular R.85 (as dated); discussion of agricultural cases from the accompanying explanatory notes (R.84, p. 4).

36 NRO X180/473; *Mercury*, 9 June 1916.

37 *Mercury*, 23, 30 June, 14 July 1916.

38 Montgomery, *Agricultural Labour Supply*, pp. 23, 40.

39 *The Times*, 24 June 1916.

40 Montgomery, *Agricultural Labour Supply*, p. 23. It was expected that Eastern Command would mobilize first in the event of a German invasion.

41 NRO X181/603, 631; *Mercury*, 14 July, 25 August 1916.

42 Above, p. 103.

43 NRO X180/473, 474, 565, 592, 593; *Mercury*, 30 June, 21 July 1916.

44 Board of Agriculture, special leaflet no. 59.

45 NRO X180/183; *Mercury*, 14 April 1916. Tee was, however, given an exemption until 31 May 1916.

46 NRO X182/1098; *Mercury*, 6 October, 3 November, 8 December 1916.

47 NRO X181/724; *Mercury*, 6 October 1916.

48 Ernle, 'Women's Land Army', p. 52.

49 NRO X182/907; *Mercury*, 5, 12, 19 May, 21 July 1916.

50 Ernle ('Food Campaign', p. 35) gives a total of 11.61 million tons in 1916 as against 14.01 million tons for 1914 (including peas, beans and potatoes). For wheat alone in the same years, Sheail ('Land Improvement and Reclamation', p. 122) gives 1.498 and 1.634 million tons respectively.

51 LGB Circular R.92 (22 June 1916).

52 NRO X182/966; *Mercury*, 15 September 1916.

53 *Interim report of the Committee to investigate the Principal Causes of the Increased Price of Commodities*, reproduced in *Journal of the Board of Agriculture* (October 1916), p. 693; Hurwitz, *State Intervention in Great Britain*, p. 215.

54 Man-power Distribution Board, 77/66/1 (25 September 1916).

55 MAF Circular A247C (5 October 1916); LGB Circular R.102 (6 October 1916), para. 5.

56 *Journal of the Board of Agriculture*, October 1916, pp. 699–701; December 1916, pp. 900, 903–904.

57 *Mercury*, 13, 27 October 1916.

58 NRO X183/1197, 1332; 184/1409; *Mercury*, 17 November 1916.

59 *Mercury*, 20 October, 17 November 1916.

60 *Mercury*, 17, 24 November, 8 December 1916; NRO X183/1351.

61 In this respect, note Sir Ryland Adkins's subsequent comment in the Commons (8 February 1917): 'I was a member of an appeal tribunal which has put back agricultural cases deliberately for months awaiting the distinct and clear guidance of the Government with regard to the spring' (5 H.C. 90:131).

62 Ernle, 'Food Campaign', p. 5. Lord Ernle was the title taken by Prothero upon his ennoblement on 1919.

63 Middleton, *Food Production in War*, pp. 83, 164–166; Defence of the Realm Act, reg. 10M.

64 *Mercury*, 12 May, 14 July 1916; NRO X183/1054; also above, p. 106.

65 Above, p. 120.

66 Defence of the Realm Act, Reg. 2L (December 1916).

67 TNA MAF 42/8/40171/D.

68 *Mercury*, 23 March, 4 May, 15 June 1917.

69 LGB Circular R.119 (30 January 1917). It was alleged in the Commons that the

War Office's demands had come as a 'staggering blow' to Prothero (5 H.C. 90:171: 8 February 1917).

70 LGB Circular R.119; Montgomery, *Agricultural Labour Supply*, pp. 24–25; Lloyd George MSS, F/15/8/3 (Prothero to Lloyd George, 11 January 1917: TNA CAB 23/1 W.C. 39 (19 January 1917); W.C. 40 (22 January 1917)).

71 Ernle, 'Women's Land Army', p. 52; Dewey, *British Agriculture*, p. 131.

72 *Mercury*, 19 January 1917.

73 CBS DC/10/38/1:Tribunal minute book, p. 110.

74 NRO X184/1947; *Mercury*, 2, 23 February 1917.

75 Correspondence reproduced in Churchill, *Lord Derby*, pp. 269–271.

76 *Mercury*, 26 January, 23 March, 15 June, 31 August 1917. See also Ernle, 'Food Campaign', p. 19.

77 NRO X197: Appeals Tribunal meeting notes (as dated); *Mercury*, 16 February 1917.

78 LGB Circular R.136, as dated.

79 The arrangement is summarized by Montgomery, *Agricultural Labour Supply*, pp. 15–17. ACI 780/1917 (15 May 1917) instructed military representatives that the release target of thirty thousand agricultural workers should not be exceeded, that no man could be taken until his existing exemption expired, and that no man below Category A could be released without the agreement of the Agricultural Executive Committees. The Instruction also confirmed that the Bath Agreement scales should continue to be applied when assessing a man's eligibility for service.

80 Douglas Thring took up the post of Bursar at Magdelene College, Cambridge, at the end of March (*Mercury*, 31 March 1917).

81 Ernle, 'Food Production Campaign', p. 30. Lloyd George (*War Memoirs*, III, p. 1310) recalled only 15,000 men so allocated, of whom, he alleged, only 2500 knew how to plough.

82 NRO X197: Appeals Tribunal meeting notes (as dated); *Mercury*, 18 May 1917.

83 NRO X186/3405; X197: Appeals Tribunal meeting notes (as dated). Across the border in Warwickshire, Rugby Tribunal's military representative wrote to his counterpart at Warwick, assuring him that he had read ACI 780/1917 in its entirety, but remained at a loss as to what to do when the local Executive Agricultural Committee had no substitutes available (WRO CR1520/62: acts and correspondence file, 1 June 1917).

84 LGB Circular R.136 (revised); NRO X197: Appeals Tribunal meeting notes, 26 June 1917.

85 LGB Circular R.144 (24 July 1917).

86 Dewey, *British Agriculture*, pp. 99–100; Montgomery, *Agricultural Labour Supply*, pp. 16–17; Ernle, 'Food Campaign', pp. 30–31. The protection voucher stated: 'This is a voucher that N. employed by N. of … is now whole time engaged on a farm in farm work as a … and is engaged on work of national importance and was so engaged on the 1st June 1917, and that consent is not given to his being called up for Military Service' (sample wording taken from TNA MH47/112/4657E).

87 Dewey, *British Agriculture*, p. 115.

88 *Mercury*, 31 August, 7 September, 2 November 1917; ACI 1441/1917 (19 September 1917). Middlesex Appeals Tribunal tersely dismissed as otiose several military 'appeals' regarding Category A men during this period (for example, TNA MH47/112/3331, 4003, 4111).

89 Ernle, 'Food Campaign', p. 35; Whettam, *Agrarian History*, p. 116; Dewey, *British Agriculture*, p. 205; Lloyd George, *War Memoirs*, III, p. 1316.

90 *Mercury*, 31 August 1917; LGB Circular R.179 (10 April 1918).

91 Dewey, *British Agriculture*, pp. 115–116; Ernle, 'Women's Land Army', p. 52; Montgomery, *Agricultural Labour Supply*, p. 13. One commentator (Grigg, *Lloyd George: War Leader 1916–1918*, p. 133) puts the total of Land Army recruits as low as twelve thousand.

92 See, for example, the report on female labour in Rutland by Thomas Hacking, *Journal of the Board of Agriculture*, March 1917, pp. 1245–1252.

93 Hurwitz, *State Intervention in Great Britain*, p. 135.

94 NRO X184/1906; *Mercury*, 22 December 1916, 26 January 1917, 6 September, 27 October 1918; *Independent*, 3 March, 8 June 1918.

95 Coming into effect two days earlier, the Military Service (No. 2) Act, 1918, Section 3, provided for the cancellation of certificates in a 'national emergency'; the proclamation gave it effect.

96 Ernle, 'Food Campaign', p. 44; Montgomery, *Agricultural Labour Supply*, p. 19.

97 NRO X193/9049–9276 (broken sequence); X197: Appeals Tribunal meeting notes (as dated); *Mercury*, 24 May 1918.

98 Sheail, 'The Role of the War Agricultural and Executive Committees', pp. 148, 152; Ernle, 'Food Campaign', p. 44. Ernle did not identify Northamptonshire by name, but these precise figures for men due and found were claimed in respect of the county by the *Mercury* in an article entitled 'The Army and the Land' (21 June 1918). In total, 361 of the men taken were said to be skilled workers.

99 LGB Circular R.207 (3 June 1918). These included farmers, market gardeners, foremen, bailiffs, farriers, wheelwrights, seedmen and grain wholesalers, saddle and harness makers, agricultural machinery erectors, repairers and operators, and land agents.

100 The Military Service (Agricultural Exemptions) Order of 11 June 1918, which gave effect to the new voucher system, cancelled certificates of exemption held by farmers on the grounds of occupation, but allowed a four days' grace period in which men could reapply to the Tribunals on personal grounds (see Sir Auckland Geddes's statement to the Commons, 1 August 1918 (5 H.C. 109:641)).

101 NRO X197, Appeal Tribunal meeting notes, 29 July 1918; NRO X194/9677, X196/10208; *Mercury*, 9 August 1918.

102 LGB Circular R.139 (revised); *Mercury*, 27 September 1918.

103 *Mercury*, 2, 9 August, 27 September 1918.

104 Dewey, *British Agriculture*, p. 203; Whettam, *Agrarian History*, p. 116.

105 Winter, *The Great War and the British People*, p. 239; Dewey, *British Agriculture*, p. 220.

6

Directing heads, sole traders and the professions

It is doubtful whether Tribunals in general had more difficult cases than these to deal with.[1]

Following the call to arms in August 1914, many businessmen responded enthusiastically, forming recruitment and drilling leagues, or joining bespoke units of like-minded men 'in a way of business'. In Leeds alone, a 1200–strong battalion principally comprising members (of all 'ranks') of the business community was formed, while the four battalions of the Liverpool Pals and the eight battalions of the Manchester Pals were drawn predominantly from their cities' commercial middle classes (as was one of the four battalions raised in Hull).[2] These were, however, headline initiatives, idiosyncratic in the manner of so many other initial reactions to the outbreak of war in 1914. More prevalent, and by definition more discreet, were the many circumspect businessmen and sole proprietors who wished to help defend the country *in extremis* but were unwilling to sacrifice their enterprises by leaving them leaderless whilst serving overseas, who chose to participate in the many Volunteer Training Corps that mushroomed in the early months of the war.[3] A majority, perhaps, committed to an extraordinary degree to their businesses, chose to regard their efforts as being in themselves sufficiently supportive of the nation at war as not to require any incremental gesture. As a species, therefore, there was little in the manner in which men of business reacted to the war that distinguished them in any way from a majority of their compatriots.

Nor did they represent a distinct interest group in the manner, for example, of the boot and shoe industry or agriculture. Their circumstances were disparate: the head of a substantial manufacturing business, for example, would feel little community of interest with the sole proprietor of a greengrocery or bakery. All, however, shared certain circumstances not typical of most men considered for military service by the Tribunals. To a greater or lesser degree, they had a financial commitment to their enterprises: an investment, whether of cash, stock and/or goodwill, that represented an asset additional to their right to wages. They also exercised an influence upon the health of their enterprise that almost always transcended that of any other individual therein. With some justice, therefore, each might have regarded himself as deserving of an incremental degree of consideration with regard to the consequences of being removed from civilian life

Few Tribunals were entirely insensitive to their predicament. A large proportion of their membership comprised men of business, or of some profession in which they held a proprietary investment. Where, therefore, a man applied for exemption on the grounds of personal hardship, it might be expected that a number of his judges would appreciate the peculiar nature of the 'loss' that enlistment threatened upon his family. More problematic, as it proved, was the issue of a man's value to his business. Claims of indispensability stood or fell upon the same criteria that applied to employed men, and where a substitute was seen to be available – a father who, previously, had retired from the family concern, a partner or qualified wife – the applicant's insistence that he alone could maintain his business was more difficult to sustain.

In the case of the sole proprietor, the Tribunals' task was complicated when his activities fell partially or fully within List D of the Certified Occupations List.[4] Was it in the 'national interest', or equitable, to keep a man out of the Army where sufficient competition existed locally to make his removal sustainable? A just balance was difficult to achieve, and what constituted 'balance' was not a constant quality. From an early stage of the conscription period, the Local Government Board urged that the cases of proprietors in the same way of business be considered 'collectively' (in that the impact of removing men from a district should be examined by reference to what should remain thereafter), and, if possible, at the same sitting. As will be noted, this proved extremely difficult to arrange.

Predictably, Northamptonshire's Tribunals were much occupied with applications from important food-distribution or retail sectors – particularly the butchery, grocery and baking trades. Even regarding less important retail and commercial sectors, the question of how the local economy was to survive the war and recover thereafter exercised many Tribunals from 1917 onwards. In the case of medium-sized concerns, where the loss of a proprietor meant the likely closure of a business, employees would lose their livelihoods and the locality their spending power. Additionally, it was feared that perceived gaps in the market might be filled by outside or even foreign businesses.[5] Clearly, therefore, it was in the local interest that going concerns should be maintained as such. Consequently, urban Tribunals in particular attempted – though not always successfully – to ensure that proprietors who remained out of uniform helped to support the businesses of their less fortunate peers.

It will be apparent from the above that cases presented to the Tribunals by sole proprietors and directing heads of businesses were rarely straightforward. Legislation recognized the 'businessman' but did little to provide clear guidelines upon how his peculiar circumstances might be addressed. Public opinion, in contrast, was not receptive to any assumption that men who already enjoyed a higher-than-median standard of living should expect preferential treatment. In April 1917, *The Times*' laconic observation of the small businessman – that 'the universe continues to revolve around his little shop' – acknowledged not only the strength of personal preoccupation but also a persistent failure to address it.[6] Difficulties arising in consideration of such cases were acknowledged frequently by the Local Government Board and Central Tribunal, but other than stressing that, in personal hardship applications, each should be considered on its own merits (as were, by definition, all cases stated on that ground), advice from the centre was confined to general statements of principle and the provision of heartening, if rare, examples of successful co-operative arrangements. Perhaps more than any other form of application, responsibility for balancing the needs of the nation with those of the local community was allowed to rest firmly with the Tribunals.

The first official word regarding businessmen (though not proprietors *per se*) was issued by the Local Government Board in March 1916, a matter of days after the establishment of Appeals Tribunals throughout England and Wales:

> Tribunals should recognize the injury that may be done to the industries and commerce of this country if managers directing important businesses ... are removed from their present employment and cannot be replaced ... The number of men who come within these classes is comparatively small, but the loss to branches of industry and commerce which supplies the sinews of war would cause damage to the economic welfare of the country out of all proportion to the gain to the Army.[7]

Clearly, the reference here was to men overseeing large or very large concerns, rather than to the more numerous family enterprises whose owners would comprise by far the preponderant type of business applicant to the Tribunals (and whose value in supplying the 'sinews of war' was less immediately obvious). A broad principle was established, but otherwise this initial guidance offered no hint, or anticipation, of the peculiar difficulties that consideration of such cases would raise. However, the issue of the scale of a business encouraged Tribunals to consider the matter of 'national interest' as much as 'national importance' in this type of case. The interest of the nation lay in part in its economic health, which could hardly be sustained by high unemployment. Naturally, local and appeals Tribunals paid particular attention to the local repercussions of releasing men in charge of significant enterprises, and Central Tribunal quickly reinforced the principle that the enlistment of a man who employed a significant number of employees, and whose removal to the Colours would probably result in the termination of his business, was not in the national interest no matter what the nature of that business.[8]

From the applicant's perspective, his role as directing head of his own business was not to be distinguished or discounted upon a point of scale but rather the depth and breadth of his personal commitment. This perception (or misperception) regarding the value of an enterprise, and its owner's indispensability both to it and the wider community, may be illustrated by a number of cases brought before Northamptonshire's Tribunals during their early sittings. Cecil Henry Rathbone, an attested man and partner of Rathbone and Sons, boot, shoe and heel manufacturers, first applied for exemption to Northampton Borough in December 1915, on the basis that the firm had lost two-thirds of its men already, and that those who remained (including himself) were vital to its continuance. His application was dismissed. Rathbone's father then sent a long, detailed letter to the Tribunal, quoting Asquith, Lord Derby and other senior members of government on the inadvisability of removing the 'indispensable' man. Northampton Borough considered the nature of the business, and the fact that Rathbone had a brother on the company's board, and confirmed their previous dismissal of his application.

On 12 March, Rathbone married, buttressing the moral (if not legal) case for his exemption.[9] Eight days later, he wrote to the newly appointed Appeals Tribunal, claiming that his father, who had returned to work at the company only since the Derby Scheme came into force, was now very ill, and that pressure of work had contributed to his decline. Their firm supplied much of the Merchant Navy's footwear needs, and the failure of the business would therefore affect both the war effort and many local families' livelihoods. 'I am sure', he concluded, 'that Lord Derby never intended his scheme to be the ruin of old established firms who have suffered as much as we have already done'. On 30 March, his appeal was dismissed, as was leave to appeal further to Central Tribunal.[10]

Interestingly, Rathbone's case was heard immediately before that of Leslie Wiggins, a man of similar circumstances who appears to have picked up a number of tips for his own, future application(s).[11] More pertinently, this was a very early case, presented at a time when Tribunals' resolve to allow businesses to 'go under' had not yet been tested. In fact, Rathbone's inference that the Appeals Tribunal was acting wilfully against the spirit and intention of legislation in being willing to threaten the existence of an enterprise would prove to be notably wide of the mark. Fears regarding the implications of local business failures were – eventually – to exercise tribunalists far more than their masters in Whitehall, even if the former were obliged repeatedly to draw a clear distinction between an enterprise as such and the necessity of maintaining a man's place within it.

Another early 'indispensable' case was that of Arthur Percy Price, junior partner in the firm of Darnell and Price Solicitors, whose senior partner frequently presented applications to the Tribunals. Price, an attested, single 28-year-old, who had stepped into his deceased father's place at the practice, first applied to Northampton Borough in May 1916, on the grounds that his expertise in conveyancing, probate and trust areas of law were indispensable to the partnership (Darnell, the senior, was principally an advocate, rarely present in their offices, according to Price). The Tribunal offered a conditional certificate, which Geldart appealed. At the appeals hearing on 25 July, Darnell, appearing as a hostile witness in effect, expressed his belief that the firm could indeed spare Price, and offered to maintain the latter's equity (and that of Price's mother) while he was serving with the Colours. The case was adjourned until 4 September, the Appeals Tribunal suggesting discreetly that some form of arbitration might take place in the meantime. Between 28 August and 9 September, a series of increasingly heated letters, copied to the Tribunal, passed between Darnell and Price, covering such issues as Price's (and, by inference, his deceased father's) financial interest in the partnership, the rights of Mrs Price to interest and equity, whether a clerk could do Price's work in his absence and, provocatively, whether the partnership or Price himself should bear the cost of his substitute's salary. On 9 September, one of the Appeals tribunalists, George Wilson Beattie, made a written intervention, attesting Price's exemplary character and strongly contradicting Darnell's increasingly overt implication that Price was a shirker. Nevertheless, the 'indispensability' claim failed: Price's exemption had finality imposed, and Darnell, having played the principal role in sending his junior partner to war, returned to the Tribunals many times subsequently to argue other men's right to exemption.[12]

Notwithstanding the failures of Rathbone, Price and other 'indispensable' businessmen, many applicants continued to regard their centrality within a concern as being in itself sufficient reason for their cases to be considered favourably. On 23 June 1916, Fred Cobb appealed against his local Tribunal's dismissal of his application for exemption on the grounds that Irthlingborough Picturedome, of which he was manager and operator, would have to close otherwise.[13] Predictably, Cobb's appeal was dismissed briskly, but misunderstandings regarding the intention of legislation persisted. As late as February 1917, the Appeals Tribunal were obliged to explain to representatives of Harpole Co-operative Society that the importance of the business itself preceded that of the man within it.[14] An enterprise had to be regarded as being in the national interest, and an applicant's role recognized as necessary to its continuing function, for the circumstances of an employment or profession to constitute – in itself – a ground for exemption.

Where, alternatively, application was made on the grounds of personal hardship, it was the degree of domestic dislocation that would result from an applicant's removal from his business or trade that alone determined his eligibility. Legislation referred in this respect to 'exceptional' circumstances, but neither it nor instructions provided to the Tribunals defined the term or offered illustrative examples. Logically, it referred to an extraordinary financial disadvantage accruing to a man's family by reason of his enlistment. But how was that disadvantage to be measured? Clearly, 'extraordinary' implied relativity: a man in a large way of business, who, by the act of going to war, left his family with far less income than previously, might not rank equally in a Tribunal's consideration with a cottage craftsman engaged in a very small way of business, much less a waged worker whose anticipated Army Separation Allowance might compensate fully for the loss of his existing income (the Separation Allowance (additional to pay) was available to the wives and dependants of all enlisted men, and calculated upon rank and the number of those so dependant. Thus, working-class men with large families were often financially advantaged by their service.) Conversely, many Tribunals were reluctant to be seen as staunch upholders of social inequality while simultaneously promoting the principle of universal sacrifice. Faced with these contradictory pressures, most struggled to implement a consistent policy and often allowed lateral considerations to influence their judgements. Mitigating factors, such as the level of an applicant's investment in his business, and its venerability, were seized upon where available, but otherwise the Tribunals' prevalent reaction to the businessman's application during the early months of military conscription was to allow an incremental period of exemption in which the applicant might settle his affairs. Their assumption appears to have been that hardship could be ameliorated or avoided entirely, given sufficient time either for an owner to dispose of a business at a going rate, or to arrange replacement management during his absence. As with their concurrent urging of farmers to ask neighbours to take on their farms, 'policy' in these cases represented little more than handwashing on the Tribunals' part.[15]

That the situation was regarded as unsatisfactory is apparent in the attention given in Parliament to the matter of businessmen and conscription during debates on the Military Service (Session 2) Act, 1916. On 11 June, it was proposed that a clause be added to the principal Act, offering exemption:

On the ground that it is proved to the satisfaction of the tribunal –

(i)   that (an applicant) is the sole head of the business:
(ii) that there is no other person available who could carry on that business on his behalf with reasonable efficiency:
(iii) that in the event of his being called to the Colours there is a reasonable likelihood of the said business being closed down:
(iv) that such a man has a wife and children dependent upon the business.

Urging support of the clause, Alfred William Yeo (a staunch champion of business proprietors throughout the conscription period) reminded the Commons that 'there are thousands of these men who are simply bewildered as to what to do. They are told when they come before the Tribunals that they must sell their businesses or get out of them. They are given a month in which to do that.' Also supporting the proposal, Sir Stuart Samuel, the member for Whitechapel, argued: 'It is all very well to tell him that his business is not of national importance. Taken in aggregate these businesses are of national importance, and it is certainly a vital matter to the man.'[16]

Instructions issued to the Tribunals with the new legislation noted that government had considered but resisted the insertion of the above clause. However, they indicated that the circumstances it envisaged should be considered, collectively, as 'exceptional' for the purposes of the principal Act.[17] Whether this direction was sufficient in itself to achieve the 'uniformity of decision and practice' anticipated by Walter Long and others must be doubted. As ever, there followed immediately a qualifying clause which removed any potential clarity: it was proposed additionally that some men falling within the circumstances outlined above might nevertheless *not* be considered suitable for exemption, while others who did not might be regarded as more deserving. Nevertheless, reactions to the new instructions indicated that some Tribunals had indeed struggled to come to terms with what constituted exceptional circumstances. At Northampton Borough, for example, Councillor Parker suggested that, in light of what they were now being told, several of their previous decisions regarding businessmen might require review.[18]

The evidence of Tribunal reports continued to indicate very different attitudes towards the problem. As Parker's comment inferred, Northampton Borough's consideration of the businessman as a collective entity had been cursory, and, in one instance at least, somewhat light-hearted. As early as 14 March 1916, they decided that already they had heard rather too many applications from hairdressers (many of whom were also tobacconists). Geldart suggested that the 'Northampton Master Hairdressers' Association for Convivial Purposes' should ensure that local businesses helped out each other, and that it might be an opportunity to weed out the 'shaky shavers'.[19]

By May, however, the Tribunal had noted and become exercised by the condition of the town's butchery trade, though at this stage their attention was not upon the traders themselves but the number of apparently indispensable slaughtermen they employed. The Master Butchers' Association had been asked to consider a system of collective slaughter that would allow the release of some men, and eleven outstanding applications by slaughtermen were stood over pending further negotiations. In the event, negotiations proved hard to arrange, and Northampton Borough's failure to pursue the matter offers an early hint of their reluctance to address the issue of small businesses collectively: a striking contrast to their concurrent, energetic efforts with regard to the local boot and shoe industry.[20]

In contrast to their larger neighbour, Wellingborough Urban Tribunal appear to have adopted a relatively early – and largely sympathetic – strategy regarding further dilution among small traders, owing in large part to the efforts of their military representative, Herbert Dulley (himself a member of a prominent local brewing family). At the end of April 1916, he urged them to review certificates issued to the town's bakers and butchers. A month later, having considered the situation of Wellingborough's butchers, he concluded that the trade would suffer locally if more men were taken; accordingly, he recommended to his Tribunal that all outstanding applications should receive certificates to 1 September. Two weeks later, he reported that he had been unable as yet to bring bakers together to discuss their own situation as a whole, but, as a stop-gap measure, urged that all married men in the trade over 30 years of age should similarly be exempted until 1 September. Wellingborough Urban agreed both proposals.[21] Their accommodation of Dulley's initiatives, moreover, seems to have reflected an empathy with local commerce that transcended issues of dilution: during a single sitting in September, they offered a certificate to 1 January 1917 to a hairdresser/tobacconist, while a female owner of a house decorating business obtained an open-ended, conditional exemption for her only employee. In neither case did Dulley appeal the decision.

During several cases concerning sole businessmen heard upon the latter occasion, Dulley pressed applicants on whether they paid income tax. Challenged by one of the tribunalists, W. Sharman, Dulley denied that he was attempting to apply different criteria to those in a 'larger' way of business (which, of course, guidance from the Local Government Board suggested he was entitled to do), but observed that a man whose earnings were sufficient to make him liable to income tax would, under the terms of the Civil Liabilities Act, be more costly to take as a soldier. In so far as the consideration allowed a further degree of ambiguity to weigh against taking a man to the Colours, it would seem that Dulley was as reluctant as his Tribunal to threaten local business interests.[22]

In contrast to Wellingborough's Urban's co-ordinated, and somewhat lenient, policy towards their small traders, Peterborough – a notably severe Tribunal in other respects – appeared to have dispensed with the incremental considerations that other Tribunals applied in considering the proprietor's case. Applications from men in a 'small way' of business were often dismissed on the basis that the loss of their concern would have no commercial and very little domestic impact. Those managing larger businesses fared little better if competition in their area meant that their loss would not impact upon distribution, or, indeed, if a business were considered to be non-essential (such as that of Walter Williamson, a boiled sweets manufacturer whose case was mentioned in the Commons in July 1917).[23] The Tribunal also looked closely at the history of a concern. A relatively new enterprise was usually considered either as having little intrinsic value to the community or as a shelter in which its owner deliberately sought to hide from military service. An association with the purveyance of alcohol was also punished, even if a trade's profits were predominantly derived elsewhere. Finally, the age of the applicant was unusually important to this Tribunal. In one case, a 65-year-old baker applied for his only employee and son, Walter Pyle, aged 20, on the basis that his removal to the Colours would mean the loss of the business and of the proprietor's life savings. The Tribunal's decision in dismissing the case was telling: 'If you disregard the fact that this is a baker ... this case is of no greater hardship than those of many other men who have been sent into the Army.' Upon only one occasion did the Tribunal appear to consider a trade in any collective sense, and that merely in passing. In March 1916, dismissing the application of Cecil Scotney, a 24-year-old master butcher and slaughterman, they observed that they had offered exemptions to several butchers already, and that, if Scotney went to the Colours, those who remained would be 'quite sufficient' to meet the public's needs.[24]

Other urban Tribunals tried – if hesitantly – to see their tradesmen in a larger light. Northampton Borough's willingness to consider trades collectively strengthened slightly in late summer 1916, though it was the town's bakers' resistance to employing women, rather than the bread supply, that triggered concerns. During the final sitting in August, a confectioner applying for his son (without whom, he claimed, the business would necessarily close) mentioned that he also had a girl assisting him. Geldart congratulated him on being the first baker in the town to offer employment to a female, and declined to challenge the six months' certificate offered by his Tribunal. A solicitor representing a journeyman baker at the same sitting warned that proposals for large-scale female substitution had been received badly by wives of the town's bakers: they 'warmly objected' to the prospect of their half-stripped husbands working among women in the pre-dawn hours, and if the proposal were carried out there was likely to be 'another war'. Two weeks later, the Appeals Tribunal encountered another perspective upon the phenomenon during the case of Frederick William Davis, a 19-year-old who assisted in his handicapped father's bakery. Captain Cook told them that he had appealed this case only to force other bakers in Northampton to employ women. Davis countered that women could hardly be expected to lift the 5 hundredweight of flour, 32 gallons of water, 5 lb of salt and 2 lb of yeast worked in a single batch. The argument failed to convince; Davis's certificate was shortened to just six weeks.[25]

If Northampton's bakers could not be trusted with strange women, the town's butchers continued to be attached to their slaughtermen. North-ampton Borough had made no further attempt to prise them apart since May; accordingly, on 20 October, their military representative attempted to inject some momentum into the process by taking several test cases to the Appeals Tribunal. 'The real truth about butchers', Geldart claimed, '[is]that they [are] all up against each other': all wanted their own, partic-ular slaughtermen, and needed them, apparently, on the same day each week. Defending existing practices, Arthur Cotton, a 26-year-old butcher, claimed that cattle needed to be slaughtered on market day, so having only two or three jobbing slaughtermen to serve the local trade would be impractical. In hot weather, furthermore, it was necessary for cattle to be killed every day. The employer of another appellant, Charles H. Ball, attrib-uted their greater workload to the reduction in imported meat since the war commenced. If he lost Ball, he claimed, one of his pork shops would have to close. Cotton was allowed to remain in his business until the end of the year, while Ball's certificate was reduced to 1 December.[26]

In announcing the latter decision, Adkins reflected the then-urgent government perceptions of a manpower crisis in asserting that 'every-thing must give way to the Army'. Three weeks later, he made the point more explicitly with respect to sole traders. A grocer and coal-merchant appealing for his only employee was told that he must expect to give up some part of his business, as a 25-year-old single man could not be spared indefinitely: 'it was very important that the ranks of the Army be kept full.'[27] Yet business, when organized, was capable of providing effective ripostes to the army's demands. A few minutes after Adkins made the latter obser-vation, J. Sheppard, secretary of Northampton and District Master Bakers' Association, rose during a military appeal against the exemption of one of his members, George Tarry, to present a letter to be read into the Tribu-nal's minutes. It claimed that so many of the county's bakers had been taken into the Army already that demand for bread – increasing because of recent prices rises affecting meat and vegetables – was now outstripping supply. Most of his members were working 16–18 hours each day; several had broken down under the strain, but conscription had made the business atmosphere so strained that no one of military age was interested in taking over going concerns. Subsequent testimony provided by Sheppard to the Appeals Tribunal would at least partly undermine this somewhat apocalyptic portrait of the trade; nevertheless, Adkins and his colleagues, relying – as yet – upon the trade's own statistics for want of corroboration, were impressed by the argument, and the appeal was dismissed.[28]

The growing problem of food availability and distribution, presenting almost simultaneously with government's heightened efforts to keep the Army up to strength, posed a considerable dilemma for the Tribunals. Continuing dilution of the agricultural workforce, while viewed seriously, threatened repercussions upon the food supply that were not capable of being tested in the short term. In contrast, the likely implications of inadequate retail food distribution were far more immediate. One derives a sense, therefore, that, by the end of 1916, Northamptonshire's urban Tribunals were looking nervously at the impact of existing manpower losses upon the food retail sector. That nothing was done to formulate a policy in the shorter term was due partly to the distraction of their concurrent, large-scale consideration of agricultural and boot and shoe applications. As will be seen, however, this was by no means the principal brake upon progress.

Reflecting the wider manpower crisis in the Army, pressure upon sole proprietors and heads of businesses was increasing in the latter part of 1916. As noted elsewhere, the Local Government Board in December instructed the Tribunals that no man under 26 years old who was fit for general service should be exempted on occupational grounds unless he was 'manifestly irreplaceable'. This was superseded only a month later by instructions that all Category A and B1 men below 31 years of age not in a certified occupation or demonstrating exceptional personal circumstances should go to the Colours immediately, or by 31 March at the latest.[29] In a separate initiative, Eastern Command attempted to curb what it considered to be misplaced localist sentiments among its military representatives. At Brixworth on 8 January 1917, Adam Cross read out instructions noting that many military representatives appeared to believe that they should not appeal exemptions offered to local businessmen:

> There is no valid reason why a man engaged in a self-centred occupation should be less liable to perform his duties to the country than those who enter into partnership with others or accept subordinate positions in even larger undertakings. The Military Service Act has been sufficiently long in force for all whose occupation is a 'one-man' business to have made arrangements for their business to be carried on in their absence, and all exemptions on these grounds should be carefully reviewed.[30]

For the War Office, 'careful reviews' were useful solely as the means by which existing certificates might be rescinded. In contrast, the Local Government Board fully recognized the complexity of the issues involving business-men's applications. In September 1916, Central Tribunal had acknowledged once more that such cases presented great difficulties, and had attempted to lay down broad criteria that Tribunals might build their policies around. They reiterated the principle that an exemption was not justified merely on the ground that a man's business would close if he went to the Colours. There also had to be 'serious hardship', which was not predicated solely upon the likelihood of a considerable loss of income (many men of more modest circumstances, taken into the Army, experienced a proportionately 'considerable' loss). More pertinent was the question of whether a business could be carried on by a relative or friend. Tribunals were also to consider the peculiar circumstances of each business: whether, once closed, it could be restarted subsequently without 'grave difficulty', the amount of capital invested therein, the age and domestic situation of the applicant, and the degree to which the business was well established or relatively new.[31]

Most Tribunals had been attempting to apply these criteria since May, so the impact of Central's advice was minimal. Conversely, their response to Eastern Command's un-nuanced initiative – which in no part recognized difficulties in adjudging business cases – was largely one of irritation and obstruction. At Towcester, several tribunalists took vocal exception to their military representative's new instructions and promptly offered an open, three-month exemption to a porcelain dealer. At Crick, two Yelvertoft bakers, married men of 35 and 39 years respectively, received open, conditional certificates (in neither case did their military representative appeal the decision). Even the Appeals Tribunal, while scrupulously interpreting the legislation regarding one-man businesses, chose to ignore Eastern Command's opinions with respect to their disposal. On 12 February, Irthlingborough's military representative appealed against a 31 March certificate given to Sydney John Meadows, a 24-year-old tobacconist, hairdresser and photographer. Meadows's brother, in business in his own right, had forfeited a three months' exemption on the understanding that Sydney would remain and manage both businesses as one. He was now the only remaining hairdresser in Irthlingborough. Initially, Adkins seemed unsympathetic: 'They must grow beards', he suggested. 'Yes, but they can't cut their own hair', replied Meadows. After brief consultation, the Tribunal not only rejected the military appeal but extended the certificate to 9 May.[32]

Clearly, therefore, local sentiment regarding sole proprietors and heads of businesses exercised a powerful influence upon the Tribunals, even during periods in which recruitment pressures were mounting. This was particularly apparent where excessive dilution had occurred already, and the remaining businessmen had made some effort to assist the enterprises of enlisted men. It was claimed after the war that such initiatives were relatively rare: that 'co-operation in the smaller towns was impossible; in some of the larger towns no real attempt was made to give assistance to businesses from which men were withdrawn.[33] There was some justice to the accusation, but it failed to acknowledge the fundamental difficulty underlying schemes that encouraged co-operation. Men given the opportunity to negotiate among themselves who should go to war and who should remain in their habitual occupations tended to exhibit a marked preference for the latter option, with the result that Tribunals' attempts to avoid the arbitrator's role rarely succeeded. The alternative – coercion – encouraged at best a sullen obstructionism on the part of all parties to an arrangement.

The occasional exception may be noted. In April 1917, the Appeals Tribunal removed finality from a certificate given to S. Warren, a widower with one child and proprietor of a large fish business (serving 300 to 350 customers each day), who had taken on two other businesses to keep them going for their enlisted owners.[34] Less edifying – and more typical – were the cases of John A. Clarke and Thomas A. Roberts, both bakers in Northampton. On 30 June 1916, each had been given conditional exemption by Northampton Borough, and Geldart appealed both. On 4 September, the Appeals Tribunal adjusted the certificates to two months, leaving it to the appellants to come to an arrangement in the meantime that would allow one of them to go to the Colours while the other undertook to preserve both businesses. Neither man wished to go off to war, however. Clarke made a formal offer to supply bread to Roberts's wife at a fixed price; Roberts offered to sell bread directly to Clarke's customers and pay him 25 per cent of the proceeds. Neither offer was acceptable to the other; hoping to sway the balance, Roberts wrote separately to the Tribunal, reminding them of his greater age (32 as opposed to Clarke's 30), indifferent health, dependent mother and four-month-old daughter. At the end of their exemption period, the Tribunal refused leave to both men to appeal further.[35]

Similarly, George Eales and Frank Marston, two bakers in Kislingbury (both Category A men), were repeatedly urged by their local Tribunal to amalgamate their businesses. Marston had offered either to sell his business to Eales or to buy the latter's bakery; Eales refused but counter-offered an arrangement whereby he would supply Marston's wife's shop with bread or allow her 5 per cent of income from Marston's customers. This, too, was refused, despite warnings from their local Tribunal that they might both have to go to the Colours. On 21 September 1917, both men went before the Appeals Tribunal and received (final) exemptions to 1 November.[36]

Occasionally, the spirit of comradely competition was entirely absent. In February 1918, the Appeals Tribunal dealt sternly with Walter E. Fortescue, a Higham Ferrers baker who had agreed to carry on the business of an enlisted man named Pollard, and to hand it back to him upon his return. Pressed by Adkins, Fortescue admitted that the net profits from Pollard's business came to some 30s.–40s. per week, but that he had not made any arrangements to pay anything to Pollard's wife. Adkins offered him the bare choice of reconsidering this policy or going to war himself; the case was adjourned in the meantime, pending confirmation from Pollard that he would be content with his wife receiving one-third of future net profits.[37]

These cases illustrate the continuing extemporary nature of the Tribunals' approach to one-man businesses. Considered on their individual merits, they nevertheless demanded that the wider issues of supply, distribution and equity should be addressed also. The arbitrary treatment of the unfortunate Eales and Marston owed much to the unlucky geography of their village, which lay less than a mile from the Harpole Co-operative business discussed above. Fortescue was probably preserved from the trenches by his existing commitment to maintain Pollard's business, and the fact that he was one of only three bakers remaining in Higham Ferrers, which, despite its proximity to Rushden, was of sufficient size to require its own bread supply. Applying the same rationale, Brixworth Tribunal gave four months' (open) exemptions to three bakers on 6 June 1918 on the basis that each of them supplied villages that otherwise would have no bread deliveries.[38] At best, such decisions were stop-gap responses to very local conditions; what was needed, but what proved enduringly difficult to arrange, was a policy that might be applied to each business sector as a whole, and to the food distribution trades in particular.

The first notable effort to achieve something resembling a policy was made by Northampton Borough in May 1917, a full year after their first, faltering attempt to persuade the town's butchers to slaughter collectively. Following the poor wheat harvest in 1916 and resulting winter 'food crisis', concern was growing regarding the number and quality of remaining baking businesses. At the end of April, a tribunalist, C.L. Lovell, reported his conversation with a journeyman baker, who argued that the businesses of smaller bakers who were coming to the end of their exemptions should be maintained as a matter of policy. Lovell noted that the town possessed three large bakeries at which the entire town's supply of bread could be produced. Together with a 'few' master bakers, there were sufficient bakers over military age to supply three shifts, each of some 48 hours per week, to work these bakeries, from which smaller, independent bakers could then obtain their bread. If some of the latter were taken for the Army, it would be relatively easy to ensure that the supply of bread to their own customers continued during their absence. Furthermore, distribution of flour supplies would be greatly simplified.

The proposal was well received, though Gribble pointed out its obvious weakness: the difficulty in getting the bakers who remained to agree to reorganize their businesses to support those of their competitors who were taken to the Colours. His Tribunal recognized that their preliminary task would be to consider the town's remaining bakers of military age at the same sitting, and that details of their medical categories should be secured in the meantime.[39] It was one thing to identify the necessities, however, and another to engage the process. Gribble's reservations were prescient: it was not until March 1918 that the Tribunal would be able to bring the town's bakers together, and even then no firm policy would be established.

Again, the problems of formulating collective solutions to cases that were necessarily considered on their individual merits were formidable. In May, the local Government Board provided examples of co-operation from several towns in England that inadvertently exposed the limitations of what was possible.[40] These noted an arrangement made by boot retailers in Birmingham to support the businesses of men already called up (one requiring no concession on their part to the recruiting authorities), and also a scheme agreed by Coventry's Master Bakers' Association, under which larger, better-equipped bakeries supplied bread to smaller-scale bakers in return for the latter working up to 54 hours per week on the premises of the former (the scheme had allowed the release of 'a number' of bakers' assistants in the town). Again, however, offering such examples was easy; the difficulty arose in attempting to utilize them as templates. In the following month, it was reported that a Metropolitan Appeals Tribunal had attempted to clear with Central Tribunal a policy regarding their local bread trade. They had concurred with their military representative's claim that the district retained more bakers than the maintenance of its bread supply required, and had refused exemptions to several with 'spare time' on their hands. Central approved their methodology; however, they also indicated that they were prepared to consider tailored options on a district by district basis only, and, in discussing the case of a sole proprietor case in the same report, rehearsed once more the many complex issues to be considered in adjudging personal hardship claims.[41] The reality was that every business had its own circumstances, and every proprietor ample opportunity to demonstrate the peculiar impact of a failed business upon his family and locality.

Northampton Borough's inability to bring their bakers collectively to the tribunal chamber may therefore have reflected, in part, a reluctance to confront the contradictions the encounter would generate. In July, an attempt to rationalize the release of butcher-proprietors in the town had resulted in no more radical step than their granting open exemptions to 14 men (all classed Category A), a decision that was modified considerably at County Hall after Geldart entered a block military appeal. During the latter deliberations, it was revealed that Northampton Borough had managed to send just two of the town's 29 master butchers to the Colours to date, and had yet to obtain any meaningful information on the remaining number of employees and older men in the trade. Sir Ryland Adkins suggested to Geldart that, if Borough had 'cut the Gordian Knot' and imposed finality upon these certificates, the information would have been made available readily enough during the individual appeals that would have ensued. Notwithstanding the implicit criticism, his own Tribunal's decision was relatively circumspect: nine certificates were adjusted to final (but not shortened) and the remaining open exemptions were confirmed.[42]

The knot proved difficult to cut. The overwhelming concentration of one-man and sole proprietor enterprises in the county lay within North-ampton Borough's jurisdiction: thus, they were particularly sensitive to the implications of their decisions. Uncharacteristic leniency towards men in a certain trade might compromise the integrity of their proceedings, but gestures that threatened to undermine – perhaps irreparably – local food distribution arrangements did not recommend themselves to the most courageous tribunalist. Nor was there any real incentive for attempting them. Requiring consideration on an individual basis, even where the opportunity existed to examine a trade as a whole, the businessman or proprietor could not be amenable to the sweeping initiatives that charac-terized, for example, the Tribunal's treatment of the town's boot and shoe trade. The result was a series of uncharacteristic half-efforts to establish a policy, followed by protracted periods in which nothing further was done to bring the initiative to a resolution. The sense of impotence that this engendered may be gauged from Northampton Borough's reaction to the perceived consequences of decisions they had made already. In August, F.O. Roberts warned his fellow tribunalists that foreigners and non-North-amptonshire immigrants were setting up concerns in the town to replace those that enlisted men had relinquished. Councillor Parker's curiously impractical response was to ask members of the Press who were present to urge the public to patronize only old-established businesses, while Gribble's rather lame suggestion that 'something be done to protect local interests' implied that he and his colleagues had neither responsibility for, nor influence upon, the trend.[43] At best, this was a tacit setting aside of the Tribunal's need to engage the issue comprehensively. At worst, it repre-sented a form of paralysis.

The enduring failure to formulate 'policy' with regard to businessmen was not unique to Northampton Borough, or to Northamptonshire as a whole. In the previous March, *The Times* had railed against the policy of Skegness Tribunal for offering long exemptions to 22 higher-category applicants, most of whom were proprietors of one-man businesses. In the following month, the same paper carried an article entitled 'Lax Tribunals: Army Requirements Overlooked', citing a stream of certificates offered to young, fit traders around the country. Concluding, it observed percipiently:

> Tribunals, judged by their decisions, are more sensitive to hints, sometimes indistinguishable from threats, of public inconvenience ... more than one chairman of a Tribunal has thrown out earnest suggestions to groups of men in specific trades to cooperate.

In October, at Bletchley in Buckinghamshire, the local Tribunal convened a special sitting to consider military appeals against exemptions held by five of the town's butchers. Following a very brief discussion, it was agreed unanimously that the town and surrounding villages could not bear further depletion of the trade.[44]

Acknowledging the enduring problem faced by the Tribunals, the Local Government Board in September offered to send a commissioner to discuss with them issues of particular uncertainty regarding sole proprietor businesses. Given that the Board itself had yet to provide more than broad generalizations on the topic, the utility of the measure must be questioned (Northampton Borough promptly took advantage of the offer, though the outcome of the discussions is not known). Certainly, no discernible initiatives materialized in subsequent months. Indeed, no trade or business was considered collectively in Northamptonshire during the remainder of 1917, a remarkable fact given the growing dilution pressures on manpower elsewhere that the faltering Passchendaele offensives were encouraging.

The next movement on the issue came from Whitehall once more. In December, the Board issued a circular addressing hardship in one-man businesses, which strongly urged that Tribunals should place the onus of examining a local trade's demographic profile upon the trade itself. It proposed that 'organisers' be appointed where a trade was not already sufficiently represented by a co-ordinating organization, to liaise between Tribunal and traders in establishing and presenting surveys of conditions locally: that is, the distribution of manpower (age and medical categorization), estimates of modern and outdated equipment in each business, and of public requirements of the trade locally. The organizer would also encourage his trade's representative organization to present schemes whereby men in high categories might be taken for the Army without adversely affecting output. It was envisaged that he would be a practising member of that trade, of over military age, or, if younger, of lower medical category, whose willing (and effective) participation might be rewarded by conditional exemption. Somewhat hopefully, it was suggested that local traders would, on their own initiative, raise a subscription fund to meet the organiser's wages and expenses. As a small *quid pro quo*, the circular suggested that, where such schemes were put into effect, the local Tribunal might wish to offer longstanding exemptions to Grade III men who remained out of uniform, subject to firm commitments on their part to maintaining the businesses and goodwill of those who were taken to the Colours.[45]

The circular marked the apogee of government's hopes for the willing co-operation of local businessmen in combing-out their own. Its effectiveness may be judged from the fact that the Board issued further recommendations regarding sole proprietors in October 1918, which, while offering some new perspectives and suggestions, largely repeated those of December 1917. From surviving records, it appears that no 'organizer' was appointed to represent any trade in Northamptonshire, and, while a number of trade-specific panel committees were to be formed on a voluntary basis during the first quarter of 1918 to provide overviews of their respective conditions, several other trades took the view that to collaborate voluntarily in the process of dilution was hardly in the best interests of their members.

The latter attitude appears to have been prevalent among Northampton's bakers, who finally came *en masse* to the Town Hall in March 1918. In mid-February, Borough Tribunal had devoted much of their sitting to discussing the report of a sub-committee to consider the outstanding matter of butchers and bakers in the town. It had been decided then to summon all men whose cases had been adjourned previously pending a 'collective' policy to be applied to their trades. On 4 March, accordingly, the butchers were seen in the morning, the bakers in the afternoon. In the first session, a brief discussion on how many days per week a butcher could be expected to help out other businesses was abruptly curtailed when Gribble suggested that, yet again, they adjourn the present cases until all the town's butchers could be summoned. The afternoon session, coming too late for that afternoon's papers, was not reported then or in the following week. However, exemptions offered to nine bakers that day were appealed by Geldart and heard at County Hall on 15 April. In a preliminary statement, solicitor C.F. Alsop explained the current manpower situation with regard to the town's bakery trade. At the outbreak of war, he claimed, there had been 228 masters and men in Northampton; by autumn 1917, that figure had declined to 87 and now stood at 75, of whom 60 were master bakers and 15 qualified operative bakers.[46] Geldart then rose to make his appeal. He claimed that every attempt had been made to prevail with the bakers, but that they had steadfastly refused to form a panel committee to present an overview of the town's bakeries. Information recently provided to him by J. Sheppard (who had put the bakers' case so effectively to the same Tribunal in November 1916) indicated that, in contrast to Alsop's assertions, there remained in Northampton – as at the end of the previous month – 66 master bakers and 52 operatives. Sheppard, who was present at the sitting, was obliged to agree that these latter figures were broadly accurate. According to a recent mayoral report (Geldart continued), the town's daily bread requirement was 4350 cwt, which indicated that there was in fact a surplus of labour available (particularly as no troops now remained at barracks to be fed). Alsop rose again to challenge Geldart, but managed only a very weak rebuttal: that the bakers had not formed a committee because they 'saw no good coming of it'. The Tribunal shortened all nine certificates, and imposed finality on five.[47]

The bakers' aversion to forming a panel committee was understandable, yet, in one sense, misplaced. The Appeals Tribunal appears to have taken evidence from such bodies impartially, rather than use them merely as devices to identify and remove the 'slack' from within a trade. A fortnight following the bakers' appearance at Town Hall, the National Service appeal against Northampton Borough's exemption of James A. Ball, a 34-year-old married fried fish and poultry seller, was supported by information supplied by the fried fish shop panel committee's recent report. It revealed that Northampton had supported 54 businesses before the war, of which 16 had since closed. The committee's unanimous opinion, presented to the Tribunal by their secretary, Arthur Adcock, was that the town could not spare more. The Tribunal concurred, and the appeal was dismissed.[48]

In fact, perceptions of dilution in the food retail trades had proceeded to the point where further paring proved difficult to achieve. The Appeals Tribunal's 'mass' adjustment of only nine bakers' certificates in April, itself an extraordinary response to a particular trade's obduracy, was their final such gesture, and the remaining months of the war brought only occasional releases – usually, of younger, high-category traders. From May, furthermore, the Tribunals' resistance to Army pressures on businessmen was reinforced by a measure designed to achieve the opposite: the Military Service (No. 2) Act, 1918.

Heads of businesses were seen to be particularly vulnerable to the new legislation.[49] Many enterprises that had lost their habitual directors now found themselves faced with the loss also of men who had 'stepped into the breach', whose removal both represented a breach of faith and threatened irrevocable closure of their enterprises and unemployment for their workers. Balanced against that threat was no more than the very small military value of taking men of this age-range into the Army, so that each such man thereafter would release just one, younger soldier for front-line service.[50] Accordingly, Northamptonshire's urban Tribunals, already reluctant further to compromise their local economies, treated the issue of businessmen falling within the 'new military age' with great circumspection. With respect to sole proprietors, the Appeals Tribunal belatedly attempted to form a perspective upon local trade conditions, and, in May, asked to see any panel committee reports previously submitted to Northampton Borough before hearing the relevant trades' appeals. For their part, the latter Tribunal on 17 June asked the press to carry notices that verified statements of stock-worth and turnover should be submitted as a matter of course by sole proprietors or heads of businesses when making applications. Following this request, they offered long exemptions, all carrying the VTC or Special Constabulary requirement, to a group of business applicants in their late 40s.[51]

Elsewhere, Tribunals' policy towards those businessmen and traders they considered indispensable amounted almost to defiance of National Service instructions. During May, Towcester (not a notably lenient body) offered two-month open exemptions to three bakers (aged 30, Grade I; 36, Grade I; and 42, Grade II), and, less controversially, open certificates to 31 August to three Grade III butchers in their late 30s. The National Service representative, Major Bairstow, appealed none of these. Potterspury went further, in regarding any sole proprietor of the new military age as having *de facto* grounds for exemption. On 18 July, they heard the application of a 47-year-old (Grade I) architect and surveyor, an occupation that their National Service representative, Major Brougham, argued could not 'in any way [be] essential to the national interest'. When the man was offered a six-month, open certificate, Brougham, with admirable restraint, commented: 'it is just possible I shall appeal'. At Towcester, five days later, certificates to 1 September or 23 October offered to four butchers proved to be the final straw for Major Bairstow, who reminded them that the war might be over by then! 'If the Tribunal [sits] with the sole purpose of exempting men', he fumed, 'there [is] no purpose in it'.[52]

However, Bairstow's superiors in the National Service Ministry had already noted the Tribunals' growing concerns regarding their local economies, and new instructions, issued in the same month, significantly undermined the efforts of their own representatives. It was conceded that many businessmen now coming before the Tribunals were themselves replacements for younger men who had joined the Colours. For the first time, it was suggested that some larger businesses were sufficiently complex to require more than one directing head (though 'sleeping partners' whose only interest was financial were of course to be overlooked in assessing an enterprise's needs). Having made these observations, the instructions prudently passed over the sensitive matter of older businessmen and asked only that Grade I men under 36 and Grade II men under 31 should not be exempted unless it was clear to Tribunals that their businesses would collapse in their absence.[53]

This was a marked change in policy, but many Tribunals had already moved from concern as to whether individual businesses might fail to whether their localities could afford to lose them. What might have been a riposte to the new instructions was delivered by Northampton-shire's Appeals Tribunal on 23 August when they considered a National Service appeal against a 31 October certificate given to John Samuel Bates, a 31-year-old, Grade I butcher and slaughterman. Bates, the only butcher in the village of Scaldwell, supplied six other villages also as well as operating a business in Brixworth. Attending the sitting, the Executive Officer of Brixworth Food Control Commission gave evidence that Bates had upwards of a thousand registered customers. The Tribunal not only confirmed the original certificate but goaded the appellant, Adam Cross, by extending it by one day. This was not an isolated gesture. In the remaining months of the war, the only occasion upon which they did not uphold or extend a businessman's certificate was in the case of an Earls Barton boot factory manager, F.S. Dunckley, a 28-year-old Grade II (married) man who made the error of stating that he also had sole control of three large retailing businesses in Ireland. Wounded imperial pride, perhaps, moved Stopford-Sackville to declare peremptorily that he 'did not think it necessary to consider the needs of Ireland just at the present time'. Dunckley's 31 October certificate had finality imposed.[54]

The National Service Ministry's closing word on businessmen (in this case, on the proprietors of one-man businesses) was issued on 10 October 1918: a comprehensive document which again offered practical examples of co-operation among traders in a number of (anonymous) towns. The circular commenced by urging – once more – that the cases of all men in a particular trade should be considered at the same time, and reminded Tribunals (if they had not yet taken the point) that 'the special position of grocers, bakers, and other men in the food trades … should be borne in mind'. Of several successful schemes then reported, one involving a district's bread trade was curiously similar to C.L. Lovell's proposal of 18 months earlier. While acknowledging that a 'fully developed scheme, under which the baking would be concentrated wholly in the best equipped bakeries, has not yet been found practicable', the circular described an arrangement whereby a town's bakers had agreed that all bread should be produced in the three largest, most modern bakeries. Bread was delivered jointly (thereby much reducing transportation costs) to each baker's place of business in proportion to a register of customers provided by him. All participants had agreed not to solicit the custom of a competitor until at least six months following the expiration of the arrangement, which had proved so efficient that night work in the trade was no longer necessary. The scheme had resulted in the release of a grand total of just four of the town's bakers to the Colours.[55] It need hardly be noted that no subsequent effort was made by Northamptonshire's Tribunals to implement a similar arrangement locally.

The businessman/sole proprietor was, and remained, the non-existent 'group'. With the possible exception of Wellingborough Urban, no North-amptonshire Tribunal made a substantive, consistent effort to address the issue in a collective manner. Their archetypal approach was an other-wise uncharacteristic prevarication, punctuated by brief initiatives which acknowledged – without seizing – the necessity of formulating a policy: one that could be applied across a trade without either diminishing it unduly or prejudicing the businesses of men who had gone to the Colours. Thus, even Tribunals who could be notably energetic in enforcing arrangements to allow large-scale industrial dilution baulked at the far more modest measures that might have streamlined the retail supply of services and commodities locally. Why was this the case?

Firstly, the trades that might have yielded the readiest returns upon the implementation of such arrangements were those involved in food production and distribution. Yet, from early 1917, Tribunals were at least as exercised by the perceived threat to the food supply as by the needs of the BEF, and while this concern encouraged greater efforts to understand the nature of local trades, it also discouraged decisive interventions that might have exacerbated the feared distribution 'crisis'.[56]

Secondly, any collective method of considering men in a particular trade required that the latter should be (or, rather, be willing to be) organized so as to allow the Tribunals to take an overview regarding dilution. Yet there was no legal obligation for traders to enter into arrangements to effect this, and organizations representing their interests appear to have assumed – correctly – that the implied threat of cancelled exemptions for 'recalcitrants' was a non sequitur: that such were the Tribunals' fears of the consequences of uncoordinated business closures that collective systems of trading would need to be in place *before* any such sanctions could be wielded. What remained was persuasion. In effect, Tribunals attempted to convince men that it was in their best interests to co-operate in furthering the cause of their conscription. The potential for success of such a strategy may readily be imagined. Around the country, organization took place within certain trades to protect the businesses of men who had gone to the Colours already, but few anticipated or encouraged dilution by formulating arrangements to assist recruitment.[57]

Thirdly, it should be recalled that initiatives to organize a trade locally represented only a preliminary measure to enable the consideration of cases on an *individual* basis. As instructions from the Local Government Board, National Service Ministry and Central Tribunal emphasized constantly, applications from sole proprietors or directing heads of business could be determined only upon their own merits. Therefore, whereas an industry-specific agreement with, for example, boot and shoe manufacturers was the culminating step in allowing large-scale, scheduled releases of men, in the case of owner-managed businesses it was only the initial stage in a process that promised no significant recruitment benefits at its culmination.

Thus, in judging the Tribunals' motivation and actions regarding the businessman/sole proprietor, the potential return upon effort must be considered. On 1 March 1917, as a result of detailed prior negotiation, Northamptonshire's Appeals Tribunal processed 334 boot and shoe appeals on a factory-by-factory basis. On 20 September 1918, 561 renewals from the same industry were considered and determined.[58] Contrast these notable successes with the protracted initiatives that brought just nine Northampton bakers to County Hall on 4 March 1918, and, indeed, with the anonymous bakers' arrangement so enthusiastically commended in circular R.227, that had allowed the release of four men to the Colours. Strenuous efforts to rationalize the trades of butchers, bakers, fried fish shop owners or, indeed, architects could provide no commensurate flood of recruits. Absent that promise, there was little incentive to the Tribunals to further burden their schedules by attempting to convince proprietors of the benefits of innovations that delivered their businesses into the hands of competitors and their persons into the hands of the Army. As a result, the businessman was, and continued to be, considered not only on a case-by-case basis (as the Local Government Board constantly urged) but almost always from a purely individual perspective also.

Notes

1 *Report of the Central Tribunal*, p. 11.
2 *The Times*, 2, 4 September 1914, 30 April 1915; Turner, *Pals*, p. 18; Stedman, *Manchester Pals*, pp. 30, 36; Maddocks, *Liverpool Pals*, pp. 24–26; Bilton, *Hull Pals*, p. 20. In Leeds, a local councillor, G. Pearson, alleged that there was a policy of excluding from the local battalion anyone who was not from the business community (*Leeds and District Weekly Citizen*, 4 September 1914).
3 Osborne, 'Defining Their Own Patriotism', p. 67.
4 'Reserved Occupations of Cardinal Importance for the Maintenance of Some Other Branches of Trade and Industry'.
5 On 13 March 1916, a master tailor applied to Northampton Borough 'because he feared that if he was taken his business would fall into the hands of Jews and foreigners'. He appears to have had little more faith in his compatriots:

'If his customers knew he had to go they would not pay what they owed him' (*Independent*, 18 March 1916).

6 *The Times*, 17 April 1917.

7 LGB Circular R.70 (26 March 1916).

8 LGB Circular R.77: Summary of cases considered, 4 (27 April 1916). The case cited was that of the managing director of a bookbinding company.

9 Section 1(1) (b) of the Principal Act provided that men who were unmarried on 2 November 1915 would continue to be so regarded. A subsequent marriage was not an occasion of escape, therefore.

10 NRO X180/20.

11 Below, pp. 162–163.

12 NRO X182/545, 846. Curiously, the case was not reported in any of the local newspapers, which may suggest that it was heard and decided *in camera* (notes of Appeals Tribunal sittings in Northampton during 1916 are no longer extant).

13 NRO X181/590.

14 NRO X184/1680: the appeal was for a butcher, William Dunkley.

15 Above, p. 104.

16 5 H.C. 82:1080–1081. The possibility of adding a clause had been debated since May. It was resisted strenuously by Lord Salisbury, who foresaw the problem of allowing exemptions to 'large' businessmen without providing the same to sole proprietors of more modest enterprises (H.L. Debates, 22–23 May 1916). On Yeo's championing of the one-man business (particularly against the allegedly favourable treatment of co-operative societies by government and Tribunals), note also his heated exchanges with Sir Auckland Geddes in the Commons, 24 July 1918 (5 H.C. 108:1791–1794).

17 Military Service (Session 2) Act, 1916, 3 (i); LGB Circular R.84 (1 June 1916), section 15.

18 *Mercury*, 9 June 1916.

19 Ibid., 17 March 1916.

20 Ibid., 19, 26 May 1916.

21 Ibid., 5 May, 9, 23 June 1916.

22 Ibid., 22 September 1916.

23 NRO X186/3118; 5 H.C. 95:1275–1275, 2095–2096. In dismissing Williamson's subsequent appeal, the Appeals Tribunal also noted the non-essential nature of his business, and were further exercised by the likelihood that the appellant's subsidiary offer to find work in a munitions factory would, if accepted, have excited accusations of special treatment locally.

24 NRO X180/118, 491, 496; X181/618; X182/788, 978, 1046.

25 NRO X182/1018; *Mercury*, 1, 8, 29 September 1916.

26 NRO X183/1224, 1229; *Mercury*, 27 October 1916.

27 However, the man for whom he applied, William Humphries, was offered a further extension subsequently (NRO X184/1483; X185/1726).

28 NRO X183/1386; *Mercury*, 17 November 1916.

29 LGB Circulars R.106, R.107 (1 December 1916), R.113, R.114 (20 January 1917).

30 *Mercury*, 12 January 1917.

31 LGB Circular R.100: summary of cases considered, no. 61 (20 September 1916).

32 NRO X184/1898; *Mercury*, 19 January, 16 February 1917.

33 *Report of the Central Tribunal*, p. 11.

34 NRO X186/3236, 17 April 1917.

35 NRO X190/6729–6730, as dated.

36 NRO X190/6687, 6688, as dated.

37 NRO X192/8768; X197: Appeals Tribunal meeting notes, 22 February 1918.

38 *Mercury*, 7 June 1918.

39 *Mercury, Herald*, 4 May 1917.

40 LGB Circular R.132 (15 May 1917).

41 LGB Circular R.139 (16 June 1917): summary of cases considered, nos 80, 81.

42 NRO X189/3421–3426, 3434, 4132, 4180, 4182, 4184, 6260, 6376, 6484; X197: Appeals Tribunal meeting notes, 24 July 1917; *Mercury*, 27 July 1917.

43 *Mercury*, 3 August 1917. On 14 January 1918, a new (DORA) regulation was announced in the Commons to limit the issue of licences to new retail businesses to prevent 'aliens' from filling gaps in the market left by enlisted businessmen (5 H.C. 101:84).

44 *The Times*, 6 March, 20 April, 1917; CBS DC/14/39/1: Tribunal minute book, p. 140 (29 October 1917).

45 LGB Circular R.167: 17 December 1917 (also NSI 35/1917: 21 December 1917).

46 This prewar figure is that recorded in the Appeals Tribunal meeting notes; the *Mercury* stated it as 224.

47 NRO X192/8916–8923, 8971; X197: Appeals Tribunal meeting notes, 15 April 1918; *Mercury*, 19 April 1918.

48 NRO X192/8930; X197: Appeals Tribunal meeting notes, 30 April 1918.

49 Cf. the comments of a former Chancellor, Lord Buckmaster, on resistance to the Act during its committee stages: '[It] has caused more acute discontent than any measure since the commencement of the War. The reason is obvious. It will embrace nearly all the effective and active men in our productive industries and in business circles' (Buckmaster to Viscount Harcourt, 12 April 1918: Bodleian Library, Harcourt MSS 448).

50 On the value of these men to the military effort, note comments made in the Commons by Asquith, Sir Charles Hobhouse and David Mason (5 H.C. 104:1491, 1521–1523, 1791–1793; 10–11 April 1918).

51 *Mercury*, 10 May, 21 June 1918.

52 *Herald*, 17 May 1918, *Mercury*, 26 July 1918.

53 LGB Circular R.220 (13 July 1918).

54 NRO X195/10157, 10184; X197: Appeals Tribunal meeting notes, 23 August, 13 September 1918; *Mercury*, 20 September 1918.

55 LGB Circular R.237 (as dated).

56 In July 1917, Sir Ryland Adkins urged that maps identifying the dispersal of the county's bread supply should be drawn up, on the basis that, if the German submarine campaign continued, food distribution in towns might come to an end, and people needed to know where to collect their own supplies (*Mercury*, 6 July 1917).

57 For example, *The Times*, 5 June 1917, 1 February, 6 June, 4 July 1918.

58 Above, pp. 77, 86.

7

Rank, deference and empathy

Extant biographies of Northamptonshire tribunalists (as given in Chapter 1) reveal an overwhelming prevalence of men of substance and standing in their communities. At the county level, the Appeals Tribunal hosted a representative selection of some of Northamptonshire's most distinguished public servants and gentry, with a leavening of genuinely aristocratic blood. Clearly, theirs was not a homogeneous group; tribunalists came from widely different backgrounds and enjoyed markedly dissimilar expectations of themselves and their immediate society. Nevertheless, most might be characterized as being of 'rank': that is, of a degree of status that distinguished them from a majority of those who applied to the Tribunals for exemption from military service.

Among them, however, were notable exceptions that weaken any assumption of the Tribunal system as necessarily comprising a collection of self-serving 'worthies'. When Northampton Borough Council sought a trades unionist to speak for the boot and shoe factory floor, a token appointment (or 'fair and just representation of labour') surely would have been almost anyone other than the self-assured and voluble James Gribble. If the County Council had wished a similar union presence on the appeals body merely to reassure labour, one, rather than two, NUBSO branch secretaries would have sufficed. And when they invited a woman to join the same Tribunal, it was almost certainly Beatrice Cartwright's extensive – and growing – experience of local issues that recommended her, rather than the fact of her sex and station alone. Nevertheless, the exceptions were just that; overwhelmingly, the Tribunals comprised men who were intended, in Walter Long's words, to 'command public confidence'. One might tip one's cap to the most exalted among them; the remainder were men to whom one would apply either for a letter of reference or a job. Above all, their status was intended to imbue the process with a necessary degree of gravitas and reassure the applicant that his concerns had been given an appropriate measure of the Establishment's attention.

This quality of 'otherness' emphasized the underlying ambiguity of the tribunalists' role and how it was perceived. To the government, often frustrated by idiosyncratic interpretations of legislation and instructions, they personified the inertial drag of local priorities. In contrast, those who stood before them in the tribunal chamber saw members of the same mechanism that worked tirelessly to take men from civilian life and place them in khaki. How tribunalists saw themselves was, of course, a matter of individual perception, but it is unlikely that any subsumed their own opinions and preconceptions entirely to the needs either of state or locality. They were required by their instructions to consider cases 'impartially, and … guided in their conclusions by a full regard for the national interests of the country'.[1] Doubtless, most, if not all, believed sincerely that they did so; but, as the *Mercury* suggested, another Solomon was needed to do their work in an entirely fair and disinterested spirit.[2] In the absence of biblical qualities, very human perspectives coloured their work. Is it possible to determine that they did so in a way that reflected either a conscious or an involuntary appreciation of social and/or economic distinction? In other words, did applicants experience an inconsistency of treatment that reflected discernibly the prejudices of their interrogators?

Certainly, there was a contemporary public perception that the playing field was not level. The *Times*, referring generally to provincial Tribunals, complained of the 'hopeless state of affairs when a bench of farmers and lawyers conspire to do good turns to one another'.[3] Auckland Geddes himself warned that 'confusion [in the application of legislation and instructions] breeds inequality of treatment … a sense of injustice … hatred of Government'.[4] The eyewitness accounts of organizations such as the No-Conscription Fellowship, and individual diarists who have left their observations to posterity, offer many vignettes in which the quality of impartiality appears to have been strained indeed. Such opinions were, unavoidably, subjective, and no massive 'organization' of almost two thousand unconnected bodies, staffed entirely by amateurs who faced peculiar local concerns and issues, could have been expected to demonstrate a unity of purpose and performance. But did some stray further than others – deliberately or otherwise – from the path laid out in Walter Long's 'mission statement' of February 1916?

In testing these questions with regard to this book's principal database, Northamptonshire's local and Appeals Tribunals, particular note will be taken of the manner in which claims for exemption based upon personal circumstance were adjudged. Previous sections have examined applications made primarily upon grounds of conscience or of occupation, neither of which offers a clear opportunity to test tribunalists' preconceptions. Obviously, these were demonstrated – if at all – regardless of the grounds upon which an application was made, but to distinguish the operation of personal prejudice from broader imperatives is often difficult. Subjective opinions expressed regarding a conscientious objection, for example, reflected a distaste which at that time transcended social and cultural boundaries. With regard to occupational applications, particularly where substantial local industries were involved, preoccupations with manpower dilution usually outweighed or disguised prejudicial opinions regarding an individual applicant. Where, however, an exemption was claimed upon the ground of personal circumstance, the applicant presented only himself and his private concerns. In effect, he was asking the Tribunal to weigh his own priorities against civic obligation. The tribunalists' personal reactions to such claims – whether sympathetic or indifferent, empathetic or hostile – were less likely to be camouflaged by wider considerations. If anomalies can be identified, they may allow us to explore the extent to which wider social dynamics were being played out in the tribunal chamber.

The vast majority of cases stated upon a 'personal' ground were made in respect of domestic and/or financial hardship. It was often the case that domestic difficulties – for example, the inability of a family to support itself adequately in the absence of the primary breadwinner – were predicated upon a financial issue. In the early months of the Tribunal system, many single young men claimed to be the only, or sole remaining, support of a widowed mother or of incapacitated parents. When married men fell within the legislation after May 1916, the financial impact of conscription upon wives and children with absent breadwinners became a paramount concern. Such stories were made more poignant – and problematic – where a man had several brothers or sons who were serving in the Colours already, or who had been wounded or lost in action, leaving him with responsibilities made more onerous by the fact of the war itself. Conversely, some applications were heard from men and women whose 'hardship' derived from the threatened loss of a final manservant or gardener/electrician, necessitating the closure of a country house or estate. Absent clear instructions from government, can it be said that the Tribunals applied the same, or similar, benchmarks to applications regardless of the individual circumstances of those presenting them?

The British experience of total war in the twentieth century suggests that perceptions of class alter, and even weaken (if only fleetingly), in times of national emergency.[5] During the First World War, the creation of the New Armies vastly increased social interaction between individuals and groups who, in peacetime, would have had little reason or opportunity to seek out each other's company. The perceived necessity of 'pulling together', of sharing both responsibility and sacrifice, was a commonly expressed sentiment. It was one regarding which aspiration far exceeded the reality, but new physical proximities could hardly have failed to lessen the strangeness of other lifestyles and concerns.

The Tribunals were not, however, part of that inadvertent social experiment. The vast majority of men who sat upon them were not of military age (at least until the Military Service (No. 2) Act, 1918, expanded the net of conscription), and few would have had first-hand experience of war as a leavening experience. Consequently, having volunteered to hear and adjudge men's claims for exemption, many were confronted by circumstances and preoccupations that remained at a substantial remove from their own. At the urban and county Tribunals in particular, this was a pronounced learning process, with cases involving dozens of often-unfamiliar gradations of the social and economic spectra. It would have been a peculiarly flexible intellect that set aside entirely its preconceptions when faced with such a barrage of new experience.

From the other side of the Tribunal table, applicants and appellants, many of whose educations had been cursory at best, were required to make a case for themselves – probably the most important case they would ever make – within an average of five minutes. They spoke, furthermore, to articulate, urbane men who might be expected to have little patience (particularly towards the end of a day's sitting) with smudged, ill-written applications and stumbling, semi-coherent explanations of circumstance. Some applicants' voices failed them almost entirely; a few, antagonized either by the adversarial format of the hearings or by some personal perception of injustice, became hostile, and, in at least one case before Northamptonshire's Appeals Tribunal, openly violent.[6] Again, it is hardly to be expected that such behaviour was ignored and the offenders' cases heard thereafter without prejudice.

But how far, and how often, did incomprehension or impatience shade into outright partiality, and how may it be measured? The obvious starting point would be to identify occasions either of palpably lenient or adversely prejudicial decisions, but even where these are evident, allowance must be made for the mood of a Tribunal on a particular day, the severity of the Army's need for men at that moment, and, most difficult to assess, the attitude and demeanour of the applicant. None of these mitigations necessarily dilutes the partiality of a judgement, but all necessitate the benefit of a doubt: that a 'bad' decision may have been predicated upon an impenetrable sense of otherness or nothing more than a fleeting dislike of an unfamiliar man's face.

A few incontrovertibly partial decisions have been gifted to us. As cited previously, Brixworth Tribunal on 6 April 1916 refused the plea of the farmer in the Yeomanry who asked to be allowed to remain on home service in order to maintain his 300-acre farm for himself and his widowed mother.[7] Minutes later, they similarly refused exemption to a boot maker and postman whose three brothers (two professional soldiers and a married man) had joined the Army previously, leaving him as the sole support of their mother. Between these two cases, they heard an employer's application: that of Earl Spencer for his forester, to whom the Tribunal promptly offered three months' exemption in order that he might arrange his domestic and financial affairs.[8] Brixworth, it will be recalled, were at this time acting against their fellow rural Tribunals' trend towards leniency in agricultural cases,[9] and it is correspondingly unlikely that a man whose occupation did not fall within the certified list would have been treated so generously had he had a less exalted employer.

In the following month, when Lord Annaly appeared before the same Tribunal to apply to have his estate carpenter, his electrician and his chauffeur exempted, the usually unbending military representative, Adam Cross, obligingly suggested they be offered certificates until the end of June. Graciously, his Lordship announced that he was 'satisfied' with this. Twelve months later, Annaly was back at Brixworth with an application for his 24-year-old, unmarried footman, previously declared unfit but now passed B1. The man was his only remaining servant, and, as a lord-in-waiting to the King, Annaly stressed that he needed a valet. The Tribunal agreed to another medical re-examination. A few weeks later, Annaly returned; his footman, having been re-examined and passed C2, was now given an open certificate until the end of the year (with leave to appeal further), conditional upon his employer's current ill-health persisting. The day's next case was that of a widowed foreman, cleaner and packer of army boots. He cared for his mother (also widowed), two children of his own and a niece, the daughter of one of his two brothers, both of whom had been lost in the *Royal Edward*. The decision was 31 October, final.[10]

As in other matters, Brixworth Tribunal represented an extreme. It will be observed that occasions of apparent deference to a superior social order were very rare (not least, perhaps, because members of Northamptonshire's aristocracy came before the Tribunals infrequently). Slightly more prevalent were instances of what might be termed the Establishment taking, or appearing to take, care of its 'own'. On 10 April 1916, the military appeal against a certificate offered to Wilfred Webb, tax collector, assessor and County Court bailiff, was challenged by a written intervention from the Lord Chancellor, which attested to Webb's indispensability to the Court Register. Without further discussion the Appeals Tribunal confirmed his three months' certificate.[11] The same Tribunal also gave a four-month exemption in July to a shepherd employed by John Williams, a county councillor, whose application had been dismissed previously by Finedon Tribunal. Technically, shepherds were within the list of certified occupations; however, Williams, who farmed 400 acres, had a labour force of four men, two youths, two women and a girl milker, which, while low by prewar standards, met the recently set labour scale requirements for his acreage.[12] Similarly, when Lady Lowther appealed for George Purse, second whip of the Pytchley hunt (whose master, Lord Annaly, did not recuse himself during the Tribunal's consideration of the case), his 31 May certificate was extended to I July, and finality was removed.

One of the more visible examples of self-serving, however justified in the 'national interest', occurred when a Tribunal offered exemption to one of its own. In October 1916, that most self-consciously 'fair' Tribunal, Northampton Borough, heard an application from the Northampton No. 1 Branch of NUBSO, supported by Alderman Pitts, in respect of their vice-president, W.P. Townley – a member of the Tribunal. He was allowed six months' exemption, though his undoubtedly relevant work as a tribunalist was not raised, or tactfully ignored, in support of the claim.[13] A slightly less deliberate example of good-fellowship was provided by Rushden Tribunal in the following year when offering conditional exemption to William Langley, JP, whose chairmanship of their Irthlingborough sister body was acknowledged openly (though his valuable work as vice-chairman of the town's council and as assistant secretary of the local NUBSO branch was cited also).[14]

Other Tribunals treated their own more scrupulously, particularly following the raising of the military age. When, in July 1918, a 50-year-old Towcester tribunalist made an application for exemption (he was not named, as was the policy of newspapers when reporting local Tribunals' proceedings), the Tribunal sent him to Potterspury to have his case heard there, 'as the chairman thought it hardly good policy for the Tribunal to deal with the case of one of its own members'. The Local Government Board sent word approving the decision. Perhaps troubled by the earlier accommodation of Townley, Northampton Borough's Councillor Parker had his own application for exemption (he came into eligibility with the Military Service (No. 2) Act, 1918) heard at Peterborough. That evidently rigorous body enjoyed a little light relief at their relatively liberal applicant's expense, when their National Service representative asked Parker whether, in view of new War Agricultural Committee guidelines, 'hoeing turnips would appeal to him'. Most notably, four tribunalists at Northampton Rural Tribunal declared that the raising of the military age to 51 rendered them unable to continue in their role, as they would be required to adjudge cases involving men older than themselves. Pressed to continue in their present roles by Hayes Fisher himself, they nevertheless stood on principle and retired in June, thereby making themselves eligible for enlistment.[15] If some tribunalists conspired to 'do turns' for their own, others pushed the principle of fairness to an extreme.

Cases in which deference was clearly displayed, or in which unusual consideration appears to have been shown towards someone with status within the local community, were relatively conspicuous, not least because local newspapers sought out and reported them assiduously. Less so were those instances where the treatment of an individual was unusual but lacked any obvious rationale. One of the more notable cases to come before Northampton Borough Tribunal – notable, that is, for the forbearance shown to the applicant – was that of Leslie Wiggins, son of the owner of Wiggins and Co., and, in his own right, director and leading shareholder of Foxon and Co. (both coal merchants' firms). Wiggins, an attested man, was to obtain an atypical degree of leeway from the Tribunal which is difficult to explain other than as a consequence of his position in the community, yet the decision eventually handed down was not notably in his favour. He first applied to Northampton Borough in January 1916, claiming that he was in a certified industry and should therefore be exempted. The case was adjourned briefly upon Geldart's request for evidence that Wiggins was in fact managing his father's depot. On 21 February the Tribunal reheard and dismissed the application, and Wiggins lodged an appeal. County considered his case in March and decided that his father's business, though having a sub-office at Northampton railway station, did not constitute a 'coal depot' within the meaning of the certified occupations list. They allowed 14 days' exemption only (that is, two weeks and two months). At the end of May, Wiggins returned to Northampton Borough, and told them that he had agreed with his partner, Mr Foxon, that, if the latter went to war, he would continue their business. His solicitor asked that his application with regard to Foxon and Co., and a further, forthcoming application with respect to Wiggins and Co., be considered as a single case. The Tribunal refused this request, but stood over the case until the Wiggins and Co. application was presented.

Three weeks later, Wiggins's Foxon and Co. application was dismissed, but he was given a three months' (final) exemption on hardship grounds in respect of his role in his father's firm (Wiggins senior was said to be very unwell still). In the last week of September, a new application was made on business grounds, as Wiggins's unfortunate father had now fractured his wrist and was unable to manage his company. Geldart objected: he did not think Wiggins indispensable, though he was willing to agree to a further month's exemption if finality was attached. The Tribunal disagreed, and stood over the case for a month. On 31 October, Wiggins came to the Tribunal with his father, who asked for yet more time to recover but stated that he was willing to accept finality on his son's certificate. James Gribble, acknowledging the scale of their business, suggested three months' further exemption, while Geldart argued for one. The Tribunal compromised upon two months, final.

That should have concluded the matter, but Wiggins wrote subsequently to the War Office, who, remarkably, took time to consider his case. In January 1917 it informed his Tribunal that it had fully reviewed his circumstances, and felt that it could not leave him in his present employment following the expiration of his present certificate. However, it accepted that he had attested under the misapprehension that he would not be able to apply for exemption otherwise, and would accede to his secondary request: to be posted to a non-combatant unit. The letter concluded 'I am to say that his conscientious objection is not to be considered an afterthought.' Following the surprised pause that doubtless ensued, James Gribble suggested that there was little point pursuing the case and they might as well let it rest. For good measure, A.E. Tebbutt reminded his colleagues that he had always suspected Wiggins to have a conscientious objection to service.[16]

Though coal merchants were semi-protected, Wiggins's role and the nature of his business had been swiftly determined to fall outside the scope of the certified occupations list. His father's original illness was not specified, though the subsequent inconvenience of a broken wrist could hardly have prevented him from running his business, and it is hard to imagine that the Tribunal would have regarded a similar injury to the father of a newsagent or hairdresser as sufficient grounds for delaying a fit young man's posting to the Colours. As a substantial businessman, Wiggins stood before a number of his peers (and, possibly, acquaintances) at the Tribunal; his preoccupations were, to an extent, theirs also – or at least sufficiently close to elicit a degree of empathy. Even the fiery trade unionist James Gribble appeared to consider the scale of the Wiggins's business as a qualifying factor without questioning its value to the war effort, and was willing to extend an already protracted exemption. Nevertheless, though lending an unusually accommodating ear to Mr Wiggins's pleas, the Tribunal did not deviate from their initial decision that he should, eventually, go into the Army.

The above cases, considered in isolation, offer evidence of the self-serving idiosyncrasies reported of tribunalists elsewhere. But how representative are they? Expectations of the system have been derived predominantly from individual excesses, advertised swiftly by the contemporary press and cited subsequently by commentators whose prior assumptions have been buttressed thereby. Conclusions derived from such a process cannot be considered definitive. It might equally be argued that the relative paucity of examples of deference and 'good fellowship' as a proportion of all cases for which information survives suggests that any accurate measure of the Tribunals' partialities must lie elsewhere.

Men whose condition was markedly different from that of the average tribunalist, whose habitual circumstances were such that an Army Separation Allowance might actually have improved their families' material quality of life, and whose social stratum provided the traditional pool of recruitment, comprised the majority of visitors to the Tribunals. It is likely that many if not most tribunalists had little experience of the acute domestic and financial issues they described, and very probably regarded them as the immutable lot of the proletariat. Consequently, any evidence that such preoccupations were accommodated – particularly where the letter of legislation and instructions was thereby tested or even stretched – must, to a degree, undermine the conventional view of Tribunals as upholders of middle-class verities.

Thus, if Northampton Borough's treatment of W.P. Townley and Leslie Wiggins suggests a certain direction to their partialities, their quixotic behaviour upon other occasions makes simplistic conclusions problematic. Their relatively progressive treatment of attested conscientious objectors has been noted already, and, even if we dismiss as prematurely flattering the *Independent*'s early judgement upon their general demeanour ('from first to last every applicant is treated with courteous consideration'), it is clear that they regarded the social implications of their work extremely closely.[17] On two issues of domestic hardship that most exercised both government and Tribunals – those of the dependent widow and the last remaining son – they located themselves firmly and consistently on the side of the applicant, in striking contrast to their colleagues at Brixworth. From surviving evidence of their proceedings, no applicant who supported a widowed mother (and whose army allowance would not be applied to her relief) was refused an exemption of some form during almost three years' sittings.[18] On the matter of families who had contributed disproportionately to the war effort, their reaction was more forthright still. If any single case might be said to have caused a near-rupture in the relationship between Town and County Hall in Northampton, it was that of an 18-year-old, former trainee engineer, Michael Verrachia. His mother, a widowed 60-year-old Italian immigrant who operated an ice-cream stall in Northampton (a baked-potato stall during the winter months), had three other sons, all in uniform. Michael, her last remaining child, had withdrawn recently from his apprenticeship to help run her business.

A.H. Geldart, the Tribunal's military representative, lodged an appeal against a three months' exemption offered to Verrachia, which was to be heard at County Hall on 17 October. Northampton Borough considered the case sufficiently important for Councillor Parker to attend personally to explain their decision, but business called him away to London that day, and their secretary, Herbert Hankinson, appeared in his place. The Appeals Tribunal, as was their policy, refused to hear him.[19] In appealing the certificate, Geldart argued that the purveyance of ice-cream was not in any way of national importance, and hinted that Verrachia had abrogated any right to an exemption by abandoning his apprenticeship. The Tribunal, satisfied that no particular domestic hardship was involved, adjusted the original certificate to 1 December, final.

Northampton Borough's tribunalists, and their chairman in particular, were furious. At their next sitting the latter berated Geldart publicly, and threatened to take up the case with the Prime Minister. Referring to Verrachia as 'this valuable boy', he observed that several local Tribunals had expressed their support of the original decision, and suggested that he and his colleagues might abandon business and go off to the seaside for two months (Tribunal: 'hear, hear'). To the attending press, he declared: 'We have a splendid test of motherhood in this case, and before I register a vote in favour of the last son being taken England will have to be in the last ditch; many will not be sitting at this Tribunal, and others will be on the coastline doing their bit.'

Parker persisted with the case. Urged on by Gribble, he wrote to Northampton's Liberal MP, Charles MacCurdy, suggesting it would be a relatively simple matter to adjust the Military Service Act to ensure that all the sons of large families should not go to war. He reported this to his Tribunal at a sitting on 9 November, after which they turned to other business. However, Parker's blood remained 'up'. A glancing reference was made to a recent, alleged comment by Sir Charles Knightley at the Appeals Tribunal, to the effect that Northampton Borough Tribunal seemed not to know what 'hardship' was. The chairman exploded; he saw no reason why they should be 'continually harassed' by comments from the body across the road, 'and he had yet to learn that Local Tribunals were to be turned into press-gangs'. Of the Appeals Tribunal's apparent rigour, Gribble observed laconically: 'Some of the old chaps over there have got into a chronic funk.'[20]

The Tribunal's anger, publicly stated and reported, reflected a genuine depth of feeling. Temporarily, it poisoned the relationship of two bodies representative of authority in the cause of a young man from an immigrant, working-class family with no local influence or social standing. Nor was the Tribunal's attitude towards Michael Verrachia in any way uncharacteristic. The anger they displayed at the Appeals Tribunal's decision was fuelled in part by another, concurrent adjustment at appeal of an exemption offered to Leonard Zephania Slinn, whose story might have been a *Boys' Own* exemplar for the dutiful child. Slinn, a 19-year-old engineer's fitter, also worked 30–40 poles of allotment (the produce from which was sold in his mother's grocery business) and was 'senior sergeant' of a drilling squad at a local boys' club. On 25 September 1916, Northampton Borough heard that Slinn's father and only sibling had volunteered for the Army 15 months earlier (leaving Leonard as the sole help for his mother), and that, of 25 members of their wider family serving in uniform, three had been killed and two others seriously gassed. The Tribunal offered the applicant an open exemption to 25 December, 'having regard to the sacrifice already made by the family'. Geldart appealed the certificate, and, on 20 October, the Appeals Tribunal reduced the exemption to 1 December (final), despite a humble yet extremely eloquent written appeal from Mrs Slinn.[21]

Northampton Borough persisted in their defence of the last remaining son, as did the Appeals Tribunal in their corrections. In the following year, a certificate they offered to a young man whose family had lost several sons was similarly shortened by the Appeals Tribunal (the latter recording, for good measure, their opinion that Tribunals were not 'courts of sympathy'). Once more, Parker could not contain his ire: 'If members of Parliament had not been asleep when the Military Service Act was under consideration ... families in [this] position would have been protected' (Tribunal: 'hear, hear'). At a sitting three weeks later, he noted a recent Central Tribunal decision which had allowed only six weeks' exemption to the youngest of five sons of a widow; his colleagues then pointedly offered a three months' (open) certificate to the last of four sons of a widow (the others were serving with the Colours), and the same to a man who had lost one brother in action and had three others in uniform. In October 1917, a mother of nine applied to the Tribunal for her fourth son. Of the three elder sons who had joined up previously, two had been killed and a third wounded twice, while the five youngest were below working age. Geldart's half-hearted attempt to play down the family's sacrifice ('I know widows who have given five sons') was dismissed curtly by the ardent VTC recruiter, W.P. Cross ('and I know conscientious objectors who haven't given one and never will'), and a three-month (open) exemption was offered.[22]

This was the Tribunal locating itself firmly within localist sentiment, oblivious to (or disregarding) the ostensible gulf of rank and circumstance that divided applicant and tribunalist. Here at least, we may discern a palpable difference of perspective between Tribunals who, in many other cases, worked harmoniously and even supportively of each other. Can it be assumed, however, that the tensions necessarily reflected different perceptions of the lives and circumstances of the applicants? Clearly, Northampton Borough were moved by compassion on the matter of youngest sons of large families who had given significantly to the war effort; the Appeals Tribunal, apparently, were less so. However, the latter were extremely sensitive to their role as final arbiter of others' decisions. The 'courts of sympathy' comment appears callous, but may have been stated defensively, and was of course correct in a literal sense. As their instructions stipulated, they were obliged, where a blurring of circumstance did not require them to exercise discretion, to apply the letter of the Act regardless of senti-ment.[23] Where other Tribunals had chosen not to do so, either inadvert-ently or in deliberately sending a message regarding a matter about which they felt strongly, the Appeals body's adjustments generated resentment and a sense that they were not in tune with local feeling.

This, and the more elevated social status of the majority of tribunalists at County Hall, reinforced a perception that they saw themselves as 'above', or at least apart from, their colleagues in the local bodies. At a single sitting in late October, two Northampton Borough tribunalists openly expressed adverse opinions of their colleagues across Guildhall Street: an unprec-edented rupture in the etiquette of the exemption process. Discussing the advisability of sending a case to appeal, F.O. Roberts referred darkly to 'the result of going to the other body, it was all too patent'. James Gribble concurred, if more circumspectly: 'we know the composition of the other Tribunal'.[24] However, we may – as Roberts and Gribble almost certainly did – place too much weight upon the implications of this elitist mindset, if such it was. If the Appeals Tribunal were, or appeared to be, less moved by sentiment than their local counterparts, it was also the case that famili-arity with rank inclined them to be less indulgent towards their peers than were, for example, Brixworth Tribunal. When, in May 1916, a prominent landowner, Major P.E.T. Hibbert, appealed against short exemptions given to two of his estate workers, he was told briskly that, while the Tribunal sympathized with his predicament (Hibbert had claimed that he would be forced to shut up his country home and return to his London residence for want of staff), the needs of the country came first.[25] Lord Erskine received the same short shrift when he came before them three months later on behalf of his market gardener and estate engineer, Walter Viney, without whom it was claimed that three-and-a-half acres of vegetables could not be cultivated. Asked if his sons could help, Erskine claimed that they did some weeding during their school holidays. He was reminded that the sons of poor people were required to work in times of national necessity, and the original certificates were confirmed.[26]

However, men who themselves employed staff were not always unsym-pathetic to the plight of the emptied estate. In July 1916, Geldart appealed Northampton Borough's decision to offer a three-month (open) certificate to William Newberry, a 24-year-old chauffeur and gardener employed by the shoe manufacturer Sir Henry Randall at Monks' Park Hall. Solic-itor H.W. Williams claimed that Newberry drove Sir Henry for business purposes only, and that he did the work of several men in the Park. Once more, it was claimed that if Newberry went to the Colours, his employer would be obliged to close up the Hall and live elsewhere. Randall's plight convinced where, two months earlier, Hibbert's had not. The Appeals

Tribunal noted that Newberry was very young and should be in the Army, but shortened his certificate by one day only.[27]

Again, cases in which the interests of men or women of great substance were involved could be expected to attract attention, as would those concerning families that had contributed greatly to the war effort already. These were headline cases in which a Tribunal's decision reflected very much upon their public image. Far more numerous, though less prominently advertised, were the relatively mundane stories of the sort of hardship that, but for the Tribunal system, would have remained the unspoken lot of the poor and misfortunate. In such cases, the removal to the Colours of a principal breadwinner might, whatever the financial compensation offered by an Army Separation Allowance, unravel an already fragile domestic situation. The prevalence of such conditions, particularly among social strata in which economic hardship was a perennial fact of life, might lead us to assume that the Tribunals would have been, or become, inured to their emotional impact.

To the contrary, however, there is clear evidence that many of Northamptonshire's Tribunals responded (and continued to respond) relatively sensitively in cases where the element of hardship – even if of a form not directly addressed in instructions – was particularly pronounced. Such sensitivity might, at times, extend no further than helping a widowed mother to 'jump the queue' to obtain an allotment;[28] at others, it was expressed in decisions which came close to defying both the letter and spirit of legislation. In May 1916, Hardingstone hesitated to release to the Army a shoe riveter with six children and wages of a guinea per week until their military representative assured them that service allowances to the family would be 8s. more. In July, Northampton Rural Tribunal gave a brewer's labourer time to find work on the land when he claimed that the Army Separation Allowance would be insufficient to provide for his 'delicate' child. At their next sitting, they offered a seemingly rigorous one-month (final) certificate to a labourer (34, Category A) with a sickly wife and six children under 12 years of age, but told him that if he managed to find permanent work on the land in the meantime they would consider a further appeal from his new employer. In November 1916, Crick Tribunal heard the application on domestic hardship grounds of a rural postman aged 30, a married man with five children. An open certificate was issued, conditional upon his finding work of national importance – but at some unspecified time after the Christmas holidays.[29]

As their reputation among other Tribunals suggested, the Appeals Tribunal seemed, superficially, to rise above such sentiment and apply the letter of legislation – or, where that was lacking, to acknowledge the military exigencies of the moment. At the end of October 1916, when pressure to improve the rate of enlistment was growing (and, at which time, to cite James Gribble, they had fallen into 'a chronic funk' regarding recruitment), an elderly, infirm widow, Mrs E. Walpole, appealed for her son, Horace, a 34-year-old, unmarried clothing presser. Horace was her only support, and had looked after her for much of the quarter-century since her husband died. The Tribunal reminded her that Walpole had received several exemptions since the previous February, and that she had been given ample time to find other help. Their decision was 1 November, final. A harrowing scene ensued: Mrs Walpole remained before them, asking plaintively, 'Can't you leave him to me?' until she was led gently from the chamber. A week later, the mother of Albert Edward Chester appealed for an extension to his exemption. Her husband was subjected to fits, while two other sons were in the Army already; with five younger children to support, Chester, a boot operative, was her only help. Stopford-Sackville told her that the Tribunal sympathized, but that a man of 19 could not be kept out of the Army. Her son was given one month's further exemption, final. On 19 December, John Charles Ridlington, a 38-year-old firewood and general dealer with a history of illness following a serious accident, appealed against Peterborough Tribunal's dismissal of his application on the grounds of personal hardship. Ridlington, who had six children aged between two and 16, claimed not to be able to work for more than short periods, but had been passed for general service by barracks. The Appeals Tribunal, unable to consider the issue of his ill-health (the ground had not been stated in the application), concluded that Ridlington's separation allowance would exceed his present earnings and dismissed the appeal.[30]

However, at times when pressure from the War Office and the Local Government Board was less persistent, the Tribunal, though self-admittedly not a 'court of sympathy', could exhibit a degree of compassion. An unmarried, 23-year-old gamekeeper, W. R. Whitehorn, appealed in May 1916 on hardship grounds against the one-month certificate offered at Brackley. He had enlisted at the beginning of the war and served for four months. His father had then died, leaving a widow with five young children (the youngest a month old) and no income. Whitehorn had been told that the Army could provide no allowance, so he had applied for – and received – a discharge. All of his wages went to his mother, whose only other income was 6s. per week from a younger brother who had now commenced work. Whitehorn told the Tribunal he 'would not mind' going back to the Army if some provision could be made for his family. The case was adjourned pending advice from Eastern Command to ascertain if this were possible: 'he had behaved well, and [the Tribunal] were anxious that neither he nor his mother should suffer'. When the Army failed to provide reassurance on the point, Whitehorn was offered a three-month certificate, which was renewed subsequently for a further two months.[31]

Upon other occasions, the same Tribunal found ingenious ways of exhibiting their empathy in a practical manner while arguing other motives. John James Lyons, a 35-year-old mineral water bottler and father of six children, had a six weeks' certificate extended to three months (open) in January 1917. Announcing the decision, Stopford-Sackville declared breezily, 'We do not desire to discourage the trade in mineral waters, as the brewers have had rather the monopoly up to now'. Similarly, in August 1917, they dismissed a military appeal against a two-month (open) certificate given to John Allen, a married, Category A boot clicker and newsagent, on the ostensible basis that his wife *wasn't* 'delicate'. Allen had lost one brother in action and another had been crippled for life, leaving their parents dependent upon him. When asked by Captain Cook if his wife was delicate (almost certainly a deliberate effort to coach him), Allen said that she was not. Cook professed surprise: 'In ninety-nine cases like this she usually is: this is the odd case' (laughter). Stopford-Sackville told Allen, 'As you have deserved so well of your country by having a wife who isn't delicate, the ... appeal is dismissed.'[32]

In September 1917, they heard the appeal of Arthur West, a 33-year-old married man with no apparent ground for challenging the finality attached to his one-month certificate from Rushden Tribunal. However, when they heard that three of his brothers had been killed in action during the previous month, they ordered that he be medically re-examined (his present rating was B1). At the time, a large backlog of referred medical cases lay before the re-forming Medical Boards, and, given that West had made no application on medical grounds, it is difficult to interpret the ruling as anything other than a deliberate attempt to keep him out of the Army. Re-rated B2, his exemption was renewed twice subsequently, and he remained in civilian life until the end of hostilities.[33]

Very occasionally, the Appeals Tribunal matched Northampton Borough's predilection for the sentimental, even quixotic gesture. Throughout 1916 and early 1917, the latter body had offered numerous exemptions to George Hopper, a 23-year-old hairdresser who helped to support his widowed mother. In 1915, Hopper's 45-year-old father had enlisted in the Northamptonshire Regiment and subsequently was killed in action at Gallipoli. Before sailing, he had – allegedly – expressed his determination that, if any of their family must die in war, it should be himself. Following his death, his widow received a pension of 12s. 6d. per week, to which her son added 16s. Geldart (who must have shared some measure of sympathy for Hopper's circumstances in allowing previous exemptions to go unchallenged), appealed the latest certificate on the basis that 'the only ground ... is sentiment and sympathy for the mother'. He admitted to the Appeals Tribunal that Hopper was a dutiful son but reminded them that he had also been passed Category A, had been the recipient of nine exemptions already, and would not now find it easy to transfer to a job that came closer to fulfilling some definition of 'national importance'. The argument was a strong one; nevertheless, in their judgement the Appeals Tribunal uncharacteristically gave great weight to the elder Hopper's alleged valediction. His son, having stated that he was prepared to work on the land, was allowed 14 days to find new employment. A week later, he returned to tell the Tribunal that he had taken up work as a nurseryman for 22s. per week. An open certificate was issued, conditional upon him remaining in his new post. Geldart, who had returned to County Hall to hear the verdict, said that his instructions obliged him to protest the decision, but that he would not do so formally.[34]

In September of the same year, Wellingborough Rural observed the letter of their instructions reluctantly and then appealed – literally – to a higher tribunal to redress their decision. Charles Lovell, an 18-year-old, Category A heel-trimmer, was refused exemption on hardship grounds, though he was the sole support of a blind father and ill mother. Explaining their decision on form R.43, the Tribunal acknowledged that Lovell's circumstances were pitiable, but that, as a young man fit for general service, they felt they could not offer exemption. However, they concluded on a plaintive note: that they would be pleased if the Appeals Tribunal 'could see their way to grant some exemption in this case'. The latter obliged: on 28 September, Lovell was offered a certificate to 1 February.[35]

The Tribunals could be compassionate; they could also be unyielding. The problem in apportioning motive lies in the indeterminable quality of decisions that were – or appeared to be – based upon perception rather than fact. Were tribunalists genuinely moved by some cases, or did they wish to appear to be so moved? Was compassion something that, being displayed publicly, assisted them in their role as arbiters of who should and should not go to war? The suggestion may be considered cynical, but, again, there is too much evidence that the Tribunals were sensitive to their public image to assume that all cases were processed with only the applicant or Army in mind. Given the extent and depth of the sacrifice that the nation was being asked to make, ensuring 'fair' treatment was a constant theme. Being held in the public gaze, usually before substantial local audiences, the Tribunals were one of the few instruments of government policy that the ordinary man and woman could witness in action. The newspapers, focusing unerringly upon those cases that reflected less than equitable treatment, did no more than disseminate more widely what was known already. If for no other reason, therefore, most Tribunals attempted to demonstrate 'fairness', and, to emphasise the point, mentioned often that they were doing just that. When public opinion was known, they took care not to set themselves against it. On almost every occasion when a local petition was presented to them in support of an applicant or appellant, Northamptonshire Tribunals either offered substantial exemptions or agreed to review previously dismissed applications.[36] It may be that this reflected a retrospective appreciation of the true value of the applicant or appellant. Equally, it suggests that tribunalists remained quite closely attuned to the local mood.

The principal of equity was paramount, therefore, and, where it was seen to be failing, notice was taken. Complaints made to the Tribunals, or anger expressed at their decisions, tended to be excited by one of two perceptions: either that tribunalists were failing to give sufficient weight to the circumstances of an application or appeal, or that others who came before them were not being treated similarly. Most of these 'others' were represented only anecdotally (such as the alleged multitude of single young men who, apparently, skulked in safety at the Wolverton carriage works), though a few were identified specifically.[37] Particular offence was taken when members of the Tribunals were themselves suspected to be above, or taking advantage of, the system. Predictably, the agricultural sector, in which the circumstances of individuals were not hidden within an industrial-scale anonymity, provided fertile ground for personal rancour. The only recorded case of attempted violence at a Northamptonshire Tribunal occurred when a farmer's son half-heartedly swung a bag (weighted with a horseshoe) at the head of W. Murland, Daventry's military representative, as he resisted the man's appeal in July 1916. The assailant, swiftly disarmed by his father and brother, heatedly claimed that widespread village gossip assumed Murland to be employing 12 men on his own farm, six of whom were of military age.

In the following February, another farmer appealed against Wellingborough Rural Tribunal's dismissal of the application of his son, Leslie Clifford Hallett. The elder Hallett, who farmed 564 acres, had three sons with the Colours already and a fourth who was incurably paralysed. The Appeals Tribunal offered a three months' (open) certificate, but the farmer remained incensed: 'I hope in the meantime some of the Wellingborough Tribunal members will soon send some of their sons.' The implied accusation carried weight, locally. When the appeal of George Knight, a 21-year-old bailiff and milkman, was challenged by Captain Cook later that month on the basis that Wellingborough, a Tribunal composed largely of farmers, had decided that Knight's farm had enough men already, the appellant's solicitor, W.W. James, explicitly challenged the integrity of that earlier judgement. He claimed that three of the tribunalists' sons had exemption certificates, that the clerk of the Tribunal was of military age, and that three of his own clients, previously refused exemptions by the same Tribunal, had been given their notices of dismissal before leaving the room (thereby facilitating their speedy calling-up).[38]

That the above clashes were reported voraciously in local newspapers hints at their atypical nature. On the whole, proceedings were marked more by an uneasy formality than personal rancour. Indeed, on the evidence of the same reports, exchanges between the military and agricultural representatives, or between the former and applicants' solicitors, were far more common – and heated – than those between tribunalists and applicants (conscience cases excepted). This may equally imply a degree of integrity in the Tribunals' work or of fatalism in those they heard, but such evidence that exists tends to suggest that the Northamptonshire public's opinion of their tribunalists did not deteriorate to that state feared by Auckland Geddes. Perhaps, in so urgently advertising their desire to be equitable, they convinced a majority that they succeeded – at least, to a degree that deflected overt criticism of their work.

Very occasionally, equity could be demonstrated to the satisfaction of (almost) all parties. The most sensational case to come before the Tribunals in Northamptonshire was that of A.F. Stanley, Mayor of Daventry. Previously, Stanley, a local businessman, landowner and grist-mill operator, had been given an open-ended exemption, subject to his attending VTC drills in the town. The relationship between applicant and Tribunal was in this case complex. The latter's chairman, J. Gardner, was also commander of the Daventry section of the VTC; Lt Col. Willoughby, the military representative in 1917 (succeeding W. Murland), was both Daventry's Town Clerk and the Commander of the First Battalion, Northamptonshire Volunteers. Another tribunalist, Councillor W. Edgar, had been Stanley's immediate predecessor as Mayor. This was a closely knit community of local officials – precisely the sort that might have been expected, as *The Times* put it, to 'do good turns to one another' in the tribunal chamber.[39] The reality, however, was strikingly otherwise.

On 30 August, the Tribunal, noting that Stanley had yet to attend a single VTC drill, wrote to him, intimating that his exemption might be withdrawn. In the following week, the Mayor sent a letter to the Tribunal, which arrived during their next sitting. Its tone was, to say the least, ill-judged. Imperiously, Stanley informed them that he could not possibly attend VTC drills whilst Mayor, but, as soon as his term expired on 8 November, he would commence drilling: 'I should not have thought it would have been necessary to have told you this; surely you all know that a business man who is elected as Mayor has got quite as much as he can do. I am inclined to think that in Daventry the position of Mayor is not looked upon with respect, otherwise I should not be subjected to this annoyance and insult.' Having briefly discussed the letter, the Tribunal, urged on by Willoughby (who, in the previous week, had written to all local Tribunals, asking them to ensure that VTC conditions attached to certificates were honoured)[40] drafted a short reply, supplied also to the Press, directing Stanley to enrol at the VTC meeting on the following Tuesday evening or risk having his exemption cancelled.

Stanley promptly refused this direction, and the Tribunal set a date for a special sitting. In the meantime, the Mayor fought his case through the local newspapers, particularly the Daventry *Express* and Northampton *Mercury* (both of which sent reporters to interview him) and nationally through the *Daily Mail*. To the *Mercury*'s reporter he stressed that he was a medical re-examination case (previously rejected under the Derby Scheme), and that, in his official capacity, he was the King's representative at Daventry. In commenting upon the case, the *Mercury* was non-committal. It noted that one of Stanley's judges, Councillor Edgar, had not performed the expected duties of special constable either during or after his period as Mayor; conversely, it also observed that Stanley was the town's only Category B exemptee who had not either drilled with the VTC or persuaded the military authorities that he was unfit for duty.

On 17 September, Stanley stood upon principle and faced the Tribunal. His defence, other than stressing the pressures of his other duties, was that not a single tribunalist had advised him personally on the matter. Willoughby contradicted this, claiming that he himself had suggested that the Mayor attend at least one drill, while the chairman reminded Stanley that they had not placed him in Section B of the VTC, as was their habit with all other Category B exemptees. Had they given him further preferential treatment, they argued, it 'would have been making fish of one and fowl of another'. Once more, they urged the Mayor to attend the VTC drill, and, once more, he refused, complaining that 'many vile things' had been said about him. Even now, the Tribunal did not withdraw the exemption. A further meeting took place on 28 September, at which the chairman took a stronger line: he admonished Stanley, reminding him that, as 'chief citizen', he was expected to be 'the pattern of law and order'. A final offer was made: if the Mayor joined the VTC within three days (they insisted now that it be B Section, which would require him to remain in the VTC for the duration of the war), the Tribunal would extend his certificate to 31 December (open). Upon Stanley's refusal, they made out a new certificate, for three days, final.

The Mayor appealed, and, on 8 October, represented by solicitor C.F. Alsop, appeared at Northamptonshire County Hall. The hearing was brief, and salutary. Adkins, Beattie and Captain Cook flung out examples of other distinguished men doing VTC drills, including the Lord Mayor of London (Cook: 'You put yourself above him?'), until Alsop, sensing the mood, intervened and asked for a brief adjournment. When he and his client returned, Stanley meekly announced he would withdraw his appeal and drill with the Daventry VTC.[41]

Stanley's case is particularly interesting in that it tested explicitly the Tribunals' frequently professed regard for 'fairness'. The Mayor's haughty disregard of the conditions of his exemption, his flamboyant overassessment of his office and willingness to fight his case outside the tribunal chamber were in themselves inflammatory. More provocative still was his underlying assumption that the rules were for lesser men: that his peers would, or should, recognize that circumstances outside the purview of legislation, predicated upon status alone, validated his stance. His inference that prior tensions among Daventry's municipal elite influenced their treatment of him is plausible, and there is evident an air of *schadenfreude* among his erstwhile political colleagues as he excavated his personal trench. Nevertheless, Stanley presented the system with a challenge it could not ignore, and, if his experience before his local Tribunal was humiliating, it became positively bruising at County Hall. Indeed, it might be concluded that the Appeals Tribunal were grateful to the Mayor for giving them the opportunity to affirm so robustly their egalitarian pretensions in the glare of local publicity.

The treatment of Stanley, and that of many others who came before the Tribunals upon personal or domestic grounds, may lead us to one or many conclusions regarding their integrity. But can any broad assumptions be valid? Tribunals were composed of more or less fallible human beings, who, having been told to be fair (by the Local Government Board) but hard (the Recruiting Department), often misjudged the balance, and with an inconsistency that makes a meaningful assessment of their motives and prejudices very difficult. At times, the conveyor-belt manner of their deliberations, when backlogs of cases required some of the busier Tribunals to sit upon three or four occasions in a single week, offered little indication that humanity played much part in the process. At others, there are glimpses of what appear to be genuine attempts to accommodate the personal priorities of men whose circumstances were significantly different from the tribunalists' own. It may be that the only substantive conclusion this discussion allows is that most Tribunals in Northamptonshire demonstrated no extreme of generosity or callousness in their dealings. Their application of 'fairness' was as inconsistent as any human quality, and as vulnerable to external stimuli. Prejudices, preconceptions, predilections, personal empathy or even a poor lunch might sway one or more tribunalists to the point at which they carried a majority of their colleagues. Conversely, occasions of apparent favouritism or harshness might have been grounded as much upon an honest and impartial appreciation of the facts of a case as upon any subjective criteria. These are, however, observations that may be made only at the most general level. It is where we move from the general to the particular that they become unhelpful.

Upon several occasions, certain Tribunals exhibited symptoms of deference or a willingness to accommodate socially prominent applicants. Others – Peterborough offers the clearest example – applied themselves so rigorously to the task of getting men into the Army regardless of an applicant's situation that one might equally regard them as admirably egalitarian or inured to mitigation.[42] Many Tribunals, struggling to apply consistency in the face of minute shadings of circumstance, handed down judgements that, from sitting to sitting, variously suggested compassion, inflexibility, sentimentality, wilfulness and near-absolute detachment. Selectively argued, a case might be made to support any prior assumption of the Tribunals' nature and motives. Consequently, existing critiques – particularly those addressing a particular aspect of the system – are often as prejudicial as the attitudes they allege.

A disinterested judgement remains elusive. The Tribunals' milieu was one in which historic class perceptions remained largely intact, despite the levelling experiences of conscription. Several of the more familiar tribunalists – the patrician Stopford-Sackville, the urbane Adkins and the rabble-rousing Gribble – conformed fully to expectations of type in their recorded pronouncements. However, as has been noted elsewhere, expectations alone may mislead. Equally, it may be recalled that Councillor Parker, an assiduous recruiter during the voluntary period (and a man who once told an applicant with varicose veins that he had seen 'horses race very well with legs like that'), nevertheless took up the cause of the last-remaining son with unaffected and abiding enthusiasm. Similarly (and against all practice, law and instructions), Sir Ryland Adkins, who had fulminated during dozens of conscientious objections, gently pushed his Tribunal to hear 17-year-old Claude Blencoe state an impromptu case on that ground when it became apparent that his mother's poorly framed hardship appeal – Claude was her sole support – was not admissible. Even Brixworth Tribunal were not beyond the exercise of compassion. Obliged in December 1917 to dismiss a builder's out-of-time application for his carpenter (a father of six children), they suggested, with the support of their equally unbending military representative, Adam Cross, that the applicant should (promptly) enter an appeal against their decision.[43]

The sum of these qualifications is that, with respect to a majority of cases, we are left with the imponderables. Mood, prejudice, external pressures and the unrecorded, unattested impression a man made in the very few minutes during which he stated his circumstances, variously (and sometimes collectively) determined the fate of his application. We may identify incontrovertibly partial, or sympathetic, judgements; we may isolate decisions that confound both logic and law. But far more prevalent are the ambiguities thrown up by often-hurried, amateur responses to the industrial-scale demands of the Tribunal system. An application that reinforced the impact of the personal in the face of those demands went some way to narrowing their influence.

To illustrate and conclude, we may contrast the cases of two local men of ostensibly similar circumstances: each with a large family, each seeking renewal of an existing certificate. On 1 December 1916, Arthur Fitzjohn, a Cooperative Society grocery manager, unsuccessful in his application to Peterborough Tribunal, appealed on the grounds of 'parental and domestic hardship':

> I am aware that I am a young man, but I would direct your attention to the fact that I have the responsibility of a young family of 6 children … whose ages range from 1 to 12 years. The fact that I have a family of 6 unequivocally demonstrates that I prove myself a more valuable asset to the State than any man who has less. And as the State directs close attention to the rearing of its future manhood it must be recognized that the welfare of 6 of tender age must be jeopardised when left to the sole control of a young wife. It is incontrovertible that the strain would be excessive to a degree inviting despair, with the reluctant risk of prospective good Citizens drifting into a state of uncontrollable persistence and all for the want of a father's guiding and chastening influence.

Having heard that Fitzjohn, if unsuccessful in his appeal, might be willing to 'try his hand' at Munitions, the Appeals Tribunal offered him a six weeks' certificate, final.

Six months later, at Finedon, a man seeking renewal of his certificate presented no other argument than to introduce the tribunalists to nine of his ten children. His exemption was extended unconditionally.[44]

Notes

1 LGB Circular R.36 (3 February 1916).
2 Above, p. 118.
3 Editorial, 27 October 1916.
4 TNA, CAB 24/GT1484.
5 Literature on the phenomenon is vast, but may be summarized succinctly by Second Lieutenant Patrick James Campbell, recalling his experience at Ypres: 'For the first time in my life, I, a boy from a public school, was doing manual work beside men who were manual workers. In a flash of revelation, caused perhaps by the flash of a bursting shell outside, I saw that instead of my being superior to them they were superior to me. But I saw something else, that it did

not matter which of us was better, what mattered was that we were working against a common enemy' (*In the Cannon's Mouth*, p. 41).

6 Above, p. 172

7 Above, p. 103.

8 *Mercury*, 7 April 1916.

9 Above, pp. 103–104.

10 *Mercury*, 19 May 1916, 4 May, 17 August 1917. The *Royal Edward* was torpedoed on 13 August 1915.

11 NRO X182/947; 14 April 1916.

12 NRO X182/809; *Mercury*, 4 August 1916.

13 *Mercury*, 15 October 1916. Townley's certificate must have been renewed subsequently (it was not reported), as he continued to serve on the Tribunal throughout the war.

14 *Mercury*, 18 May, 1917.

15 *Mercury*, 31 May, 23 July, 9 August 1918; *Herald*, 31 May 1918; *Independent*, 29 June 1918. Regarding Parker's ordeal at Peterborough, the *Independent* excoriated 'the flippant tone of those placed in brief authority'.

16 NRO X180/20; *Mercury*, 2, 26 June, 29 September, 3 November 1916, 26 January 1917; *Herald*, 29 June 1916, 26 January 1917.

17 *Independent*, editorial, 18 March 1916; see also above, pp. 38–39.

18 In passing, it should be noted that even the most deserving case of the 'sole remaining son' could be ruined by bad presentation. On 16 September 1916 at Middlesex Appeals Tribunal, Joseph Haynes pre-emptively spoiled a convincing argument (he was the sole support of a widowed mother subject to severe fits, with three brothers fighting in France) by stating on his form R.43: 'I also wish to appeal on the ground of being a criminal of an infamous character' (TNA MH 47/21 M1849). The appeal was dismissed.

19 Above, p. 21.

20 NRO X182/1052; *Mercury*, 8 September, 20 October, 3, 10 November 1916.

21 NRO X183/1228.

22 *Mercury*, 6, 28 July, 14 October 1917. The latter case was curiously similar to one heard by East Ham local Tribunal (reported in *The Times*, 10 March 1916). Here too, of an applicant's three elder serving brothers, two had been killed and a third wounded twice; a three-month exemption was offered to the applicant, with notice that they would consider his future applications favourably. On W.P. Cross, see below, p. 201.

23 As late as June 1918, the Central Appeals Tribunal considered and rejected a widow's appeal for a sole surviving son of military age (two brothers had been killed in action) on the basis that the fact of one or more bereavements was not in itself a ground for exemption (LGB Circular R.209: Summary of cases considered, 100 (13 June 1918)).

24 *Mercury*, 3 November 1916; *Herald*, 3 November 1916.

25 NRO X182/953, 954; *Mercury*, 12 May 1916.

26 NRO X182/894; *Mercury*, 25 August 1918.

27 NRO X181/753; *Mercury*, 21 July 1916.

28 This was the Appeals Tribunal's placatory offer to Mrs Verrachia for the loss of

her son (*Mercury*, 20 October 1916).

29 *Mercury*, 26 May, 14 July, 1 December 1916, 2 February 1917.

30 NRO X182/986, X183/1015; X184/1490; *Mercury*, 27 October, 3 November 1916. Contrast the Appeals Tribunal's policy with respect to the sole support of mothers with that of Warwick District Appeals Tribunal, who, though relatively unbending on other matters, appear to have had a habit of extending exemptions where such cases were appealed by the military (for example, WRO CR1520/59, 116 (Thomas Steggle), 131 (William Sharp) and 134 (Thomas Greenfield)).

31 NRO X180/326, X182/885; *Mercury*, 12 May 1916.

32 NRO X184/1667; X197: Appeals Tribunal meeting notes, 5 January 1917; X189/6552; *Mercury*, 12 January 1917, 10 August 1917; *Daventry Express*, 11 August 1917.

33 NRO X197: Appeals Tribunal meeting notes, 28 September 1917; X190/6785, 7433, 9757; see also below, p. 189–190.

34 NRO X186/3142; X197: Appeals Tribunal meeting notes, 19, 25 April 1917.

35 NRO X190/6890; X197: Appeals Tribunal meeting notes, as dated.

36 NRO X197: Appeals Tribunal meeting notes, 2 July 1918; *Mercury*, 12 May, 18 August 1916, 19 January, 22 June 1917.

37 On the Wolverton Works, see above, p. 88.

38 NRO X184/1555, 1966; X197, Appeals Tribunal meeting notes, 5, 19 February; *Mercury*, 28 July 1916, 9, 23 February 1917.

39 Above, p. 157.

40 Below, p. 208.

41 NRO X197/6977; *Mercury*, 31 August, 7, 21 September, 5, 12 October 1917.

42 Above, p. 139.

43 NRO X196/10879; *Independent*, 28 July 1917; *Mercury*, 20 September, 14 December 1917.

44 NRO X183/1344; *Independent*, 19 May 1917.

8

Fitness to serve

The fifth ground for exemption laid out in the Military Service Act, 1916, and its successors was the demonstrable ill-health or infirmity of the applicant. Though the median fitness of the British male had been an obsessive concern in some quarters since the South African War (during which large numbers of volunteers had been rejected as physically inadequate to the task of soldiering), the peacetime Army, a small, professional force, had been able to maintain its strength from an adequate reservoir of fit young men between the ages of 19 and 30. However, the massive wave of volunteers reporting to the recruiting offices during August and September 1914 overwhelmed existing medical examination facilities, and most were processed with no more than a cursory regard for their levels of fitness. Anticipating that the traditional age-limits on recruiting would be too narrow to satisfy the Armed Forces' demand for men, government raised the upper limit to 35, though so pronounced was the short-term flow of manpower into khaki that the Army soon had the luxury of being able also to raise the minimum height requirement from 5 ft 3 in to 5 ft 6 in (this was swiftly brought down once more to 5 ft 4 in as the flood of volunteers subsided during October 1914).[1] Thereafter, with the average monthly recruitment falling to a rate much below that which Kitchener envisaged as necessary for the raising of his New Armies, medical examinations of volunteers did not err on the side of doubt. If a man seemed upon superficial criteria to be fit he was assumed so, and was enlisted. The process was weighted towards failing the minimum number of men, with doctors attending the examinations being paid a shilling for every man they passed and nothing for those they rejected (an arrangement that *The Times* at least considered to be both reprehensible and counter-productive).[2] Nevertheless, the process remained relatively uncontroversial – by definition, a volunteer wanted to be in uniform – and mistakes or deliberate misdiagnoses made by the medical officers were exposed only at the front line.

The implementation of the Derby Scheme in the latter months of 1915, under which more than 1.1 million men attested their willingness to serve, imposed a massive new burden upon medical officers, and previously brief examinations became positively fleeting. Many men unsuitable for any sort of military life were waved through as fit for front line service, and returned, in due course, to add to the Tribunals' workloads. With the introduction of compulsion, it became apparent that a more methodological approach was necessary in order to allocate men, based upon their level of fitness, to where they might serve best. Accordingly, from January 1916 until late 1917, men who passed their medical examinations were placed into one of three categories: A, B or C, allocating them to active, support or sedentary service.[3]

Clearly, it was in the Army's interest to secure the greatest number of general service, or front-line, men, and as the county medical boards were chaired by Army doctors (though comprising also a minority of civilians), there was little chance that their work would do other than complement Army policy on recruitment. This was not necessarily apparent to the Tribunals in the shorter term. Pressure of work during the frantic early months of their sittings, and the tribunalists' relative unfamiliarity with the practices of the Medical Boards, almost certainly hindered a full appreciation of the incidence of poor or inadequate medical examinations. However, their attention was seized, after September 1916, by a drastic reduction in the number of men rejected by the Boards, a reflection of the Army's urgent need to replenish manpower losses in the aftermath of the Somme battles. Nationwide, a 'fail' rate of 30 per cent in the first two weeks of September fell to 6 per cent by November and just 3 per cent in the first quarter of 1917, while in the same period the proportion of passed men rated as fit at the highest level, A, doubled.[4]

By the beginning of 1917, the Tribunals had lost much faith in the competence and motives of the Medical Boards. In many cases, re-examinations were being ordered where there was any doubt as to an applicant's state of health, with little regard to the complaints of the military representatives (whose task, of course, was to minimize 'leakage' of men already in the recruiting system). This divergence accelerated following the implementation of the Military Service (Review of Exceptions) Act in May 1917, which resulted in thousands of palpably unfit men, previously exempted, being rated 'A' and rushed into uniform. The political furore that ensued brought pressure to reform the recruiting system in general, principally by removing it from the purview of the War Office. The recommendations of a Parliamentary Select Committee (the Shortt Committee) resulted in the creation, in November 1917, of civilian-staffed medical boards under the control of the new-constituted Ministry of National Service. Thereafter, the number of cases referred for re-examination dropped sharply, though some obvious misdiagnoses still occurred.

The profile of medically related cases coming before the Tribunals in Northamptonshire very much reflected these national trends. Additionally, though this was not a significantly urbanized county, the Tribunals were faced with certain local health issues. The workforce of its major manufacturing industry, the boot and shoe trade, was susceptible to phthisis, or pulmonary tuberculosis, owing to the prevalence of dust particles in the workplace and, apparently, male workers' pronounced habit of expectorating frequently. A notable black spot (or, perhaps, merely one for which accurate statistics were available) was Irthlingborough, which had an infection rate of 2.75 per 1000, compared to the national average of 1.25 (the town also had the dubious distinction of possessing the country's highest infant mortality rate: a massive 157.8 deaths per 1000 births, more than 50 per cent higher than the contemporary average).[5] Figures for the industry as a whole at this time are not extant, but Northampton's two NUSBO branches alone recorded 1394 members receiving sickness payments – for a range of ailments – during 1916.[6]

The county's large agricultural workforce, though ostensibly enjoying a healthier lifestyle than their urban compatriots, were endemically exposed to a high rate of occupational injury which often lessened their value as front-line troops. However, there were relatively few medically contentious cases heard by the Tribunals that concerned farmers, skilled agricultural employees or even farm labourers. The first two were protected under the certified occupations lists; of the latter, most of those rendered unfit by their work of necessity ceased to be employed on farms prior to the question of their fitness to serve being raised.

Finally, it should be noted that the Medical Board system prior to the reforms of late-1917 was very much devolved, making local variations in the quality of examinations an important factor in the Tribunals' work. In this respect, Northamptonshire was unfortunate in having had the services of Colonel Thomson, chief medical officer at Northampton Barracks, whose idiosyncratic medical judgements and acute distaste for the Tribunals' work would reflect the worst of military practice.

The advent of conscription brought hundreds of thousands of men into the recruitment net. Even so, the occasion appears to have tempted some recruiting officers to revisit previous failures, rather than concentrate upon their new bounty. In the Commons on 20 January 1916, Sir Ryland Adkins urged the Under Secretary for War to issue a circular to all Home Commands, reminding them that where men had taken and failed a medical examination under the Derby Scheme they could not now be enlisted against their will.[7] The message was not heard clearly; despite a lengthy clarification by Lord Newton on 24 February regarding the rights of rejected men, the practice continued. In March, *The Times* reported the observation of MP Donald Maclean, chairman of the City of London Appeals Tribunal, that many such attestees, resubmitting themselves for examination in ignorance of their rights, were being recategorized as fit for service.[8]

Notwithstanding such evidence of institutional malpractice, there were few cases brought before Northamptonshire's Tribunals during their early months that turned primarily upon an applicant's fitness. Mention was made occasionally that a previously rejected man had been accepted either as a 'Derby' volunteer or conscript, but such statements were almost always supplementary to the principal ground of application or appeal. A farm worker, applied for by his employer at Northampton Rural Tribunal in May, claimed to have been examined but rejected three times before being accepted under the Derby Scheme. Alfred Turner, a market gardener who, in the following August, appealed a short certificate on the grounds that he was in a certified occupation, claimed that, though unfit for service, he had been passed 'A' at Northampton Barracks recently, upon which occasion he had been told to 'keep his eyes open and his mouth shut'. Turner was the first man to be sent by the Appeals Tribunal for a second medical examination before his case was decided.[9]

One reason for the dearth of references to poor diagnoses during the early months of conscription was that, in many cases, an applicant's medical examination had not yet taken place when he appeared before the Tribunals. The shortage of military doctors on Home Service meant that the county's sole medical examination facility was seriously overstretched, and men receiving their call-up papers were usually given an attendance date falling later than their appointments with the Tribunals. It was claimed by one solicitor, furthermore, that requests that men applying to the Tribunals be given priority at the Medical Boards had not been well received. Indeed, after May 1916, the latter had good reason to afford conscripted men a relatively low priority. The Military Service (Session 2) Act, 1916, gave the Army Council the right to call for re-examination of any man rejected for service since the outbreak of war. Though instructions to recruiting officers emphasized that they should exercise this right with discretion, the Medical Boards had been given a strong incentive to 'queue-jump' second-chance cases in preference to those of already enlisted men trying to avoid service via the Tribunals.[10]

The situation in Northamptonshire contrasted with that of more highly urbanized districts, where relatively ample medical examination facilities highlighted the issue of misdiagnoses at an earlier stage. The City of London's Appeals Tribunal appear to have lost any trust in their Medical Board as early as April 1916, declaring it an 'economy in the public interest' that obviously unfit men be exempted whatever their medical certificates declared.[11] In a sense, therefore, the refusal of Northampton Barracks to expedite Tribunal examinations minimized interference in, and understanding of, their work for several months.

Consequently, the problem of tardy medical examinations was not resolved quickly. As late as 22 September 1916, the Appeals Tribunal were obliged to conclude that they must assume every man who appeared before them to be fit until a medical certificate from barracks told them otherwise – a decision that cost at least one man who claimed to be unfit (and had a civilian doctor's certificate to that effect) his appeal that day.[12] The situation was recognized to be unsustainable – in effect, it made redundant one of the principal grounds for exemption – yet the only measure available to the Tribunal in the short term was to ask the press to carry a reminder that all men attending should have a medical certificate prior to their cases being heard; in other words, to place responsibility firmly upon those called-up.

This paucity of medical facilities placed a further burden upon already overworked Tribunals, who, in turn, recognized the inconvenience to their applicants. Kettering Urban Tribunal calculated that the necessity of sending every man to Northampton for examination had cost the boot and shoe industry alone some two thousand man-hours of lost production in the final three months of 1916 (during which time Army orders were mounting quickly). Consequently, the Tribunal asked that medical officers might be sent to attend their sittings. This was refused curtly; few doctors were available, they were told, and Eastern Command had turned down similar requests from towns larger than their own. The War Office was similarly unhelpful when Kettering Urban Tribunal's clerk made a visit to Whitehall to press the request. Reporting this, the *Mercury* also suggested what must have been becoming clear already to the Tribunals: that 'the authorities fought shy of civilian doctors'.[13]

In doing so, the Medical Boards appear to have been defying the Army Council itself, which had recommended the use of civilians where necessary.[14] However, one of their stated objections to doing so (other than the anticipation that civilians would fail to match the enthusiasm of their military counterparts in meeting recruitment targets), was that men who personally knew their patients might be reluctant, where there was any doubt, to pass a man fit for service. Sir Ryland Adkins declared publicly that he considered this to be little more than an evasion, as doctors could be assigned readily to districts other than their own to certify men. The Medical Boards, in his – almost certainly astute – opinion, were not interested in finding solutions.[15]

Despite official obfuscations, Tribunals in Northamptonshire were beginning to take note of their Medical Board's idiosyncratic methods. On 1 December, a miller's packer, twice rejected for service but now passed B2, came before Northampton Rural. He alleged that, during his latest visit to Barracks, Colonel Thomson had told his subordinates: 'It's no use throwing a man like him out altogether: look at his muscles.' The Tribunal postponed the case, pending a further examination by the Central Medical Board (appointed in the previous September to adjudicate cases where the results of Army Board examinations contradicted those of civilian doctors).[16] During the next case they heard, the employer of a farm bailiff who had attended barracks on the same day as the previous applicant expressed surprise that his man had been passed A, as he had been so poorly the previous summer that his doctor had warned him not to ride his bicycle. At the Appeals Tribunal a month later, it was revealed that John Barratt (appealing on personal grounds) had been passed B1 by Thomson even though he suffered from epileptic fits. Pointedly, the Tribunal gave Barratt three months' (open) exemption without requiring a re-examination.[17]

In fairness to the Medical Boards, the inherent suspicion of 'shirkers' that shaped their attitudes had some foundation, and men appealing for re-examination were not always the innocent victims of misdiagnoses they claimed to be. In October 1916, the Army Council fulminated against the alleged 'now too-prevalent practice of men who have been examined by one medical board going on to another and being re-examined without revealing the fact of the previous classification'.[18] Clearly, given that they had a single recourse to (military) medical examination in their county, Northamptonshire men were not among the guilty parties, but the practice, if evident elsewhere, could only have fuelled the uncertainties and mistrust that poisoned the relationship between the Tribunals and Northampton Barracks.

Nevertheless, copious evidence of the latter's cavalier treatment of examinees continued to arrive before the Tribunals. During the winter of 1916–1917, medical examinations at Barracks became even more superficial (in line with the countrywide trend), and several men who were palpably unfit for any form of service were declared to be front-line material. In February 1917, Hardingstone Tribunal heard the application of a motor mechanic who had attested but been rejected for service in London in September 1915, yet who, subsequently, had enlisted successfully. Soon after, he was discharged unfit, though he had attempted to remain in uniform on lighter duties. Briefly, he had worked in munitions (until replaced by female labour) and had applied to an aeroplane factory, where the circumstances of his discharge had been considered 'ambiguous'. This brought him to the attention of the recruiting officer once more: a visit to barracks determined him to be Category A, though his solicitor showed the Tribunal two certificates from doctors declaring him to have a hernia. Once more, the applicant was referred to the Central Medical Board.[19]

By this time, when presented with discrepancies between civilian and military diagnoses, most Tribunals in Northamptonshire placed their trust in the former. In January 1917, Northampton Borough's Councillor Parker, commenting upon a case in which a man with acute deafness had been sent back to barracks for a further examination (only to be told there that the Army did not re-open cases), stated frankly that he preferred to take the expert opinion of a doctor who had known the applicant all his life. At Brixworth, two months later, an insurance office clerk who had been rejected under the Derby Scheme, passed Category A by Colonel Thomson and then referred to the Central Medical Board, was recategorized 'C' by the latter. Pointedly, the Tribunal gave him six months' exemption (open), an unusually generous certificate by their standards. In the same week, the Appeals Tribunal heard the case of Bernard Bonham, a boot operative who had attested and been declared sedentary at his Derby Scheme medical examination. Though having a badly diseased lung (phthisis), Bonham was called up and declared fit for general service. The Tribunal, preferring the weightier testimony of his civilian doctor, handed the case to the District Tuberculosis Officer.[20]

Upon occasion, the personal associations of individual tribunalists, particularly in the rural districts, exposed the Army Medical Board's misdiagnoses without need of a civilian doctor's testimony. On 26 March 1917, Oundle Tribunal (not a notably lenient body) rejected outright the Category A classification given to a 37-year-old plumber when several tribunalists protested that the man had been treated for pleurisy, and recently had been at 'death's door'. Their chairman, J. Rippiner, gave him two months' exemption 'as a protest at the way the Army Medical Board treated such cases'. Similarly, Hardingstone reacted strongly to the case of a chauffeur/electrician who had been rejected four times and now passed 'A' at barracks. His employer claimed that, years earlier, the man had been kicked by a horse and had since been unable to walk more than a short distance. One of the tribunalists, T.J. Hakes, who knew the man personally, considered that he was no more fit for the Army than a 70-year-old.[21]

The final collapse of confidence in Northamptonshire's Army Medical Board followed the introduction of the Military Service (Review of Exceptions) Act 1917, coming into force in April of that year. The legislation dragged a host of previously exempted men back to Northampton Barracks for re-examination. Colonel Thomson and his staff, already indifferent both to local opinion and to the Tribunals' responsibilities to the letter of legislation, processed their latest charges on the basis that any man in possession of a civilian medical certificate was, by definition, a shirker. The Tribunals responded robustly. On 7 June, Potterspury Tribunal offered five months' exemption to an 18-year-old Hartwell ploughman, passed B1 at barracks, who proved his unfitness for service by the simple expedient of removing and holding up his glass eye. At Northampton Borough in the same week, the Tribunal heard several new applications from men previously exempted on medical grounds but now supposedly fit for active service, during which further evidence of Thomson's methods emerged. A 25-year-old train driver, hospitalized for several weeks and incapable of working, was passed 'A'. He had shown his medical certificate to Thomson, who had exploded: 'Certificate be hanged; do you think I am blind? Are you a Tribunal case? You are A1, and you can put some grease on your boots.' A clicker, likewise passed fit for general service upon re-examination, presented a doctor's certificate stating that he was unfit for any military service. 'This is another one', a sergeant dourly told Thomson, who again dismissed the man without even the most cursory examination: 'You go to the Tribunal with these tales, but we don't want them; we know what's the matter with you. You can go in A1, and you can tell the Tribunal what you like.' Several other civilian doctors' certificates were defaced by Thomson: one had 'incorrect' written over the original diagnosis, while another was partially obscured by a scrawled 'exaggerated statement'.

Several applicants at Northampton Borough during the same sitting were represented by H.W. Williams, who complained that, if half his clients were telling the truth, the system was a farce. Men had been 'treated like dogs', the Tribunals had been insulted and medical certificates scoffed at. He was aware that he was speaking strongly, but wanted to be heard 'under oath'. James Gribble, who, until that moment, had listened with uncharacteristic reserve, observed that several boot and shoe operatives examined at barracks and subsequently called up had suffered from consumption; one, who had been discharged subsequently as unfit, had died in hospital: 'If half I hear is true', he concluded, 'Colonel Thomson ought to be sent to Germany.' The *Mercury*, reporting proceedings, noted that the statement was 'vigorously applauded' by the applicants. Every case heard that day as a result of medical re-examination was adjourned, and the Tribunal decided that all future such cases would be heard with both a representative of the Army Medical Board and a local practitioner present, handing to Colonel Thomson a *fait accompli* he could hardly ignore if all his medical judgements were not to be overturned.[22]

Encouraged by Northampton Borough's example, or similarly exasperated by the decisions emerging from barracks, the Appeals Tribunal drew its own line in the sand later that month on a point of arrogant incompetence. Edward Manning, a married, 34-year-old epileptic, had been passed 'A' upon re-examination. Williams, his solicitor, alleged that a civilian doctor's certificate had not been presented during the process. Captain Cook claimed that this was not possible, as he, personally, had sent the certificate to barracks, pinned to Manning's medical history sheet. Adkins suggested that someone from the Medical Board should attend to explain where it was. Cook replied that he did not think anyone from barracks would come to the Tribunal to discuss medical matters. 'That is the model of official evasion', fumed Adkins, and adjourned the case. A week later, Cook admitted that the certificate had been 'possibly mislaid'; in any case, Colonel Thomson had told him that epilepsy was difficult to diagnose, and that Manning's tongue had shown no signs of being bitten. Effectively ignoring this testimony (and the Army Medical Board itself), the Tribunal instructed the appellant to obtain and present to them a new civilian doctor's certificate. Returning to the Tribunal with this on 20 July, he was given an open exemption to Christmas.[23]

Even notably conservative Tribunals showed themselves willing to make gestures that pushed the limits of their authority when confronted by medical misdiagnoses. On 26 July, one of Wellingborough Rural's tribunalists, J.C. Turner, drew the attention of his colleagues to the case of an applicant whose employer had withdrawn an appeal made on his behalf. The man, rated B2, had been examined by three civilian doctors, all of whom had declared him unfit for any form of service. Turner asked his fellow tribunalists whether they might offer to consider a further application from the man on personal grounds. His chairman, W.S. Gibbard, said that he strongly objected to unfit men being taken, and agreed that the case should be heard. When the Tribunal's secretary, Hugh Jackson, pointed out – correctly – that the Tribunal had no power to do this, Gibbard declared 'That is your red tape. I think we should defy it.' To further goad Colonel Thomson, they decided to return the man's medical certificate to barracks and inform the Medical Board of their decision.[24]

The chasm of mistrust between Army Medical Board and Tribunal was reflected throughout England and Wales. Commencing in July, the public hearings of the Shortt Committee exposed a vast catalogue of administrative and technical incompetence within the existing medical examination system.[25] The results were as much to the disadvantage of the Army as to those processed by the system. Giving evidence to the Committee, Surgeon General Bedford, Deputy Director of Medical Services, offered a lurid glimpse of the consequences of cursory medical practices:

> I have been inspecting many recruits who have recently joined Labour Units in the Command, and am shocked to see the specimens of humanity which have been accepted as of potential value to the Army; men almost totally blind; deformed dwarfs of the poorest intellect; men with extreme Oedema of both legs almost unable to stand; cases of very severe and marked Rheumatism; cases of marked Paresis which rendered locomotion almost grotesque; several cases of insanity, which told their own tale at a glance.[26]

The Committee's preliminary recommendation, made on 19 July (while it was taking evidence still), was unequivocal:

> That the chairman be authorized to inform the Prime Minister that the Committee are of opinion, in view of the evidence already taken, that a change of system should be made at once, and recommend that the whole organisation of Recruiting Medical Boards and of the medical examinations and re-examinations should be transferred from the War Office to the Local Government Boards.
>
> That the Committee are of opinion that in order to restore public confidence this change should be made at the earliest possible moment, and be not delayed until the committee present their full report with their terms of reference.[27]

Lord Derby himself, sensitive to GHQ's complaints regarding the quality of supposedly fit men they were receiving, fully supported the recommendations, and urged, furthermore, that the entire recruitment process be placed into civilian hands. He declared himself to be 'badly let down' by the Medical Boards, who, he alleged, had gone much further than the Act intended. His intervention was of great consequence in the debate that resulted in the creation of the Ministry of National Service in the following November.[28]

However, the process of reform was far more protracted than the Shortt Committee had anticipated. The new civilian Medical Boards did not commence work until mid-November, and, in the meantime, Colonel Thomson's work at Northampton continued.[29] His antipathy to the county's Tribunals was such by now that he and his colleagues attempted, if clumsily, to ignore legislation and bypass entirely what they considered to be a malignantly obstructionist element of the recruitment process. Even as the Shortt Committee was hearing damning evidence of the Medical Boards' malpractices, one of Northampton Borough's tribunalists, T.S. Hornsey, reported to his colleagues that several men holding certificates from the Tribunal had been ordered to report to barracks thereafter for examination, which was clearly contrary to the Act. Councillor Parker asked reporters present at the sitting to ensure that their newspapers carried notices to the effect that all such orders should be ignored.[30]

On the Tribunals' part, awareness that the medical examination system was about to be overhauled inclined them to ignore Thomson and his staff, and to adjourn or refer cases where there was some dispute as to an applicant's health. By September, Rushden seem to have washed their hands entirely of the medical issue, referring to the Central Medical Board all cases in which an applicant produced a contradictory (that is, a civilian) doctor's certificate. This appears to have been a common strategy in other regions, which suggests that Thomson's regime was by no means exceptional. When, in the following month, Sir Ryland Adkins asked his Tribunal's military representative whether they might refer the case of a Wellingborough clicker, Frederick Johnson, to the Central Board, Cook replied that the latter's workload of similar referrals was such that they were not taking on any new cases at present. Johnson's appeal was simply adjourned until such time as the new civilian Medical Board was established.[31]

The final medical case of note to be considered under the old regime in Northamptonshire offered ample testimony as to why it departed unmourned. Crick Tribunal, ignoring Thomson's 'A' grading of a baker with a weak heart, postponed a decision upon the case pending the applicant's re-examination by one of the new civilian Medical Boards, when constituted. Their military representative appealed this, and the Appeals Tribunal referred the man's case directly to Central, who rejected him outright. Northampton Barracks' response to public criticism of their conduct in this case was to deny that Colonel Thomson had illegally adjusted the man's civilian medical certificate (as the latter had claimed at his original hearing), and to complain that the local Tribunal might have considered the matter more carefully before allowing it to come to the attention of the newspapers. Crick Tribunal's chairman, the Reverend Mitchison, took a different view: 'he thought they might congratulate themselves on what they had done'.[32]

By mid-November, the new civilian Medical Boards had started their examinations. Administratively, the country was divided into eight regions; these, in turn, were sub-divided into areas, each having a Medical Board staffed entirely by a rota of part-time civilian doctors (paid five guineas per attendance or session, plus expenses). A new recruit was examined in turn by four physicians, who measured physical proportions, identified any deformities, tested vision, hearing and reflexes, examined chest and abdomen, enquired of any previous medical conditions and formed a (necessarily provisional) judgement of mental health. Following this, their conclusions were discussed with the President of the Board and a collective decision made regarding the examinee's status under the new medical grading system (I–IV, the latter a 'rejected' classification). To prevent fatigue-related misdiagnoses, a limit of 60 such examinations per session was established, though in times of high recruitment (for example, during the implementation of 'clean-cut' provisions in 1918), this figure was, inevitably, exceeded.[33]

Was the new system significantly more effective than the old? Certainly, the notable reduction of public disagreements between Northamptonshire's Tribunals and the new Boards suggests that the civilian bodies represented a marked improvement upon Colonel Thomson's regime.

Statistics correlated soon after the war ended indicate that the percentage of men examined by the new Boards and determined to fall within Grade I was just 31.8 per cent in the region covered by Eastern Command (36 per cent for England and Wales as a whole), a striking reduction to the rate of Category 'A' assessments made by the Army Medical Boards immediately prior to November 1917. For Northamptonshire in particular, the new regulations carried one welcome directive: no man diagnosed with any form of tuberculosis could be considered as fit for military service and should be designated as Grade IV.[34]

However, the system remained undermanned, with only 2500 doctors in England and Wales participating in the system. As late as mid-December, the House of Commons Appeals Tribunal noted that cases they had sent for medical re-examination at the start of November had yet to be processed, due to 'a great deal of congestion'.[35] It was inevitable, therefore, that misdiagnoses were not eradicated from the process. The new (civilian) Medical Appeals Panels considered 33,000 re-examination cases during the final year of the war. This represented a tiny percentage of the (2.5 million) medical examinations carried out under the new regime, but, as each of them required permission from an Appeals Tribunal to proceed, it is clear that there were seen to be problems still.[36] Despite the provision for far more comprehensive examinations than previously, it was stated in the Commons in June 1918 that examinees were complaining of their hurried and cursory nature, the lack of opportunity to discuss ailments, the lack of tests to determine physical fitness and the continuing dismissal of family doctors' certificates.[37] Birmingham Appeals Tribunal referred to their Appeals Panel at least 51 cases for medical re-examination after November 1917, while at least one other County Tribunal – Middlesex – held almost as poor a view of the reconstituted civilian facilities as they had of their military predecessors (and Middlesex had led the field in criticism of Mill Hill Barracks' medical staff, perhaps the exemplar of the pre-Shortt Boards).[38] During 1918, they referred some 1565 men for re-examination: at a single sitting on 25 July, they gave leave to 147 men to challenge their diagnoses.[39]

In Northamptonshire also, there was evidence of continuing problems. During December 1917, the Ministry of National Service exhibited symptoms of old thinking when instructing its representatives to make all efforts at Tribunal hearings to get Grade III men into the Army without making any specific commitments regarding work to which they would be assigned thereafter. As late as June 1918, Stopford-Sackville noted that his own Tribunal had received 'a large number' of requests for re-examination. Many of these may have been last-gasp efforts by healthy men to avoid enlistment; however, it should be noted that, in the same period, a rumour circulated in the boot and shoe trade that many older workers, trained to replace those who had been taken by the Army but now within the 'new military age', were being medically upgraded (in many cases to Grade I) by the re-formed Boards and sent to the Colours.[40] At Hardingstone in July, the Grade I rating of a 36-year-old edge-setter who had undergone two major operations only weeks earlier drew from the Tribunal the observation that 'there were either some very clever men at the barracks or some fools at the Hospital'. The *Independent*, which had only cursorily criticized the older system, carried three editorials during 1918 lamenting the apparently large number of regradings that took place following appeals to the Tribunals.[41]

Against such evidence of continuing malpractice, there are equally strong indications of systemic improvements. Instructions sent to the Medical Boards regarding examinations of older men following the implementation of the Military Service (No. 2) Act, 1918, emphasised how far theories on the treatment of recruits had progressed since Thomson's day. The Boards were urged to examine men over 41 years old separately from younger recruits, to ensure strict privacy for individuals, with separate cubicles in which they could dress and adequately heated facilities. Examinations were to be made with due regard to the age of the attendee, and any medical certificates presented were to be considered carefully in arriving at a grading.[42] Notwithstanding the general discontent of Tribunals and public alike regarding the enlistment of older men, the new intake appear to have been examined and graded with sufficient sensitivity and accuracy to avert criticism, though, clearly, this was due in part to National Service Instructions directing that older men should be categorized as non-combatants whatever their physical condition.[43]

Despite the problems that continued to mark the process, the issue of medical misdiagnosis of recruits was much less rehearsed at Northamptonshire Tribunals' proceedings during the final year of the war than previously. Whether this in itself was evidence of better practices is not clear; it may be that, having made a firm stand upon principle, tribunalists allowed themselves to be satisfied that the switch to a civilian-staffed arrangement had effectively closed the matter (unlike their colleagues on the Metropolitan Tribunals, who continued actively to advertise the system's many failings).[44] However, the above observations aside, the only notable instance of overt disagreement between Medical Board and Tribunal regarding a man's medical condition arose during a sitting of Northampton Rural on 26 June 1918, when a 30-year-old farmer produced medical certificates to show that he suffered from pleurisy and heart trouble, claiming that these had been ignored during his recent examination. The case was adjourned pending the result of his approach to the appeals panel.[45]

The standard set by the Medical Boards was so low that men once recognized as altogether useless in any military capacity were frequently passed as fit for the actual fighting line ... looking back upon this disagreeable business I am satisfied that the public were under obligation to the Tribunals for the stand they made in defence of the poor remnants of personal liberty left to the men of military age.[46]

The work of the Army Medical Boards between January 1916 and November 1917 has received little favourable assessment. Excoriated by the public, the Tribunals, and, eventually, by government and the Army itself, the Boards were tasked with the contradictory responsibilities of ensuring that the BEF had the right men for the job and of failing as few recruits as possible. Overworked and understaffed, their organization entirely inadequate to the industrial-scale supplying of men to the Armed Forces, it is apparent that the median quality of their work, never very high, fell significantly during periods of accelerated recruitment.

Upon occasion, however, they exhibited a quality of arrogant self-confidence that cannot be explained solely by reference to the difficult conditions they faced. Believing that Army life was just what 'shirkers' needed, they often treated civilian diagnoses of serious illnesses as frivolous, wrong or at best over-stated, and ignored them accordingly. In this, they were strongly supported by the War Office, notwithstanding the frustrations of front-line commanders obliged to accept the consequences of the policy. Army Council Instructions regarding the Military Service (Review of Exceptions) Act 1917 decried the 'not infrequent practice to manufacture evidence that men are affected by certain diseases, when, in fact, they are not', and listed symptoms of pulmonary tuberculosis, disorders of the heart, epilepsy and diabetes, when presented to the Medical Boards, as 'counterfeit' diseases.[47] The Surgeon-General of Eastern Command, Major General F.J. Jencken, who had ultimate authority for medical examinations of recruits in Northamptonshire, expressed before the Shortt Committee his personal belief that tuberculosis – the county's most prevalent industrial disease – could be ameliorated and even cured by military training and discipline.[48]

Dissenting voices to such palpably misguided beliefs were regarded with hostility and disdain. The many reported utterances of Jencken's subordinate, Colonel Thomson, indicate that he regarded civilian doctors, recruits and Tribunals as co-conspirators in a plot to confound the needs of the Army and nation. Upon occasion, his Board's misdiagnoses had a quality of wilful disregard that hinted not so much at error under pressure as outright defiance of what he believed to be the usurping authority of the Tribunal system. Consequently, the necessary link of trust between Northampton Barracks and the Tribunals deteriorated rapidly and irreparably, to the point at which bodies that, habitually, were content not to exercise leniency in other cases found themselves giving the benefit of the doubt on medical grounds.

A medical examination was intended to be an administrative detail in the process of transferring suitable men from civilian life into the Colours. Yet the paucity of facilities in Northamptonshire, Northampton Barracks' firm belief in the infallibility of their Medical Board and the Tribunals' growing unwillingness to dismiss evidence that contradicted military diagnoses slowed, rather than facilitated, that process. The hiatus between the report of the Shortt Committee and the implementation of its recommendations further stalled much-needed reforms. Thereafter, the county's civilian Medical Board performed at least sufficiently well (despite sporadic complaints regarding their diagnoses) to avoid the volume of adverse publicity that had illuminated the malpractices of their predecessors at Northampton Barracks.

From one perspective, the issue of medical examination was an aside to the far more substantial issues that faced the Tribunals. In Northamptonshire, dilution within the boot and shoe trade and cyclical demands upon the agricultural industry represented far greater tests of the tribunalists' resolve and judgement than a problem that, by definition, affected men on an individual basis. Nevertheless, the developing relationship between the Tribunals and Army Medical Boards affords more than a series of salutary anecdotes regarding military incompetence and arrogance. In effect, the Tribunals became the public voice that ensured that private injustices should not disappear within the vast anonymity of the recruitment process. Their robust defiance of local Medical Boards, even at the height of recruitment initiatives, offers the clearest refutation of the charge, laid by pacifist organizations during and after the war, that the War Office and Tribunal were twin pillars of the same militaristic edifice.

Notes

1 Winter, *The Great War and the British People*, p. 50; 'Military Fitness and Civilian Health', p. 215; Beckett and Simpson, *A Nation in Arms*, pp. 8–9. The decision to raise the minimum height (and chest) requirement had been Kitchener's; according to Leo Amery, it 'killed recruiting entirely' (Barnes and Nicholson, *Leo Amery Diaries*, 12 September 1914).

2 Editorial, 24 February 1916.

3 See the note on p. vii for a more detailed explanation of medical categories.

4 Parliamentary Papers (PP) 1917–1918, III, 327, q. 4383 (Shortt Committee Report), appendix 1.

5 NUBSO Branch Reports, July 1916, pp. 468–469.

6 Ibid., pp. 71–83.

7 5 H.C. 78:734.

8 5 H.L. 21:200–201; *The Times*, 16 March 1916.

9 NRO X184/762; *Mercury*, 19 May, 4 August 1916.

10 Military Service (Session 2) Act, 1916, 3 (2); ACI 1071/1916.

11 *The Times*, 12 April 1916. In the same month, Accrington Tribunal's chairman, Mayor Barlow, reflecting upon their local Medical Board's obstructionism, observed grimly 'I should like to have a quarter of an hour at them' (*Accrington Observer and Times*, 29 April 1916).

12 NRO X183/245; *Mercury*, 29 September, 1916. The unfortunate appellant was James Lincoln, a poultry worker.

13 *Mercury*, 22 September 1916. Problems created by the lack of adequate medical facilities were not confined to Northamptonshire. In south Buckinghamshire during July 1916, attested men wishing to be medically examined in advance of their groups being called up were being directed to Cowley Barracks, Oxford (CBS DA/10/38/1; Eton Rural Tribunal minute book, pp. 41–42). Note also Lord Salisbury's comments in the Lords (18 May 1916) regarding the urgent need for more examination stations (5 H.L. 21:1080).

14 ACI 1017/1916 (17 May 1916): 'In order to avoid unnecessary expense in travelling, the services of a local medical practitioner should as far as possible be employed where a men resides at such a distance from HQ of the recruiting area in which he lives as to make such a course economical.'

15 *Mercury*, 29 September 1916. Note also Adkins's subsequent comments in the Commons (20 March 1917): 'The tribunal of which I am a member found the greatest difficulty in dealing with the very large number of men who had not been medically examined or re-examined under the existing law ... When we came to inquire how it was that case after case that came before us had to be adjourned, sometimes indefinitely, for want of medical examination, we found that it was because there really was not a large enough staff of military medical authorities to deal with the cases promptly' (5 H.C. 92:659–660).

16 TNA WO 27/5702/A.G.28 (15 September 1916).

17 NRO X184/1746; X197: Appeals Tribunal meeting notes, 13 January, 1917; *Mercury*, 1 December 1916, 19 January, 1917.

18 ACI 1819/1916 (20 October 1916).

19 *Herald*, 23 February 1917.

20 NRO X185/2500; *Mercury*, 12 January, 16 March 1917.

21 *Mercury*, 23, 30 March 1917; *Herald*, 30 March 1917.

22 *Mercury*, 8 June 1917.

23 NRO X197: Appeals Tribunal meeting notes, 22 June 1917, 3, 20 July; X187/3620.

24 *Mercury*, 27 July 1917. Note also Adkins's comment in the Commons (21 June 1917): 'I say there can be no doubt whatever that the carrying out of [medical re-examinations] is in most, if not all, its particulars, most unsatisfactory' (5 H.C. 94:2043), and, at the same sitting, that of Sir Godfrey Baring, chairman of Hampshire Appeals Tribunal (5 H.C. 94:2008): 'It is astonishing that our Appeal[s] Tribunal has long since lost any faith, not only in the competence, but in the good faith, of some of these medical boards.'

25 Winter, *The Great War and the British People*, pp. 51–53; 'Military Fitness and Civilian Health', p. 218; Grieves, *Politics of Manpower*, pp. 131–132.

26 Shortt Committee, minutes of evidence, 22 July 1917.

27 Shortt Committee, Draft Special Report, p. 7.

28 Winter, *The Great War and the British People*, p. 53; Churchill, *Lord Derby*, p. 222.

29 LGB instructions regarding the revised medical gradings and rights of appeal against the new Medical Boards' decisions (R.157 and R.155 respectively) were issued on 3 November 1917.

30 *Herald*, 20 July 1917.

31 *Mercury*, 21 September, 19 October 1917; NROX192/8994. Middlesex Appeals Tribunal adopted a slightly more creative interim policy: from June 1917, they accepted provisionally the evidence of civilian doctors' certificates but required their appellants to find work in local munitions factories or aeroplane workshops (cf. TNA MH 47/56/M3700, M3801, M3952, M3979, M3988, M3991).

32 *Mercury*, 2 November 1917.

33 Winter, *The Great War and the British People*, pp. 54–55; 'Military Fitness and Civilian Health', pp. 219–222.

34 Winter, *The Great War and the British People*, p. 57; NSI 3/1917 (2 November 1917).

35 *The Times*, 11 December 1917.

36 NATS/1/12/M/36.

37 5 H.C. 106:2337–2338 (13 June 1918).

38 WRO CR1520/2. In his memorandum summarizing the work of Middlesex Appeals Tribunal (21 November 1918), their chairman, William Regester, wrote: 'The question of the old Medical Boards is now a matter of history ... Unfortunately, it has been proved by facts that the examinations carried out by the new Medical Boards have been far from satisfactory' (TNA MH47/5: Tribunal Minute Book 7). One of his colleagues on the Tribunal, Sir Herbert Nield, MP, had long expressed a very personal animosity against Mill Hill Barracks (and, in the Commons, against the examination system generally); his own son, who suffered from weak eyes, had been passed B1 by them and sent to Egypt, where the sun tormented him constantly (*Daily News*, 31 August 1916). Both *The Times* and the *Daily Telegraph* ran occasional columns headed 'Stories from Mill Hill' in which the lamentable quality of medical examinations were highlighted.

39 TNA MH 47/113: register of cases; MH 47/5, Minute Book 7, as dated. The Tribunal's medical histories file (TNA MH 47/117, unfoliated) offers ample evidence of continuing problems. For example (one of many), R.F. Greenshields, 44, was passed Grade I at Conduit Street Medical Board on 21 May 1918; re-examined on 24 June, he was diagnosed as having fistula, haemorrhoids, varicose veins, oedema of legs and feet, and severely restricted vision.

40 Winter, 'Military Fitness and Civilian Health', p. 220; NRO X197: Appeals Tribunal meeting notes, 25 June 1918; NATS 36/1917 (21 December 1917). The accusation regarding re-grading of boot and shoe operatives was made during the anti-'industrial conscription' meeting of 25 June 1918 at Trade Hall, Northampton (above, p. 85).

41 *Mercury*, 5 July 1918; *Independent*, 30 June, 6 July, 5 October 1918.

42 NATS 88/1918 (29 April 1918).

43 NATS 218/1918 (11 July 1918). Category equivalents for men over 41 were: Grade
I = BI; II = BII; III = BIII. Men graded BI were not to be considered fit for front-
line service. See also Sir Auckland Geddes's explanation of older men's gradings
to the Commons: 5 H.C. 108:17 (8 July 1918).

44 For example, the contributions of Sir Donald Maclean and Sir Herbert Neild in
the Commons debate on the issue, 27 June 1918 (5 H.C. 107/1283–1284, 1306).

45 *Mercury*, 28 June 1918.

46 Cartmell, *For Remembrance*, pp. 83–84.

47 ACI 1196/1917 (5 July 1917).

48 Winter, 'Medical Fitness and Civilian Health', p. 218.

9

The Tribunals and the
Volunteer Training Corps

Born in the early days of the war from the widespread urge to 'do something' to protect the homeland from a German invasion, the Volunteer Training Corps, or VTC, had a protracted gestation. The early proliferation of small, independently organized groups, the heterogeneity of opinion regarding their role, the enduring conviction of the War Office that they represented both a diversion of men from fighting units and an expensive frivolity ensured that 'something' long remained an undetermined quality. A degree of early consolidation and rationalization took place under the leadership of Lord Desborough of Taplow, who became President of the Central Association of Volunteer Training Corps (CAVTC) in September 1914.[1] However, it remained an organization of sovereign entities (and not all VTCs were affiliated), holding widely differing ideas on how they should prepare for a German invasion and in what attire. The CAVTC, rather than become a fulcrum for the whole, acted principally as an advisory clearing-house for the multitude of queries and suggestions that poured in from local corps, and as a (largely unsuccessful) lobbying body dedicated to extracting from government a commitment to define the role of the VTC.

As with the Local Defence Volunteers of the Second World War, the VTCs did not enjoy a high reputation within their communities. 'Bank Holiday Stalwarts' (one of the kinder epithets) made easy targets for those who watched them drilling without arms, uniforms or discernible purpose.[2] Later, at the Tribunals, many complaints were made of men who had escaped service in the VTC mocking the martial skills of those who had not. This was a rare issue upon which the preconceptions of the War Office and public were quite closely aligned. Throughout the period of voluntary enlistment, it was the received wisdom in government that men of military age who participated in the VTC were at best misguided and at worst shirkers whose removal to the Colours was, or should be, a priority. This was to entirely dismiss the original spirit of the VTC, participation in which had been an expression of individuality, not an obedient nod to official policy on what constituted a 'volunteer'. Mistrust of motive and lack of faith in the Corps' potential remained strong both at Whitehall and Home Command; nevertheless, there was a slow move during 1915 towards instituting a semi-official identity for the VTC, as Lords Lieutenant attempted (with varying degrees of success) to bring local groups within county regimental structures.

Ironically, the advent of conscription brought a rationale for the corps beyond that of being a last, forlorn hope against a German invasion. Men who were exempted only temporarily from enlistment would be expected, at some point, to join the Army and commence military training. If some part of that training might be anticipated during the exemption period, the time and resources required to get a civilian to where he might best assist the war effort would be usefully reduced. Properly founded and organized, the volunteer corps would provide a necessary structure without (it was hoped) placing too many demands upon conventional resources. Accordingly, in February 1916, it was announced that the VTC would henceforth fall within the ambit of the 1863 Volunteer Act, and be organized on a formal, territorial basis under the direct control of the War Office and Home Command. The Volunteer Act of December 1916 authorized the outfitting of the VTC in khaki, one-off grants to participants, a standardized training programme and a requirement that all volunteers attend a minimum number of drills each year.[3]

In the half-year from January 1917, separate sections of the VTC were created, to which various categories of volunteers would be allocated. Section A was established for men over military age, of Category C1 fitness or better, who, in times of national emergency, would leave their civilian occupations and serve full-time in uniform. Section B was reserved to men of military age, exempted by the Tribunals, who, similarly, would leave their employments in an emergency. Section C was for youths over 17 years of age but not yet liable for military service. Section P would contain men who were also Special Constables, while Section R was reserved to volunteers from government departments. Finally, Section D was established in May 1917 for men who were unsuited (and often unwilling to commit themselves) to any other section.[4]

Sections A and B were intended to be qualitatively distinct from the others. Men joining them were required to serve for the duration of the war, to undertake 14 drills per month until 'efficient' (that is, in general drilling and marching, musketry and bayonet fighting), and ten per month thereafter. Those in other sections were required to drill only ten times per year, and might resign from the VTC subject to 14 days' notice. There was no obligation for men in Section D to become 'efficient'.[5]

Though the VTC remained, as the name suggested, a collection of regional volunteer forces, government determined that, if it should continue to exist in an age of conscription, voluntarism alone could not be relied upon to keep it up to complement. Accordingly, the Tribunals were advised that they could, at their discretion, attach a 'requirement' that a man being offered an exemption certificate should join the VTC, though the requirement in itself should not constitute the condition of the exemption. Many Tribunals followed this recommendation from an early stage in their proceedings, though the Northamptonshire bodies were noticeably tardier. It has been suggested that an important factor in the spread of the practice was awareness of neighbouring Tribunals doing the same.[6] If this was the case, perhaps Northamptonshire's tribunalists were not well connected to the grapevine, though there are other potential reasons for their hesitation. Firstly, despite the mooted changes to the structure of the Corps, the county's local volunteer force was not formally reconstituted as a regiment until July 1916.[7] Until then, the amateurish nature of arrangements may have discouraged the Tribunals from taking its pretensions seriously. Furthermore, the circumstances of the county's principal industries – agriculture and boot and shoe – did not, as noted, accommodate readily the VTC condition. In the former, working hours were intrinsically long and the 'workplace' usually located far from drill halls. Given the relatively benign attitude towards agriculture of most rural Tribunals during their early sittings, it is hardly remarkable that the option was not considered actively. The boot and shoe trade's commitment to war production – rising steeply throughout the first half of 1916 – was difficult enough to maintain in the face of manpower dilution without the added burden of evening exertions for the dwindling workforce.[8] Neither industry, eventually, was able to escape the blanket imposition of VTC attachments to conditional certificates, but the Tribunals approached the matter cautiously, and some remained convinced that forcing a man in dawn-to-dusk employment to take on the further burden of drilling was both unfair and impractical. Finally, as will be seen, a lack of firm guidance from the Local Government Board as to the circumstances under which the Tribunals could, or should, require men to join the VTC when offering exemptions encouraged each to apply their own understanding to the issue, and to long postpone any decision regarding sanctions for non-compliance.

Nevertheless, by May 1916 some of the county's Tribunals had begun to attach the VTC requirement to certificates, though as late as June Northampton Borough remained so unfamiliar with the ethos and purpose of the Corps (and of the tenets of pacifism) as to try to persuade several conscientious objectors to drill with them as a condition of their exemption.[9] Others saw it as an unnecessary complication to the already difficult task in hand, or as an unfair attempt by the military to 'have a second go' at men. When, on 23 June, Wellingborough Urban's military representative, Herbert Dulley, suggested that they might ask men to drill with the Corps, he was told that they hardly had the right to oblige men whom they regarded as being entitled to exemption to undergo military training.[10]

The very nature of the local VTC was changing, however, and this, together with further pressure from the LGB and War Office, encouraged a swift *volte face* on the part of local Tribunals. At a sitting of 3 July, Northampton Borough were addressed by W.P. Cross, chairman of the Executive Committee of the Northamptonshire VTC, who told them that 'important developments' in the work of the VTC were imminent (three days later, the Corps was reconstituted as the First Battalion of the Northamptonshire Volunteer Regiment under the command of Lieutenant Colonel F. Willoughby; the Second Battalion, eventually commanded by Lieutenant Colonel G.S. Eunson, came into being on 11 August).[11] The Tribunal were congratulated by Cross on having sent 204 men to the Corps to date, and told that those concerned were taking a 'keen interest' in their work. That assertion was implicitly and immediately contradicted, however, when Cross urged that those who had refused to fulfil their commitment to drill should be threatened with cancellation of their exemptions. With Geldart's support, the principle was approved, if cautiously, by Alderman Campion, chairing the sitting that day.[12]

On 7 July, the *Mercury* noted that several other Northamptonshire Tribunals (including the previously reticent Wellingborough Urban) had already reacted to the the VTC's changed status by asking applicants to join the Corps, and, in some cases, in such a way as to appear to have made it a condition of their exemption.[13] Yet there remained widespread uncertainty regarding the legitimacy of their authority in this respect. On 6 July, Walter Long attempted, with characteristic opacity, to clarify the situation. He cautioned tribunalists that they should not as a matter of course require membership of the VTC of men receiving certificates, but that: 'in granting exemption from Military Service, it is open to a Tribunal to impose any condition that is reasonable to require.'[14] A month later, the War Office added its own understanding, reassuring the Tribunals that a requirement for exempted men to drill was made entirely at their discretion.[15] What the recipients of this advice made of it depended upon the relative weight they accorded to its contradictions, but if it was not clear that they might make exemptions specifically conditional upon VTC membership, it was equally unclear as to what extent they could wield the threat of withdrawal of certificates for non-compliance. The effect of the instructions (and the uncertainty they engendered) was to slow the adoption of any consistent policy regarding either imposition of the option or effective measures against defaulters.

Nevertheless, having taken up the VTC's cause, most were now reluctant to regard it as an occasional or exceptional recourse, though again, attitudes varied widely from Tribunal to Tribunal. Northampton Borough discovered a sudden and marked enthusiasm for attaching the requirement to their certificates. A fortnight after hearing W.P. Cross's report on the state of the county's Corps, they invited him to join the Tribunal as a permanent member. In response to Councillor Parker's welcoming enquiry as to whether the Corps could accommodate usefully all the men they were now 'shovelling in', Cross urged even greater efforts to persuade employers not to resist the trend, and, to reinforce the point, offered a list of men sent by the Tribunal who had not yet turned up for drills.[16]

That list – a constantly lengthening one – testified to the unpopularity of the VTC among exempted men, whatever Cross's claims to the contrary. At the start of August, Northampton Borough were obliged to revisit the question of their authority, or lack of it, regarding sanctions to be imposed upon their (now two hundred) defaulters. It was agreed that their military representative had the right to ask for a review of certificates in such cases, but it seemed to them inequitable that exemptions might be considered automatically rescinded merely by the fact of a man's refusal, or inability, to attend drills. James Gribble suggested that cards be sent to each of the defaulters, allowing them three or four days to comply with the requirement or risk having their exemptions withdrawn, and this was agreed.[17] The success of the measure cannot be established; however, no existing certificate was withdrawn for non-attendance at drills by this or any other Northamptonshire Tribunal for more than a year following the first threat of sanctions.

Being the court of second resort, the Appeals Tribunal were not deeply involved in the early struggle to establish a consistent VTC policy (though at least one of their number – Stopford-Sackville – was a keen recruiter for the VTC in his own time).[18] The condition had usually been attached (or not) to a certificate before they adjudged cases, and they were content in most instances to respect the decision of local Tribunals. When they did begin to require men to join the VTC, it was as an occasional device, intended as much as a test of the appellant's willingness to 'do something' for the war effort as to swell the local Corps' complement. The first man they asked to participate as a condition of an extension to his (one-month) exemption was William George Drage, a naturalized Canadian citizen and one of six sons of a Northamptonshire widow, who had returned to Britain to care for her when the last of his brothers died. Caught up in the conscription process, he found in the Appeals Tribunal a sympathetic appreciation of the unfortunate consequences of his being a 'good son'. The VTC requirement they imposed effectively provided the means by which the principle of universal sacrifice could be reconciled to natural justice. Originally offered for three months, Drage's exemption (of 28 July 1916) proved enduring: as late as 15 March 1918, Thrapston's National Service representative's appeal against its latest renewal was dismissed.[19]

On other occasions, the Appeals Tribunal imposed a VTC requirement when no other device appeared to be available to them. On 18 August 1916, Frank Lewis, managing director of a Kettering agricultural implement manufacturers, supported his appeal against his local Tribunal's dismissal of his case with a petition signed by eighty farmers in his district who attested to his vital input to their work, and, more obliquely, with the record of his brother, who, in Australia, had raised four hundred volunteers for the Colours. The Tribunal adjourned his case until Kettering Urban had considered that of his fellow director, but asked him to attend the VTC in the meantime to show good faith.[20]

This use of the VTC requirement pending, rather than appending, an exemption, was not unique to the Appeals body. At the end of August, while waiting for the Local Government Board to respond to their urgent representations regarding changes to the certified occupations list for the boot and shoe industry (and for the War Office to clarify what new boot orders they intended to lodge with local factories), Northampton Borough were obliged to make an interim decision affecting several hundred men. They agreed to adjourn all outstanding industry cases due to be considered by schedule until 25 September (the trigger date for the amended list), subject to the men concerned attending VTC drills in the meantime.[21]

By autumn 1916, use of the VTC option was habitual among almost all Northamptonshire's local Tribunals, though, again, no consistent policy can be discerned. Rural Tribunals in particular were torn between the urgings of their military representatives and the realities of life outside the urban centres, which made the required number of attendances at drills highly problematic. This was not an issue unique to Northamptonshire (in Buckinghamshire in October 1916, the VTC's Acting Adjutant noted the practical impossibility of farm workers attending drills miles from their farms),[22] but the highly centralized nature of the county's VTC establishment exacerbated the issue. Men required to drill were obliged to finish their day's work and travel either to Northampton or Wellingborough (after March 1917, Northampton alone) and to find their own way home thereafter. At Potterspury, on 23 August 1916, the VTC option was discussed in respect of a farm labourer, a 28-year-old single man. One tribunalist pointed out that if he attended drills he would not be home before 11 pm, and urged upon his colleagues the general principle that farmhands should not be obliged to join the Corps. Such had been Major Brougham's efforts to get the man into khaki, however, that the Tribunal, while agreeing that entirely with the sentiment, felt obliged nevertheless to append the requirement to his (four months') exemption.[23]

In contrast, urban Tribunals showed considerably more readiness to require their applicants to commit to drilling. Northampton Borough, egged on by the diligent Cross, came to regard the VTC condition as an indivisible component of the exemption process. A bespoke boot maker who produced 20 pairs per week and repaired a further 20 pairs applied to renew his exemption at the Tribunal at the beginning of September. Having heard that he worked from 8 am to 10 pm and also had a country round, they extended his certificate by three months – subject to his drilling with the Corps. How he might find time to do this was not considered.[24]

It is evident, therefore, that in Northampton at least, VTC drilling was becoming a *de facto* condition of exemption, notwithstanding (half-hearted) instructions to the contrary. The requirement to undergo military training was seen as a relatively convenient way for men to demonstrate a personal sacrifice for the wartime nation in a manner less disruptive than changing employments, and certainly less onerous than taking a cut in wages. Furthermore, given that the vast majority of exemptions offered by this and other Tribunals were temporary, it was in the interests of the nation that men who were, eventually, to go to the Colours should gain at least the basic soldiering skills in advance. The inherent contradiction of making men 'volunteer' for the VTC did not undermine its perceived advantages in the short term.

However, the policy of imposing the requirement in every case could not be sustained indefinitely. Evidence that many men found the commitment excessively difficult to fulfil caused concern, not least because it under-mined rather than (as had been intended) reinforced the principle of equity that Tribunals proclaimed to be inviolable. The process of tempering policy was, however, tentative. On 11 September, James Gribble asked his colleagues if it was reasonable, where a man clearly could not fulfil the VTC requirement, that his employer should urge him to approach them with a view to having it removed. Cautiously, Parker concluded, 'I think it may be taken that it is so.'[25] As a trade unionist, Gribble was almost certainly thinking of the industrial implications of an exhausted workforce rather than of individual injustices, but his intervention reveals a degree of self-reflection, or at least pause, among the most enthusiastic 'VTC' Tribunal. A further cautionary note was sounded in October, when Walter Long once more urged that VTC membership should not be made a condi-tion of exemption unless it was 'advisable in the public interest and fair to the man'.[26] This was no less ambiguous than his previous contribution, but the phrase 'fair to the man' held at least a hint that the VTC option had sometimes been taken up over-zealously.

By this time, many more men were experiencing a taste of life with the VTC, and its former image as a home for elderly enthusiasts was diminishing. Nevertheless, anecdotal evidence suggests that the organization, if not the obligation to serve therein, continued to be regarded less than seriously. A Northampton greengrocer who had applied successfully to Central Tribunal to reinstate his exemption was asked by them to accept the VTC requirement. Apparently regretfully, he told them that he was obliged to decline because Tuesday, when he was expected to attend drills, was also his wife's washing day (the exemption was not rescinded). Many others turned up for a token first drill and were not seen again, while some played the Tribunal system shrewdly by volunteering for the VTC before their hearings – to forestall the requirement being attached to certificates – and resigning promptly thereafter, exemption having been obtained.[27]

Despite the best efforts of W.P. Cross and the Corps' officers, some tribunalists and even military representatives seemed to share a slight sense of the ridiculous regarding the VTC's reputation. When a carpenter and undertaker, applying for his only employee, told Wellingborough Urban that the man would be no good in the VTC as he had sciatica and could hardly walk, Herbert Dulley told him (to some apparent amusement in the tribunal chamber), 'Never mind; we are going to have a cripples' section'. A 40-year-old village sexton and gravedigger who also farmed 10 acres, cleaned the village school and did odd jobs was given a six-month exemption by Towcester Tribunal but asked if he might take on the VTC also 'to fill up his spare time'. Even Cross himself was sometimes moved to see his raw material in a humorous light. An applicant's solicitor objected to the VTC requirement as his client 'only takes light exercise'. 'Well, that's all he will get', Cross promised, to general laughter from his colleagues.[28]

There persisted a contradictory perception of the Corps as both a pretend army (despite a high-profile inspection of the Northamptonshire Volunteers' Regiment by Lord French on 19 November, which, owing in part to heavy rain, lacked almost any civilian audience) and a necessary expression of civic duty from those securing exemption from 'real' service.[29] Consequently, Tribunals placing men with the VTC considered themselves to have done their duty but expected little from what resulted. Such low expectations, perhaps as much as uncertainty regarding their authority to impose sanctions, discouraged for many months any strong initiative to deal with the enduring problem of defaulters. Nevertheless, the fact that some men publicly flaunted the directions of the Tribunals remained a matter of concern, as their non-compliance advertised an inequality of sacrifice. Where such inequalities occurred on an individual basis they might be tolerated, but, where the fate of entire workforces was being considered, the self-excused man became prominent, and provocative.

It seems not to be a coincidence, therefore, that Northampton Borough took a lead among the county's Tribunals at least in *considering* sanctions against VTC defaulters whenever dilution pressures upon boot and shoe industry were most pronounced. This reflected their view of the utility of the option. Notably resistant to the War Office's attempts to further comb out the industry, yet obliged to apply the criteria of ever more stringent reserved occupations lists, the Tribunal exercised the VTC requirement to emphasize that men permitted to remain in the factories owed a gesture to those who went to the Colours. Thus, recruitment pressures and the Tribunal's irritation regarding defaulters mounted concurrently. In the same week in November in which they drew up their 'first proposal' to release a tranche of younger workers by 31 December, they also considered W.P. Cross's latest list of (110) VTC defaulters. Yet again, it was suggested that an example might be made of a number of them. Gribble asked that the VTC's officers should call before them those named and ask why they had not complied, after which a decision might be made on which men to pursue. It was agreed that the sanction could in theory be withdrawal of an exemption or, in the case of lesser defaulters, the imposition of stricter conditions, with drilling to take place three times each week.[30]

Yet again, however, Northampton Borough's attitude towards the VTC was tempered by the persistent question of who could, and who should, drill. In principle, they regarded every exempted man as potentially liable, and, as noted, imposed it as a blanket 'request', particularly on those whose exemptions were considered by schedule rather than individually. Nevertheless, whenever they returned to a moment of decision regarding sanctions, they were obliged to consider the specific: to acknowledge the unreality of requiring a man in manufacturing or agriculture to find hours in his day that were simply not available to him. During the implementation of their 'second proposal' upon the boot and shoe trade in February 1917, Gribble noted that Lt Col. Willoughby had circulated drilling cards to the Tribunals. These were to be issued to men required to train with the VTC, and, once signed by the recipients, committed them to drilling ten times per month. How could boot and shoe production targets be met, he asked, or more food grown on the land, if the men concerned were constantly drilling? His colleagues acknowledged the point, and even Cross thought it best to await 'clarification' from Willoughby before distributing the cards.[31]

In the same month, Section B of the VTC was formed. Within weeks, of 1641 men in the Northamptonshire Volunteers' Second Battalion, 1268 (or some 77 per cent) had been transferred thereto (in contrast, Buckinghamshire VTC's Section B contained only 50 per cent of the county's volunteers in February 1917, while the corresponding figures for Cheshire and

Leicestershire were 43 per cent and 49 per cent respectively).[32] The initiative for this appears to have come from barracks rather than the Tribunals. Predictably, it was Gribble, with his close contacts among exempted boot and shoe workers, who first noted the trend. On 27 March, he informed his colleagues that men they had sent to the VTC were being told by company commanders that they 'must' join Section B. This was wrong, he suggested, unless specifically required by the Tribunal. Councillor Parker admitted that he was unaware of what authority was being exercised, but weakly expressed confidence that Lt Col. Willoughby would stop the practice. Gribble raised the pertinent point that, when temporary certificates carried the requirement to drill with the VTC, the requirement itself should likewise be temporary; but a man's direction to Section B attached an enduring obligation that the Tribunals would thereafter be powerless to alter. It seems that W.P. Cross himself had been unaware of the situation: asking for explicit evidence, he promised to correct the practice 'within an hour' of leaving the sitting.[33]

The result of his intervention is not known, but Northampton Borough, similarly to other Tribunals in Northamptonshire, quickly acknowledged the logic of having men become 'efficient' if they were, eventually, to be released for service with the Colours. At a sitting of 30 April, they agreed a broad policy with regard to those they exempted: all in Categories A, B1 and C1 who had not reached their thirty-fifth birthday would be required to join Section B, while other classes would go to the 'ordinary' section (Section D was not constituted until 12 May, when an Army Council Instruction circulated to that effect).[34] Other Tribunals imposed similar distinctions. In September 1917, during their most celebrated case, Daventry alleged that Mayor Stanley, alone among the town's Category B exemptees, had escaped posting to Section B.[35] In the event, although the vast majority of Northamptonshire's volunteers were in the Section by the end of the war (in Second Battalion, of 944 volunteers of all ranks who attended a final exercise on 30 November 1918, 882 were 'B' men), only one in ten had been transferred to the Regular Army, possibly because a very high proportion were skilled boot and shoe workers upon whom the Contracts Department relied heavily.[36]

Even with regard to Section B, there remained a strong contrast between the Tribunals' willingness to place men therein and their reluctance to take practical measures against defaulters. As late as mid-1917, not a single Northamptonshire certificate had been cancelled by reason of its holder's failure to attend drills. At a sitting of 25 May, the 'old theme' (as the *Mercury* termed it) was discussed once more at Northampton Borough, specifically regarding some two hundred exempted boot and shoe operatives who had yet to turn up for a single roll-call. Alderman Campion, chairing the sitting that day, suggested a review of their exemptions; Geldart, to whom the task would have fallen, protested: 'It's easy to say in ten seconds, but this would mean 200 reviews.' For want of any more effective alternative, the Tribunal decided to send yet another round of threatening notes to defaulters, though allowing themselves the option also of making an example of one person from each factory involved if this did not produce the required rush to barracks. Having committed themselves so decisively, they adjourned the matter until a full list of defaulters could be drawn up; a task, they anticipated, that could not be completed before Whitsuntide.[37]

However, the 'example', when finally made, was upon the Appeals Tribunal's initiative, though such were the circumstances that its deterrent value must have been negligible. In July, the certificate of a Northampton boot and shoe operative, C. Skeers was reviewed. Skeers claimed that he did a lot of heavy lifting at his factory and stayed later than other workers. When first he had received notice to attend drilling, he wrote to the Town Clerk to explain his position but had received no reply. The hearing was adjourned briefly while Geldart was summoned from Town Hall. When the latter told the Tribunal that Skeers had not only failed to attend drills himself but persuaded a number of his workmates to do likewise, his certificate was shortened – from an original end date of 12 August to 1 August.[38]

No further examples were made in the short term – a further indication, perhaps, of the general aversion to having VTC issues dominate business. On 29 August, Lt Col. Willoughby wrote to the Tribunals, reminding them of the official responsibilities of men in Section B. He asked that they should apply the VTC requirement consistently throughout the county, and ensure that employers of men failing to attend the required number of drills were notified that certificates might be withdrawn.[39] Few Tribunals rushed to comply. Northampton Borough discussed the letter, but concluded only that it would be best if the War Office allowed Willoughby the flexibility to excuse men engaged on short-term boot and shoe orders for the Army. At Wellingborough Urban, the chairman, J.H York, thought it the military's responsibility to apply for reviews of the cases of some hundred local defaulters, rather than expect the Tribunal to take the lead (when, on 15 October, applications were duly made in respect of some 65 certificates, York dismissed them without exception, declaring it 'a wicked shame' to have wasted the men's time by bringing them to the Tribunal). The Appeals Tribunal were slightly more responsive: at a sitting of 21 September, Adkins suggested it would be 'helpful' when considering whether men's certificates should be renewed if appellants brought with them certificates, signed by their VTC officers, confirming that they had attended the requisite number of drills. The only other measurable effect of Willoughby's intervention was to cause Daventry Tribunal to initiate their campaign against Mayor

Stanley, which, eventually, would provide a far more salutary example than that made of the unfortunate Skeers.[40]

However, the long prevarication regarding sanctions was about to end. Nationwide, the press, forewarned of measures being contemplated to punished men not fulfilling their VTC commitments, urged that they should be effective.[41] On 12 September and again on 18 October, the Army Council issued instructions to the military representatives to press their Tribunals for the cancellation of defaulters' certificates.[42] On 29 October, Northampton Borough, perhaps galvanized by the case of Mayor Stanley (who had succumbed very publicly three weeks earlier), announced that some two hundred defaulting boot and shoe men would be called up 'immediately', with 60 receiving their notices within the coming week. The force of the announcement was softened somewhat by a further direction that Geldart should warn the men involved of the impending action before issuing notices (presumably to give the offenders a final opportunity to attend drills), and that all concerned had seven days in which to appeal following the cancellation of their certificates.[43] Nevertheless, the initiative reflected a growing willingness among the Tribunals, however reluctantly, to settle a long-festering matter. Even Wellingborough Urban took up the cause, and in as uncompromising a manner as they had previously defended their exempted men. On 5 November, John Miller, a 38-year-old married man, B2, appealed against their cancellation of his certificate. He drove a mail cart from 4 am to 9 pm every day excepting Sunday, and therefore had no feasible opportunity to drill. The Appeals Tribunal reinstated his exemption (to 5 February 1918), and pointedly removed the VTC requirement.[44]

The timing of this more stringent policy did not entirely complement efforts by the War Office to improve the quality of the VTC as a whole. Inspections of volunteer-manned defences in the southern counties revealed many shortcomings of efficiency and inadequate equipment (many local forces depended upon private subscriptions still to equip themselves), encouraging a view in government that the number of Volunteer regiments might usefully be reduced, with Section D men being released to allow more 'efficients' (Section A and B) to be trained up. Lord Scarbrough, Director General of the VTC, successfully resisted any absolute reduction in manpower but accepted the need to find a more productive role for Section D men. He suggested that they be required to serve for the duration, and to commence the full drilling programme by the end of February 1918 or have their exemption certificates rescinded. This was not taken up (probably because the initiative would put further pressure upon existing resources), and Section D continued to provide both a source of refuge for 'shirkers' and of ire for Lord French and others who considered them lost soldiers.

Moves to disband the Section entirely in the early months of 1918 failed, not least because many 'D' men, fearing transfer to Section B, resigned and thus by default eased pressure upon resources. The Section was not finally abolished until August 1918; however, at the start of December 1917, Lord Scarbrough hastened its passing into relative irrelevance when he circulated a letter to the Tribunals, reminding them that exempted men of military age – particularly in the new medical Grades I or II – were needed urgently to give the country an effective home defence force. Less fit men, he urged, should be asked to join the Special Constabulary or to assist upon allotments, rather than be sent into Section D where they would contribute nothing to the war effort (his suggestion was supported, if tardily, by the Local Government Board in May 1918).[45]

As noted, Tribunals in Northamptonshire who imposed the VTC requirement had overwhelmingly directed fit men into Section B almost since its creation in January 1917, and Scarbrough's request did not significantly alter local policy regarding where a man should go. However, despite further guidance in January 1918 from the Local Government Board, which supported the Director General's recommendation regarding men graded I or II, use of the VTC option continued to vary widely. In the third week of January, correspondence between the county's Tribunals revealed that while certain bodies (notably Kettering and Northampton Borough) imposed the requirement wherever it was considered 'reasonable', others – Rushden was cited in particular – used it only infrequently, and hardly ever in respect of boot and shoe men. The most pronounced result of this tentative move towards consistency was to foster a sense of indignation among the more rigorous Tribunals that they were merely disadvantaging their local boot and shoe factories and risking future contracts (the revelation inclined Northampton Borough to 'grass' on Rushden both to the Local Government Board and the county's Appeals Tribunal). Otherwise, agreement was reached only upon a conclusion that the Local Government Board's latest instructions were permissive but advanced no understanding of what constituted appropriate policy regarding the VTC.[46]

Little more was said on the matter for some weeks thereafter, but the example made of some exempted men in the previous November had not removed the problem of defaulters. At the end of March, Councillor Parker declared himself 'fed up' of the seemingly endless complaints from Lt Col. Willoughby and others. Again, he warned that examples should be made, and told one applicant for renewal that if he did not attend drills 'he would find the last word had been said on the matter'. Two weeks later, the Appeals Tribunal, hearing a large, scheduled list of boot and shoe appeals, entered into their minutes a National Service Ministry letter, again reminding representatives to ensure that all exempted Grades I and II men be sent to Section B. Following this, it was held that all men given open exemptions should, as far as possible, commence drilling. They noted also that Northampton Borough were now insisting that any Grade I men previously exempted and serving with Northampton's volunteer fire brigades should resign and drill with firearms immediately.[47]

In May, the Military Service (No. 2) Act, 1918, strengthened the Tribunals' power to impose the VTC requirement. Section 4(6) made membership of Section B compulsory for all men who received exemption, subject to specific direction otherwise by a Tribunal. Importantly, it also specified that, where the requirement was attached, it should be in force for the duration of a man's exemption. Men so exempted were required to attend Barracks with their National Service Registration Card and exemption certificate within seven days of receiving the latter. Subsequently, the Volunteer Force (Tribunal Exemptions) Order, 1918, applying to all men exempted after 1 May but not placed in Section B, required them to serve at least 12 hours of 'military duty' each week or otherwise to join the Section.[48]

The legislation, intended in part to end (unjust) criticism that exempted men were being allowed to remain in Section D to keep them out of the Army, was too successful.[49] Across the country, Tribunals, having finally been given firm guidance, sent applicants in droves to their local Corps until no more could be accepted. The Northamptonshire bodies were no exception. Throughout June, Northampton Borough attached the requirement to all certificates issued to men in Grades I and II. Peterborough Tribunal did likewise, and with farcical consequences. On 9 July, they wrote indignantly to Lt Col. Eunson of Second Battalion, complaining that they had four hundred exempted men waiting to join the local regiment, who could not be accepted for want of resources. They had no intention, they stated, of obliging a crowd of exemptees to attend barracks, if they were not to be clothed and equipped. They also threatened to withdraw the VTC requirement from some 250 exempted men who had already gone into the battalion, on the basis that it was hardly fair for them to serve if others could not do so for want of adequate resources. They concluded with asperity: 'Of course if the military situation is so satisfactory that these men need not be trained, or if it is not practicable in the present emergency to deal with them, then this Tribunal have no further observations to offer, beyond expressing their profound astonishment that such should be the case, in the face of the Act of Parliament.'[50]

The War Office's response to this and similar complaints elsewhere was to inform Volunteer Regiments around the country that, notwithstanding recent legislation which provided otherwise, they should refuse to take on any more exempted men.[51] This initiative resulted, on 20 July, in an extraordinary meeting of the Northamptonshire Territorial Forces Association, which many tribunalists and other local worthies attended, its proceedings reported by the *Mercury* under the headline: 'An Awful Muddle'. An embarrassed Lt Col. Eunson told them that his battalion had an establishment of 900 men (down from its initial intake of some 1600 men). Previously, the War Office had implied that it might be expanded to a complement of 2000, but had since informed him that his absolute limit must be 938 men of all ranks. Nevertheless, he had taken on men in excess of this number sent recently by the Tribunals, though they were drilling without equipment or uniforms. Ruefully, he added that he expected to be 'hauled over the coals for swearing them in'. From the floor, Councillor Parker reassured him that he had done the right thing in difficult circumstances, but Eunson persisted gloomily that he 'should have it in the neck one of these days'.

Less conciliatory than Parker, Alderman Campion condemned the War Office's attitude as 'an exhibition of colossal stupidity', while Major-General Viscount Downe (who, in July 1916, had taken a lead in raising the Second Battalion) noted darkly that the government 'had done many things like this'. It was emphasized that the War Office's direction was a direct contravention of the terms of the Act. Particularly, the situation wherein older men drilled while newly exempted youths mocked their efforts (to considerable ire locally, it was alleged) undermined every principle of equity that they had sought to uphold. A resolution lamenting the confusion created by the War Office, and demanding measures to correct the situation, was proposed by Campion and seconded by the shoe manufacturer Sir Henry Randall. It was agreed that this should be sent to Lloyd George and the Secretary of State for War, with a copy provided to Sir Ryland Adkins with which to canvass his fellow MPs in the House.[52]

Lt Col. Willoughby, who was present at the meeting but not called upon to answer for the War Office's initiative, seems to have maintained a number of vacancies in his own battalion, and, in contrast to the unfortunate Eunson, tried to fill them. In the same week, word that four exempted men had been excused VTC duty by Northampton Borough (as per the War Office's instruction) did not reach barracks via the National Service representative. Accordingly, Willoughby sent out a squad to arrest the 'defaulters' and escort them under arms through the streets of Northampton, an uncharacteristically harsh measure which aroused local feeling and prompted a chastened Tribunal to notify the terms of all future exemptions directly to the battalion.[53]

During the final months of the war, Northamptonshire's Tribunals responded very differently to the dilemma. The Appeals Tribunal stood on principle: legislation had been enacted, giving them a very clear duty that neither circumstance nor the War Office should be allowed to obstruct. Their policy, therefore, was to proceed as instructed and let the Home

Army deal with the consequence of their masters' refusal to provide adequate facilities. Accordingly, on 20 September 1918, when offering long (renewal) certificates to 561 men at their final major boot and shoe sitting, they ordered all Grades I and II men to report to barracks for drilling.[54]

Other Tribunals seem rather to have been content to shrug off an option they had never embraced enthusiastically. Men asking to be excused VTC duty when receiving their certificates were often obliged – such as the 'well-known' Wellingborough organist turned munitions worker, who had his exemption extended by six months on 24 September. More usually, the requirement was entirely ignored in considering an application. Press reports of sittings during the final three months of the war do not mention the imposition of a single VTC requirement (the Appeals Tribunal's last defiant gesture aside), though some renewed exemptions carrying existing obligations to drill are noted. The final VTC matter discussed before the Tribunals was a predictable one: in the first week of December, at the winding up of Northampton Borough's business, James Gribble asked about the position of men whose exemption certificates carried the VTC requirement. It was decided to send out notices to all concerned, directing that they consider their obligations suspended.[55]

The final tally of men in Second Battalion, Northamptonshire Volunteers, was drawn up on 30 November 1918, following their final field exercise.[56] Of 944 men of all ranks serving, 882 were in Section B, while 32 long-serving, senior stalwarts remained in Section A. Twenty-seven 'men' (that is, youths who had not reached their eighteenth birthdays) were attached to Section C, with three boys (presumably eager volunteers who were too young for formal admission) unallocated. However, of the total establishment, only 512 were fully 'efficient', 189 had not passed the required levels of expertise in any discipline, while the remainder had passed variously in musketry, bayonet fighting and drilling, or a combination of any two. This was hardly the effective unit envisaged by those who had long urged that every exempted man be pushed into Section B.

Officially, the regiment was disbanded on 29 January 1920. The War Office had authorized the disbandment of all volunteer forces (other than the motor units) as early as September 1919, but the demobilization process was slow and confused, with men reluctant to hand back weapons and uniforms. Accordingly, clearance certificates permitting the formal dissolution of units were issued months later, and in a piecemeal fashion[57] However, the vast majority of volunteers effectively disbanded themselves at the cessation of hostilities; ostensibly, they took with them the thanks of a grateful nation, but in reality were so little considered by the government that a decision to issue a volunteers' service medal was postponed and then quietly dropped in 1921. The King's letter of thanks to former members of the corps ignored the contribution of the real volunteers (those who had joined of their own volition prior to May 1916); presumably, this reflected the abiding official view that anyone of military age who had willingly joined the VTC was a shirker. One less than grateful recipient of the communication called it a 'printed letter of lukewarm thanks, signed with a facsimile of an undecipherable signature':

> ... I wish to take the opportunity through you of conveying my high appreciation of the services rendered by all ranks of the Force, and also by all who, by their willing support, contributed to its success.
>
> I cannot forget the self-sacrifice and patriotism which inspired so many subjects, who from reasons of health or age were unable to serve abroad, to come forward and train themselves for any eventuality in the hour of their Country's need.
>
> George R.I.[58]

The imposition of the VTC 'requirement' upon exempted men fully exposed the anomalies of government's hands-off attitude both towards the corps and the Tribunals. The latter were of course amenable to the principle that those not conscripted should demonstrate some form of sacrifice, but, while they largely welcomed the initiative, putting it into practice proved troublesome. Having imposed the requirement as directed, they discovered that they were obliged to police the consequences. To discharge such a role elsewhere – for example, with respect to those relatively few conscientious objectors whose certificates were predicated upon their continuing to do work of national importance – was not an onerous task. To do the same with regard to hundreds of boot and shoe operatives and farm workers was wholly impractical. So too was the requirement itself in many cases, as the Tribunals discovered when men returned in great numbers to complain that there were not sufficient hours in a day both to work and to drill. The gap between what government wanted, and what reality permitted, was left to the Tribunals to bridge. Not surprisingly, most failed to meet the challenge adequately.

Had there been the political will to see the experiment succeed, their task might have been simplified; but Whitehall insisted that exempted men should train usefully with arms without ever committing sufficient resources to facilitate the aim. Clearly, improvements occurred during the conscription period. The 'volunteers' of 1918 (though, of course, very few of them actually *were* volunteers in the literal sense by that time) bore little resemblance to the mobs in mufti who had so alarmed Sir John French when first he took up command of Home Forces in January 1916.[59] Inevitably, the evolution of the Royal Defence Corps from 1916 had the effect of dragging up its least respected component, the VTC. Two years later, the latter had a military command structure, weapons, uniforms and premises – though often occupied, cuckoo-fashion, in the absence of their habitual Territorial Force residents. But the improvements were relative, and fell far short of ensuring what had been declared to be the goal. A great deal of effort, of the Tribunals' time, of the evening hours of hard-working men, had been expended in creating a resource whose utilization was never contemplated seriously by GHQ. Other than the minuscule number who, in June of that year, answered the call to man coastal defences, or served briefly in France in supply or communications units, none of the men whose participation had given the Tribunals so much incremental business contributed even marginally to the war effort.[60] Any rationalization of their diversion into the Corps might stand only upon a single merit: that they had, in return for their exemptions, been able to demonstrate a rather impractical sacrifice to those who had gone to the Front.

Notes

1 Osborne, 'Defining Their Own Patriotism', p. 67; Mitchinson, *Defending Albion*, p. 69.

2 Popular variants included 'George's Wrecks', 'Gorgeous Wrecks' and 'George's Relics', all derived from the GR armlets worn by volunteers (Beckett and Simpson, *A Nation in Arms*, p. 15).

3 Osborne, 'Defining Their Own Patriotism', p. 71; *Daily Telegraph*, 19 December 1920.

4 ACI 84/1917 (13 January 1917), ACI 86/1917 (22 January 1917), ACI 765/1917 (12 May 1917).

5 Mitchinson, *Auxiliary Forces for the Land Defence of Great Britain*, p. 252; NRO ML1540/119.

6 Mitchinson, *Auxiliary Forces*, p. 248.

7 Above, p. 201.

8 Above, pp. 67–68.

9 *Mercury*, 23, 30 June 1916; also above, p. 46.

10 *Mercury*, 23 June 1916. In the previous month, in Buckinghamshire, the local VTC officer had urged Eton Rural Tribunal only that they should 'suggest' the option of drilling to men receiving exemption certificates (CBS, DC/10/38/1: Tribunal Minute Book, p. 32).

11 NRO ML1540/3. Originally based at Wellingborough, the Second Battalion (excluding its Peterborough Company) was transferred to Northampton on 8 March 1917 (ibid., 49).

12 *Mercury*, 7 July 1916.

13 At Wellingborough Urban on 4 July, Herbert Dulley asked that all conditional certificates should have the VTC condition attached, with the threat of review for non-compliance (*Mercury*, 7 July 1916).

14 LGB Circular R.95 (as dated).

15 TNA WO 70/42/9/VF/83 TF2 (15 August 1916).

16 *Mercury*, 28 July, 4 August 1916.

17 Ibid., 4 August 1916.

18 Stopford-Sackville's recruitment activities in the voluntary period have been noted previously (above, p. 19), but his work continued following the advent of conscription. On 15 May 1917, for example, addressing a meeting on behalf of the Thrapston and District Company of Second Battalion, Northamptonshire Volunteer Regiment, he urged the audience to join them, to learn the 'tricks of bombing and trench digging ... which had been a surprise not only to the Germans but to the British nation' (*Mercury*, 18 May 1917).

19 NRO X183/777, X185/1296, X192/8766.

20 NRO X184/875.

21 *Mercury*, 1 September 1916; also above, p. 70.

22 Beckett, 'The Local Community and the Great War', p. 511.

23 *Mercury*, 25 August 1916.

24 Ibid., 8 September 1916.

25 *Mercury*, 15 September 1916.

26 LGB Circular R.102 (6 October 1916).

27 *Mercury*, 22 December 1916, 12 January 1917.

28 *Mercury*, 8 September, 6 October 1916; *Herald*, 22 September 1916.

29 NRO ML1540/53–55; *Northampton Independent*, 21 November 1916: 1383 men of First Battalion and 1291 of Second Battalion (including 399 men of the Peterborough Company) turned out for the Field Marshal.

30 *Mercury*, 1, 15 December 1916.

31 *Mercury*, 16 February 1917.

32 NRO ML1540/67; Mitchinson, 'Auxiliary Forces', p. 259.

33 *Mercury*, 30 March 1917.

34 *Mercury*, 4 May 1917; ACI 765/1917 (as dated).

35 Above, p. 174.

36 NRO ML1540/119. On 17 February 1917, Lt Col. Eunson wrote to the Secretary of the War Office, noting that Second Battalion's Section B men were almost exclusively boot and shoe workers (ibid., 65). Peterborough Tribunal later commented that '[we] are disposed to grant no exemption from the statutory obligations of Section B except for very substantial reasons' (NRO X4237: letter of 9 July 1918, entered into the minutes of the Territorial Forces Association, 20 July 1918).

37 *Mercury*, *Herald*, 25 May 1917.

38 NRO X189/6453; X197: Appeals Tribunal meeting notes, 20 July 1917.

39 NRO ML1540/75 (as dated).

40 NRO X197: Appeals Tribunal Notes of Meeting, 21 September 1917; *Mercury*, 21 September, 19 October 1917; also above, pp. 173–175. The Wellingborough Urban review list also included medical rejection cases and those of men who, with the military representative's approval, had remained in the Special Constabulary rather than transfer to the VTC.

41 Cf. *The Times*, 19 September 1917; *Manchester City News*, 22 September 1917; *Oldham Chronicle*, 24 September 1917. The former mentioned Mayor Stanley in discussing the problem of defaulters.

42 ACI 1414, 1577, 1578/1917 (as dated).

43 *Mercury*, 2 November 1917.

44 NRO X191/7096; X197: Appeals Tribunal meeting notes, as dated.

45 Mitchinson, *Defending Albion*, pp. 174–175; 'Auxiliary Forces', pp. 281–284, 308–309, 357; TNA WO 32/5048(39A): *Future Policy as Regards the Volunteer Force* (27 November 1917); *Mercury*, 7 December 1917; *The Times*, 28 January 1918; LGB Circular R.184 (2 May 1918).

46 LGB Circular R.169 (18 January 1918); *Mercury*, 25 January, 15 February 1918.

47 NRO X197: Appeals Tribunal meeting notes, 10 April 1918; *Mercury*, 29 March, 12 April 1918. Willoughby was not as inflexible regarding defaulters as his many 'complaints' suggest. In February 1918, he told employers that, while he could release no man from drills in advance, a defaulter with a good excuse regarding his employment commitments would not be reported (*Mercury*, 15 February 1918). His approaches to Parker were probably in respect of persistent offenders.

48 TNA WO 70/42; NATS Circular R.185 (25 April 1918); Orders in Council, 25 June 1918; ACI 913/1918 (16 August 1918); Army Form V 4031.

49 Lord French's complaint was reported in *The Times*, 28 January 1918.

50 NRO X4237: Minutes of the Territorial Force Association, 20 July 1918).

51 TNA WO 99/625 (T.V.I.).

52 *Mercury*, 7 July 1916, 26 July 1918. Of the flood of 'volunteers', the *Independent* (25 July 1918) reported that battalion commanders were 'at their wits-end to know what to do with them'.

53 *Mercury*, 26 July 1918. In London, the VTC was so overwhelmed that the National Service representative at the Appeals Tribunal's City division asked that, in future, exempted men should be sent to the London Ambulance Unit instead (*The Times*, 27 July 1918).

54 *Mercury*, 27 September 1918. Also above, p. 86.

55 *Mercury*, 27 September, 6 December 1918.

56 NRO ML1540, 119. Figures for First Battalion are not extant.

57 TNA WO/99/N/214 T.V.R., WO/99/859 A.G.I.; NRO ML1540/135; Mitchinson, 'Auxiliary Forces', p. 369.

58 Mitchinson, 'Auxiliary Forces', pp. 367, 372–374; *Defending Albion*, p. 200; NRO ML1540/127 (excerpt).

59 Mitchinson, *Defending Albion*, p. 123.

60 Nationwide, some nine thousand VTC men had (very reluctantly) met the Army's request for fifteen thousand volunteers (Osborne, 'Defining Their Own Patriotism', p. 72).

10

Conclusion

The task entrusted to the Tribunals was laborious and formidable, especially to men who, as a rule, had many other claims upon their time and energies. It called in a high degree for the exercise of patience, sagacity and impartiality. The decisions of cases involved grave responsibilities from which members of Tribunals might not unnaturally have shrunk if they had not placed the country's need before all other considerations. The work of the Tribunals was unostentatious; but it has played a vital part in securing the Victory and Peace which have been achieved.[1]

The last thing a man ought to do who cares for personal popularity, is to become a member of a local tribunal. In the nature of the case he has the opportunity of making many enemies and very few friends.[2]

Between January 1916 and the Armistice, some 2.5 million Britons went to the Colours, of whom 1.35 million were taken via the mechanism of successive Military Service Acts.[3] Of the latter, it may be assumed that an indeterminable number would have enlisted eventually without compulsion; of the remainder, many went into uniform with varying degrees of reluctance but did not apply for exemption. The total number of applications made to the Tribunals during the conscription period cannot be calculated, owing to the early destruction of the greater part of the database. During the early months of the conscription period, it has been noted elsewhere that, of 1.2 million single men of military age who were deemed by the Military Service Act, 1916 to have enlisted, approximately 750,000 sought exemption.[4] Official statistics compiled after the war also give a snapshot total of 779,936 men, married and single, holding exemption certificates as of 30 April 1917.[5] Clearly, such numbers far exceeded those anticipated by the architects of conscription, and expert, if anecdotal, opinion indicates that no subsequent amendment to the principal Act came close to securing the numbers of men anticipated by its drafters. The Tribunals could take no blame for men lost to reserved occupations, or for the median ill-health of the nation, but their perceived 'leniency' towards higher-category men was a persistent irritant both to government and to GHQ. At no point after

June 1916 did recruitment by compulsion make good the wastage of general service men;[6] unsurprisingly, successive Directors of Recruiting unerringly identified the principal cause of the shortfall to be the band of amateurs who applied localist preoccupations, flawed understanding of legislation and ill-judged sentiment in deciding who should go to war.

It is readily apparent, therefore, what yardstick the War Office applied in adjudging the success (or otherwise) of the Tribunal system. For the historian, however, the question of its utility is more difficult to determine. A study that examines the processes by which tribunalists perceived and confronted the many issues arising during the course of their sittings must, in part, be judgemental. But was 'success' predicated upon the efficient processing of fit young men from civilian life to the Colours, the mainte-nance of local economies in the face of periodic large-scale manpower depletion, the exercise of a humane perspective in inhuman circumstances, or a balance which sought to deliver a measure of each?

We might begin to address that question by rehearsing the surviving statistics of the appeals process in Northamptonshire. The County Tribunal heard their first case, at Northampton, on 24 March 1916; their last, at Peterborough, on 5 November 1918 (a further Northampton sitting had been scheduled for 12 November, but was cancelled for obvious reasons).[7] During a total of 162 sittings they heard 12,150 cases, comprising 6801 original appeals, 4154 renewals, 880 applications for leave to appeal further (the majority rejected) and 315 applications for medical re-examination.[8] By comparison, Middlesex Appeals Tribunal considered 11,307 cases during the conscription period, of which 8791 were original appeals.[9] The higher proportion of renewals coming before Northamptonshire's appeals body might suggest, superficially, that it had more 'lenient' instincts than did Middlesex (that is, fewer of their certificates appear to have had finality attached). However, different circumstances pertaining to each Tribunal's jurisdiction make broad conclusions of this nature difficult to sustain. Middlesex did not, for example, deal with large numbers of scheduled cases from a particular industry, which alone might account for the statistical variance. As to motive, it might equally – and contrarily – be argued that the relatively few (15) applications for leave to appeal to Central Tribunal granted by Northampton reflects a harsher, or more assured, policy than that, for example, of the corresponding Dorsetshire body, which responded positively to such applications on 266 occasions.[10]

Elsewhere, the variegated manner in which the work of Tribunals has been expressed in surviving statistics makes useful comparisons problem-atic. In passing, it may be noted that Birmingham district Appeals Tribunal heard 7333 cases during the conscription period, of which 2427 were 'allowed', in that decisions of local Tribunals were adjusted in favour of the appellant (whether enlisted man or military representative).[11] Birmingham City's far busier local Tribunal heard a total of 90,721 cases, of which 34,760 were dismissed outright; of the remainder, 3549 were offered temporary certificates, 4191 conditional and a mere nine absolute.[12] Bristol City local Tribunal, during the course of 821 sessions, heard more than 41,000 applications, of which 17,000 were dismissed outright. Bristol District Appeals Tribunal sat upon 258 occasions, hearing some eight thousand cases; at the time of the Armistice, a mere 683 certificates offered by them remained in force.[13] During 315 hearings, Leicester City local Tribunal heard 52,385 applications, of which it was claimed – surely erroneously – that only 898 were appealed.[14] Finally, the less-than-overwhelmed Newport Pagnell local Tribunal heard a grand total of 593 cases (attested and conscripted men) between December 1915 and October 1918–a function, perhaps, of their proximity to that notorious haven for shirkers, the Wolverton Rail Works?[15] The meaning of any of these figures, absent a full understanding of the context of the proceedings to which they refer, can hardly be determined. What particular circumstances, prevailing in any Tribunal's jurisdiction, should be considered in judging their temperament and policies? It is hardly controversial to assume that a majority of men who obtained temporary exemptions went into the Army eventually, but can 'eventually' inform estimations of rigour or leniency? All that may be said with certainty is that absolute exemptions were relatively few, that conditional certificates endured as long as the conditions attached thereto and that temporary exemptions – the vast majority of those granted – were offered under infinitely varying circumstances.

Consequently, it may be argued that few meaningful *comparative* deductions can be drawn from the fragmentary statistics of the Tribunal system. Even where identifiable, the proportion of exemptions to outright dismissals, of exemptions lengthened upon appeal to those shortened and/or having finality imposed, of short to long exemptions, or of absolute to conditional exemptions, tells little of the policies of each Tribunal, much less of the 'system' collectively. It is only in the examination of cases individually, and of tribunalists' responses to the wider stimulae of legislation, conflicting pressures from government departments and the developing military situation, that differences in policy become apparent.

In Northamptonshire, idiosyncratic distinctions between certain Tribunals are readily discernible, and these often determined the likelihood of an application being heard sympathetically. A Brixworth farm worker, for example, appears to have had less chance of obtaining an exemption by reason of his employment alone than did his Hardingstone counterpart. A Northampton boot and shoe operative, benefiting from the industry's robust representation on his local Tribunal, was more likely to stay out of uniform than an employee in a Rushden factory (though, paradoxically, he was much more likely to be required to join the VTC thereafter than was a Rushden boot and shoe exemptee).[16] While none of the county's Tribunals displayed any particular animus towards the youngest brothers of men already serving with the Colours, it is almost certainly the case that their best opportunity for a sympathetic hearing lay at Town Hall, North-ampton.[17] And it is hardly unjust to the memory of Peterborough Tribunal to suggest that an applicant of whatever occupational, domestic or moral circumstance would have been well advised to have resided somewhere other than in their jurisdiction.

Though readily identified, such variations of temperament are neverthe-less difficult to explain satisfactorily other than by reference to the flaws within the mechanism itself. This was a process of human judgement made upon the basis of facts, allegations and perceptions; each Tribunal was composed of individuals, each of whom, in turn, had a different under-standing of his or her role. A dominant personality – Sir Ryland Adkins at the Appeals Tribunal, for example, or Councillor Parker at Northampton Borough – might seem to have exercised a disproportionate influence on his colleagues, and, in expressing his views volubly, appear to be 'speaking the mind' of the Tribunal.[18] Yet how far was this the reality? In assessing the relative contributions of James Gribble or Alderman Campion, it is easy to measure either agreement or dissent with their Tribunal's 'policy' because they took particular care to voice both. Conversely, the opinions of many of their colleagues, who attended for duty's sake but confined their participa-tion to voting, are, and will remain, lost to us. A vote, one way or another, says little of the processes that shaped it. A Tribunal was a collective and therefore of unequal parts, moving haphazardly, rather than instinctively, towards consensus.

An effective military representative, such as Adam Cross at Brixworth and Herbert Dulley at Wellingborough Urban, was similarly able to influence day-to-day 'policy' regarding exemptions. Others seem to have done little more than to lodge an occasional appeal when their Tribunals' decisions wandered too wantonly from the spirit of their instructions. An endearing example of the latter, R.G. Scriven at Hardingstone, almost certainly had a genuine aversion to sending men into the Army (a prejudice he shared substantially with his Tribunal). A world – yet only three miles – away was the day-to-day experience of Northamptonshire's busiest military repre-sentative, A.H. Geldart, who had the misfortune also to serve the county's most quixotic body, Northampton Borough, and who laboured hard for poor returns and thin thanks. A recurring, implicitly damning comment from the Tribunal was that they appreciated he was 'only following orders'. On more than one occasion, his care to follow the letter of those orders inclined them to take an obstructionist course as a gesture of their frustration or ire.[19]

Thus, the diversity and relative strength of personalities were potentially major factors in setting policy. Beyond the impact of the idiosyncratic, however, it has been observed that an individual Tribunal's policy could shift notably during the conscription period. Legislative milestones were the principal cause of this, but government priorities were variously impacted also by short-term military exigencies, anticipated harvest failures, 'submarine threats' to food distribution and, of course, enduring perceptions within Whitehall that the Tribunals themselves were not fully cognisant of their intended role and thus needed herding.

In fact, misapprehensions were mutual, and this fundamental symptom of a flawed system governed the relationship between Tribunals and Whitehall even beyond the establishment of the National Service Ministry in November 1917 and the formulation, on paper at least, of a co-ordinated manpower policy. As envisaged by their architects, the Military Service Acts were intended to secure as many men as possible for the Armed Forces. Nothing in their provisions acknowledged the competing claims of the domestic economy, of personal circumstance or of moral exception *except* the discretionary mechanism they provided to the Tribunals. In effect, the sole potential brake upon the War Office's intention to remove the vast majority of men of fighting age from civilian life was relinquished by government and placed into the hands of men who stood entirely outside the process of balancing the nation's resources for 'total war'. This was not so much the privatization as the surrender of public policy-making.

How then were the Tribunals – even those which sought assiduously to subordinate personal opinion to duty – to interpret their role? The several grounds for exemption provided by the Act ostensibly indicated official anticipation of who was to be taken for the Army and who should remain in civilian life, but the letter of legislation was often misleading. Despite the apparent breadth of provisions for exemption, government did not make apparent an overarching intention: that each of the stated grounds envisaged a relatively exceptional degree of the circumstance it outlined. Considerable chagrin was evident among enthusiasts for conscription when the reality of the exemption process replaced theory. Setting aside the stark misjudgement of the extent of conscientious objections to military service, the volume and complexity of cases made to the Tribunals went beyond anything envisaged by Lord Derby and his fellow compulsionists. The logic of their case had been built entirely upon demographic considerations, the exceptions in their legislation upon a cursory assumption of atypical circumstances or events. What they did not anticipate were the consequences of permitting the expression of a million human preoccupations within an industrial-scale process.

For the Tribunals, the revelation came swiftly. Effectively overwhelmed by Derby Scheme and military service applications during their early sittings, they discovered that the letter of legislation barely scratched the surface of circumstance, obliging them to apply considerable initiative when considering all but the most straightforward cases. The results, predictably, did not please government, yet urgent efforts to redress the unexpectedly high proportion of exemptions had little success. The incidence of absolute exemptions was curtailed sharply, but this was one of the few issues upon which Whitehall and most Tribunals concurred. Elsewhere, attempts to clarify legislation often created further ambiguity, leaving tribunalists to establish their own measures of what constituted median and extreme circumstance.

Industrial applications and/or appeals subject to consideration by schedule aside, each case was judged upon its merits; but each of the various grounds for exemption reflected, or created, incremental issues that impacted upon a Tribunal's policy. Applications in respect of domestic or personal hardship – excluding those made by businessmen or sole proprietors, which generated their own difficulties – were perhaps the least problematic cases. Though often involving relatively harrowing circumstances, several mitigating options were available which blunted the impact of conscription. Nothing could soften the dislocation of forcible removal from domestic life, but Army Separation Allowances ameliorated the financial blow for low-income families, while the principle of universal sacrifice in wartime, when seen to be applied rigorously, blunted the worst criticisms of the system. Gestures could be (and were) made regarding the most obviously deserving cases – the sole support of a widowed mother, the last remaining son out of uniform – which validated judgements elsewhere. Some Tribunals stood on principle most firmly in these cases because they allowed fairness to be demonstrated at little cost to recruitment efforts.

In contrast, the ground of conscience was odious to many Tribunals during the early conscription period, as copious evidence of their ill-tempered incredulity indicates. However, despite the claims of the No-Conscription Fellowship and their allies, attempts to deal with conscientious objectors were more nuanced than the well-publicized exceptions suggest. Some religious groups (the Quakers, most notably) fared relatively well, their moral stance being well understood. Others, such as Christadelphians and Seventh Day Adventists, were treated less gently, though growing familiarity with their doctrines eventually removed most Tribunals' mistrust of their apparent contradictions. Communicants of the Established Church, being somewhat handicapped by their bishops' prevailing support for the war, were almost always unsuccessful before the Tribunals unless a particularly long-standing objection to militarism could be demonstrated. Applicants of any denomination were not so strenuously tested, or so often denied exemptions, as those who professed a moral, as opposed to doctrinal, objection to service. Even here, however, as the case of Harold Croft indicates, a Tribunal might move some way to accommodating conscience without surrendering to the pacifist message entirely. What they did not, nor could, accept was the principle that the 'absolutist' moral position must of right transcend what was seen to be the national interest.[20]

Perhaps more than with respect to any other form of application, the ambiguity of legislation impacted upon the Tribunals' reaction to conscience. The Local Government Board's intentions regarding exemption were nowhere more confused or misleading than in these cases, as Walter Long's bewildering utterances during March and April 1916 attest. Outside Northamptonshire, some Tribunals gave a spate of absolute exemptions on this ground and were duly excoriated by government; the remainder shunned an option that, exercised freely, almost certainly would have caused public outrage. Given no clear guidance on which of the alternatives most appropriately dealt with conscience, many Tribunals, simultaneously hostile to the application and nervous of the implications of being 'soft' on pacifism in wartime, treated early cases relatively harshly, offering at most the non-combatant option. However, the shocking novelty of the conscientious objection faded, and it has been shown that the treatment of those exempted on this ground evolved into little more than a mechanical monitoring of their conditions of exemption. The Tribunals did not wish to hear cases of conscience; having heard them, they had little urge to revisit the experience unnecessarily.

The ground of ill-health should have been relatively uncontroversial to process, but the Army's Medical Boards laboured to make it otherwise, to the point at which the War Office and GHQ regarded their efforts with as much frustration as did the Tribunals. Though a relatively minor aspect of the exemption process, misdiagnoses were regarded with strong dissatisfaction by tribunalists, who, in taking care to publicize their ire, acted as the public voice of local opinion. Nowhere was the unspoken *quid pro quo* of equity for sacrifice more blatantly traduced than when a palpably unfit man was obliged to appeal a Category A certification. Such episodes squandered both time and goodwill, and local barracks were made very aware of the strength of feeling against them. The wholesale reform of the medical examination system in November 1917 (to the benefit of applicants and Army alike) would not have occurred had not the Tribunals taken the lead in confronting, head-on, its excesses.

Setting aside the rarely brought case of a young man wishing to complete a course of education, there remains the most complex and problematic ground for exemption allowed by the Act: that of occupation. No other form of application involved more than a fraction of resources that the Tribunals devoted to this ground; no other aspect of their work located them so firmly as arbiters in the struggle between local and national interests. This book has examined the issue by reference to different industries, trades and occupations, but the Tribunals were obliged to consider all in light of the same concept: that of 'national interest'. This was perhaps the broadest, most opaque concept to confront the system, inviting a different understanding from every person, party and community having a concern in the utilization of the nation's manpower. Again, it is almost certainly the case that the phrase's author(s) envisaged a limited, narrow interpretation, to be informed overwhelmingly by sensitivity to the national emergency. And again, they omitted to share their intentions with the Tribunals in such a way as to ensure consistency of practice.

To the latter, 'national interest' was often indistinguishable from local interest. In Northamptonshire, the two major employers – agriculture and boot and shoe – were partially protected by certified occupations lists but increasingly subjected to combing-out. Some Tribunals, acutely aware of the damage that excessive dilution might inflict upon the boot and shoe trade (which already had lost the greater part of its peacetime domestic market to American interlopers), concluded agreements with manufacturers that significantly exceeded the latitude the government believed it had given to them. Northampton Borough's 'second proposal' of December 1916 in particular, adopted by the county's other urban Tribunals (Rushden excepted) and approved by the Appeals Tribunal, was implemented despite explicit objections from the Army Council, as was their subsequent extension of existing exemptions to higher-category men in February 1917.[21] On both occasions, 'expedient in the national interest' proved to be more than a straightforward calculation of the level of substitution necessary to release all remaining fit men to the Colours. It required also consideration of the likely loss of, or delays to, contracts for millions of pairs of Army boots that the War Office had insisted should be completed as soon as possible. It was the Tribunals, rather than Whitehall, who appreciated the broader perspective here.

A central issue with regard to occupational applications was the 'indispensable' man. During 1916, many Tribunals heard claims of indispensability with justifiable scepticism, particularly where they involved very young, healthy men. As late as June 1917, the Appeals Tribunal acted decisively to restrict the boot and shoe industry's estimation of Category A and B1 men they regarded as special cases. Increasingly, however, dilution left a diminishing core of military-aged men whose skills, once relatively common, had become commensurately vital to their trades and industries. Again, the boot and shoe trade offered the most striking examples: as early as January 1917, A.E. Marlow had alleged that every further machinist taken to the Colours would put ten female closing-room operatives out of work.[22] Many Tribunals became progressively more reluctant to put such calculations to the test.

The War Office – its Army Contracts Department apart – did not share this perspective. As the recruitment process degenerated of necessity into a barrel-scraping exercise during 1917, each higher-category applicant to the Tribunals became a prize worth fighting for. In October of that year, Auckland Geddes estimated that, of some 270,000 men between the ages of 18 and 25 remaining out of uniform yet fit for general service, only ten thousand were not in some form of protected occupation.[23] It is hardly surprising, therefore, that military representatives were ordered to challenge all certificates offered to these men regardless of their circumstances. Yet their efforts, however necessitous, incited some Tribunals to suspend all business until the policy was reversed. Such gestures might appear melodramatic, but the principle at stake was an important one. Blanket military appeals implicitly rendered inconsequential the balance established by legislation; in effect, the needs of the Army were being argued as ranking superior to both statute and circumstance. It is significant that the Appeals Tribunal consistently sided with, and supported, their local counterparts during such confrontations, no matter how military exigencies pressed.

However, the same Tribunal could be simultaneously sympathetic to claims of indispensability and scrupulous in testing them, as their most successful (or, perhaps, their most familiar) appellant, William John Hewitt, might have acknowledged. A 37-year-old print compositor, Hewitt obtained an open-ended exemption on 5 July 1916, conditional upon his remaining in that employment (his firm's principal client was a munitions firm). Challenged by his local Tribunal's military representative, the certificate was reduced at appeal to three months, open. Hewitt returned to the Appeals Tribunal upon a further nine occasions, the last on 1 November 1918, when his exemption was renewed until 1 May 1919. At each visit, his employer was obliged to update the Tribunal as to Hewitt's present indispensability – which, predictably, increased as every other compositor with the firm went to the Colours. Upon receiving his fifth renewal in November 1917, he was ordered to go before the new Medical Board before next attending the Tribunal: there, he was passed Grade III.[24] The Army did not get Hewitt (and, probably, no longer wanted him once the results of his examination were known), yet the system's strongest critics could hardly claim that his circumstances had not been tested rigorously. Nor could it be alleged that Hewitt had been the victim of a cursory, uncaring process that sought only to place men in uniform.

The Tribunals were obliged to deal with complex and varied issues, and to do so with despatch, detachment, fairness and rigour. Solomons were needed; few were found. Many subsequent assessments have identified the shortcomings of those who volunteered to serve as tribunalists, yet have failed also to acknowledge the variegated responsibilities that the task imposed, or to appreciate the uncertain, shifting brief that government passed on. The legislation that brought the Tribunals into being was, to their generation, entirely unprecedented: the culmination of a fractious debate that long predated the war. It was enacted by an administration that was largely fearful of innovation and loath to accept responsibility for its potential social consequences. Hence, the degree of autonomy built into the Tribunal system, no less than the ambiguous, broad-principle advice provided thereafter, detached Whitehall from the day-to-day resentments generated by selective compulsion. The strategy, whether deliberate or incidental, was largely successful. Even politically sophisticated opponents of conscription could allow government's manufactured disinterest some credence – as did, for example, the No-Conscription Fellowship, who condemned the Tribunals for not making full use of legislation they had been gifted by politicians apparently more progressive than themselves. Less worldly perspectives – those of the many failed applicants for exemption – were hardly likely to look further than the men who signed their forms R.41 or R.43 in identifying the architects of their misfortune.

This is not to suggest that tribunalists were hapless scapegoats, reluctantly implementing a policy with which they fundamentally disagreed. The human connections between the local recruitment organizations of the voluntary period and their Tribunal successors are many and apparent, and the sense of duty that informed the day-to-day business of deciding who should go to war was not noticeably leavened by heart-searching. Stories of inordinate sacrifice by a single family, or the plight of a frail widow dependent upon a sole surviving son, could elicit strongly sympathetic reactions from the Tribunal bench. Equally, commonly expressed frustrations regarding domestic circumstances entirely disrupted by the call to arms were met often with stony reserve or a brief lecture on the part that others were playing. Few tribunalists volunteer their services to slow or confound the conscription system; they were there to do their bit within a process whose necessity they acknowledged and whose implementation they undertook diligently.

However, willingness to serve does not necessarily indicate enthusiasm for the many ambiguities thrown up in the gap between intention and the letter of legislation. As tribunalists became familiar with the detail of their work, there was apparent a growing self-confidence and a corresponding willingness to challenge or override the more glaring anomalies and injustices they confronted. Northampton Borough Tribunal were defying the letter of their instructions as early as May 1916 by offering exemptions to attested conscientious objectors.[25] Similarly, Army Council Instructions to military representatives in 1917 that exemptions to all A and B1 men should be challenged caused Rushden to suspend their sittings, while on the same issue both Northampton Borough and Wellingborough Urban Tribunals voted against strike action by the narrowest margin. The latter's acting chairman, W. Sharman, offered the press an unequivocal view of his duty following that vote: 'The Tribunal was there to represent Wellingborough, and they should do their duty, give their decisions, and take no notice of the military.'[26] For Peterborough Urban, perhaps the least 'lenient' body discussed in this book, few ambiguities in legislation proved troubling. Yet in July 1918, even they, confronted by the insupportable consequences of having applied rules regarding the VTC precisely as government intended, rebelled and threatened to remove the requirement from hundreds of exempted men (and, for good measure, wrote to Lloyd George to inform him of their displeasure).[27] Seemingly wilful changes to policy were provocative to most Tribunals, particularly when they encouraged an impression of bad faith, unfair dealing or plain incompetence.

The Military Service Tribunal was envisaged as a safety valve for the anticipated grievances of a society unused to, and suspicious of, coercive recruitment. Yet, given a degree of autonomy by legislation, tribunalists exercised it in ways that recognized more and wider imperatives than keeping the BEF's fighting strength at levels deemed by GHQ to be non-negotiable. That process took time. Unfamiliarity with their role during the early months of the conscription period made some Tribunals wary of committing themselves to policies that challenged too forthrightly the preoccupations of the War Office. A few, nervous of the effect of their deliberations upon local opinion, sought to keep proceedings entirely hidden from public scrutiny. Interest in the system was intense, however, and, as the Tribunals' experience developed, so too did a deeper perspective upon the role they had undertaken. This was the accessible – the only accessible – mechanism of official recruitment policy, enacted in a forum that laid open the dramas of thousands of otherwise anonymous lives. As leading actors in that theatre, tribunalists became acutely sensitive to their primary, if unstated, responsibility: to provide the accountable face of the 'unBritish' necessity that was conscription.

This is not the traditional view of the Tribunals' work. The vignettes offered by strongly critical works – particularly those devoted to the plight of conscientious objectors – portray them at their worst. Partial yet largely unchallenged, their evidence implies that Edwardian militarism, social exclusivity and cultural disdain for the uneducated man hung over the process like a late-Imperial haze: an Old World wilfully detached from the horrors of the New. The perspective has a superficial credibility. Few if any of Northamptonshire's tribunalists were pacifists, and the biblical impartiality expected of them by Walter Long remained elusive; but most came to recognize, to varying degrees, that compulsion was a social contract requiring the visible demonstration of fairness in its implementation. Though obliged (and undoubtedly willing) to take fateful decisions during an unprecedented national crisis, most were neither ignorant of nor inured to the consequences of their decisions. Nor is the generally accepted view of tribunalists as overawed by, or collusive with, the military authorities sustainable (a view, incidentally, with which very few contemporary recruiting officers would have concurred). As James Gribble, former professional soldier and exemplary war-fundraiser, robustly reminded a visiting military representative in June 1916, he and his colleagues 'sat in the interests of the people and not ... of the military. It [is] not for the Tribunal to act as recruiting sergeants.'[28]

Notes

1 Lloyd-George to the Tribunals (extract), 1 September 1919; copy in NRO Quarter-Sessions, Misc., 368, 1/1.

2 Cartmell, *For Remembrance*, p. 86.

3 *Statistics of the Military Effort of the British Empire*, p. 364; PP Cmd 1193: *General annual reports on the British Army ... 1913–1919*, p. 60. The total figure includes enlistments both for the Regular Army and Territorial Force, and recruitment under the Derby Scheme.

4 Above, p. 24.

5 *Statistics of the Military Effort of the British Empire*, p. 367; Dewey, 'Military Recruiting and the British Labour Force', p. 215. Another, local, snapshot, provided 17 days later by Brigadier-General Grove, OC No. 7 (Warwick) District, noted that, of 40,831 applications made to that county's local Tribunals since the beginning of 1917, only 10,348 had been refused outright. Of these statistics he wrote indignantly: 'Is this a good record? Is this the way to end the war?' (WRO CR1520/62: acts and correspondence file: 17 May 1917). Grove, or his superiors, ensured that his letter had a wide circulation; Eton Rural Tribunal received a copy in the same month (CBS DC/10/38/1: Tribunal minute book, p. 116). A more rigorous policy was implied by Sir Donald Maclean in respect of his own Appeals Tribunal (City of London) in a statement to the Commons on 17 January 1918 (5 H.C. 101:527), in which he claimed that, of forty thousand individual cases heard since the commencement of the conscription period, only three thousand exemption certificates remained in force at that date.

6 *Statistics of the Military Effort of the British Empire*, pp. 84–85, 369–374.

7 NRO CE351: Beatrice Cartwright, *Diary*, 6 November 1918.

8 NRO Quarter-Sessions, Misc., 368, 1/3. To place a local perspective upon these figures, over a slightly longer period, and during 363 sittings, Northampton Borough Tribunal heard 25,951 cases of all types. Every sitting was attended by their most assiduous (yet otherwise anonymous) tribunalist, T. Sargent. Councillor Parker attended 343 sittings, while James Gribble, who joined the Tribunal some three months after its establishment, attended upon 312 occasions (*Mercury*, 6 December 1918; *Independent*, 7 December 1918).

9 TNA MH47/5, Tribunal Letter Book 7.

10 *Report of the Central Tribunal*, pp. 16–17.

11 WRO CR1520/62: clerk of the Tribunal's report.

12 Brazier and Sandford, *Birmingham and the Great War*, pp. 29–30. Possibly, the great discrepancy between the total number of cases stated and the offered breakdown may be explained by renewals and applications for medical re-examinations.

13 Stone and Webb, *Bristol and the Great War*, pp. 117–118. The original records from which these statistics were drawn by the authors are no longer extant.

14 Armitage, *Leicester, 1914–1918*, p. 169.

15 CBS DC/13/39/43: Tribunal register of proceedings. On the Wolverton works, see above, pp. 28, 88, 172.

16 Above, pp. 68–69, 210.

17 Above, pp. 164–166.

18 The minute book of Bletchley Urban Tribunal in Buckinghamshire shows a remarkable preponderance of cases in which a decision is noted as 'carried unanimously' (CBS DC/14/39/1, *passim*). An uncanny coincidence of temperament, or one or more dominant voices speaking consistently for the whole?

19 No Tribunal in Northamptonshire achieved the affectionate relationship that Middlesex Appeals Tribunal enjoyed with their (third) military, and, later, National Service representative, Captain H.O. Carter, whose health in July 1918 caused them acute anxiety. While promising to forgo their own summer break that year, they informed the National Service Ministry that Carter 'needed a rest' and asked that arrangements be made to allow him a holiday. In a parting letter to the Tribunal (21 November 1918), Carter recalled: 'As regards myself, mere words cannot express my great gratitude for, and appreciation of, the manifold kindnesses and the unusual consideration which has been shown to me both by yourselves ... It would be impossible for anyone to have received better treatment, or to have been given more assistance, and I can truthfully say that my connection with the Tribunal has been a source of pleasure, and will remain a very pleasant memory in my life' (TNA MH 47/5, Minute Book 7, unfoliated).

20 Above, pp. 47–50.

21 Above, pp. 71–75.

22 Above, p. 74.

23 TNA CAB27/8 G.T. 2295 (13 October 1917).

24 NRO X196/779, 1404, 1943, 3464, 6694, 7146, 7412, 8984, 8694, 11093.

25 Above, p. 45.
26 *Mercury*, 22 June 1917.
27 Above, p. 211.
28 *Mercury*, 2 June 1916.

Appendix 1

Appeals Tribunal files, minutes, register books held at the Northamptonshire Records Office

File sequence

X180: Case 1 (12.15) – 598 (16.06.16)

X181: 602 (16.06.16) – 799 (13.07.16)

X182: 800 (13.07.16) – 1099 (20.09.16)

X183: 1102 (20.09.16) – 1398 (28.10.16)

X184: 1400 (28.10.16) – 1999 (07.02.17)

X185: 2000 (16.02.17) – 2798 (06.03.17)

X186: 3000 (16.03.17) – 3458 (28.04.17)

X187: 3610–3624 (all 04.05.17), 3907–3923 (all 08.05.17); 4105 (10.05.17) – 4571 (19.05.17)

X188: 5261 (22.05.17) – 5300 (22.05.17); 6118 (25.06.17) – 6299 (26.06.17)

X189: 6301 (26.06.17) – 6587 (26.07.17)

X190: 6606 (31.07.17) – 6898 (20.09.17)

X191: 6900 (20.09.17) – 6923 (20.12.17), then 7000–7493 (31.12.17), 7900–7923 (10.01.18)

X192: 8716 (14.01.18) – 8996 (10.04.18)

X193: 9000 (08.04.18–9599 (26.06.18)

X194: 9600 (28.06.18) – 9826 (01.08.18)

X195: 10139 (02.08.18) – 10211 (20.08.18)

X196: 10877 (21.08.18) – 11153 (28.10.18)

X197: Northampton (01.17–11.18) and Peterborough (03.16–11.18): working notes of Appeals Tribunal meetings

X198: Boot trade appeals 2307–7901 (broken sequence)

X199: Adjourned cases 8789 (c. 05.18) – 11102 (15.10.18); agricultural cases 3915 (03.09.17) – 9004 (03.18): War Agricultural Committee certificates; some correspondence on individual cases

X200: Appeals Tribunal Lists, 1916, 1917: typed, some (pencilled) decisions in right-hand columns

X201: Boot trade (military) appeals, filed by local tribunal, considered in batches from 2916–2982 (14–15.03.17) to 5724–6118 (26.05.17); some late 6000 series (09.17)

X202: Boot trade appeals: two large files of cases heard in 04.18 and on
   20.09.18. One file of nine cases, all conscientious objectors (cases nos
   71, 143, 209, 262, 263, 264, 866, 1041, 5260)
X203: Boot trade appeals
X204: Northampton and Peterborough appellants lists, 1916–1918.
X205: Boot trade appeals; summary appeal sheets; appeals register books
   (alphabetical)

Note: The numerical sequence is preserved consecutively only in respect of first
appeals. Where an appellant returned to the Tribunal, his previous forms were
bundled with that presented at his final visit. Dates given above which fall earlier
than the establishment of the Appeals Tribunal refer to Derby re-grouping cases
held over owing to time-constraints upon Central Tribunal.

Appendix 2

Central and Middlesex Appeals Tribunal files, minute books, registers etc. held at the National Archives

All MH 47/:

Central Tribunal

1. Minute Books 1915–1917
2. Minute Books 1917–1922
3. Selected case papers and copy of Tribunal's supplementary report
4. Veterinary Tribunal selected case papers

Middlesex Appeals Tribunal

5. Minute Books 1915–1918
6. Rough duplicates of 5.
7. Register of appeals of non-attested men, 1916–1918 ('M' series)

8–52: case papers of the non-attested appellants

8. M1–174
9. 176–338
10. 339–506
11. 507–661
12. 662–799
13. 800–930
14. 931–1061
15. 1062–1202
16. 1203–1306
17. 1307–1410
18. 1411–1540
19. 1541–1644
20. 1645–1759
21. 1760–1863
22. 1864–1993

23. 1994–2123
24. 2124–2227
25. 2228–2321
26. 2322–2425
27. 2426–2529
28. 2530–2631
29. 2632–2734
30. 2738–2854
31. 2855–2960
32. 2961–3080
33. 3081–3196
34. 3197–3330
35. 3331–3462
36. 3463–3570
37. 3571–3668
38. 3669–3807
39. 3808–3960
40. 3961–4110
41. 4111–4260
42. 4261–4400
43. 4401–4550
44. 4551–4650
45. 4651–4770
46. 4771–4960
47. 4961–5080
48. 5081–5230
49. 5231–5370
50. 5371–5600
51. 5601–5917
52. 5918–6024

53–65: non-attested men, exemptions (all 'M' prefix)

53. 96–2395
54. 2413–2892
55. 2900–3299
56. 3304–4092
57. 4101–4642
58. 4655–4949
59. 4953–5159
60. 5161–5366
61. 5371–5500

62. 5501–5660
63. 5661–5869
64. 5871–5989
65. 5990–6023

66–68: case papers, conscientious objectors ('M' prefix)

66. 5–694
67. 705–2102
68. 2130–5914

69. Non-attested men, adjourned cases M1220–5598
70. Non-attested men, adjourned cases 5990–6023
71. Register of appeals, voluntarily attested men ('V' series)

72–103: Voluntary attested men, case papers

72. V1–190
73. 191–388
74. 389–560
75. 561–780
76. 781–970
77. 971–1150
78. 1151–1300
79. 1301–1420
80. 1421–1570
81. 1571–1720
82. 1721–1900
83. 1901–2020
84. 2021–2160
85. 2161–2280
86. 2281–2430
87. 2431–2572
88. 2573–2705
89. 2706–2837
90. 2838–2995
91. 2996–3130
92. 3131–3290
93. 3291–3435
94. 3436–3599
95. 3600–3750
96. 3751–3930
97. 3931–4090
98. 4091–4260
99. 4261–4440

100. 4441–4620
101. 4621–4770
102. 4771–5000
103. 5001–5264

104–110: Voluntarily attested men: exemptions

104. 434–2508
105. 2529–3548
106. 3620–4756
107. 4802–5019
108. 5031–5140
109. 5141–5219
110. 5220–5275

111. Voluntarily attested men, adjourned cases 979–5261
112. Agricultural cases: non-attested M3326–5158; attested V3039–4970
113. Registers of medical re-examination
114. Medical assessor cases, disposed of nos 1–667
115. Medical assessor cases, disposed of nos 680–1487
116. Medical assessor cases, refused and adjourned, nos 8–1563
117. List of appeals on medical grounds, medical histories, grading, etc. Cases referred to Middx Tuberculosis officer
118. Cases where appeals made to courts, or where legal questions raised
119. Cases submitted to Central (attested and non-attested)
120. Papers relating to exempted men, and applications of employers seeking exemption for employees
121. Tribunal correspondence, in-and-out, Feb – Dec 1916
122. Tribunal correspondence, in-and-out, Jan 1917–Sept 1919
123. Letters from local Tribunals, Mar – Dec 1916
124. Letters from local Tribunals, Dec 1916–Nov 1918
125. Correspondence with Central re: conscientious objectors; letters to MR
126. Lists of cases with some decisions noted, 1916
127. Ditto, 1917
128. Ditto, 1918
129. As above, but with case histories attached, Mar – May 1916
130. Ditto, Jun – Aug 1916
131. Ditto, Sept – Dec 1916
132. Ditto, Jan – Apr 1917
133. Ditto May – Sept 1917
134. Ditto, Oct 1917–Mar 1918
135. Ditto, Apr – Oct 1918
136. Card Index A – Cha

137. Che – Ga
138. Ge – Jo
139. Ju – Par
140. Pas – So
141. Sp – Z

142. Circulars and pamphlets issued by Local Govt Board, printed Acts, Booklets, etc

143. Statistical returns (incl. Middx appeals trib. stats) and lists, summary of Tribunal sittings, attendance of members

144. Misc. memoranda, Parliamentary questions, lists, press cuttings, legal papers, etc., 1916–1917; Minutes of evidence of Select Committee on Military Service, with summary of proceedings and the Report, 1917

145–162: Letter books of the Tribunal

145. Missing
146. 16 May – 20 July, 1916
147. 20 July – 5 Sept 1916
148. 6 Sept – 16 Oct 1916
149. 17 Oct – 24 Nov 1916
150. 24 Nov – 4 Jan 1917
151. 4 Jan – 1 Feb 1917
152. 2 Feb – 12 Mar 1917
153. Missing
154. 18 Jun – 2 Aug 1917
155. 2 Aug – 5 Oct 1917
156. 5 Oct – 17 Dec 1917
157. 14 Dec – 15 Mar 1918
158. Missing
159. 28 May – 19 July 1918
160. 18 July – 29 Oct 1918
161. 29 Oct – 11 Dec 1918
162. 18–23 Oct 1919

163. Central Medical War Committee, minutes Aug 1916–July 1917

References

Primary sources

Northampton Record Office
CE351: Appointments diary of Beatrice Cartwright, 1916
ML1540: Northamptonshire Volunteer Regiment Papers
X180–X205: Northamptonshire Appeals Tribunal files, working notes of meetings, summaries of scheduled cases, register books, 1916–1918
X4237: Northamptonshire Territorial Force Association Papers
Quarter-Sessions, Miscellaneous, 368: partial statistics on Appeals Tribunal sittings, some departmental papers, boot and shoe data

The National Archives
MH47: Central Tribunal Minute Books, selected case papers and supplementary report (1919); Middlesex Appeals Tribunal files, registers, memoranda, statistical returns, minute books, correspondence
MSA: Military Service Acts, 1916–1918
ACI: Army Council Instructions
CAB: Cabinet papers, correspondence and reports, 1915–1918
LGB: Local Government Board, circular and instructions
MAF: Ministry of Agriculture and Fisheries, circulars and instructions
NATS: National Service Ministry, circulars and instructions
WO: War Office Instructions, correspondence and papers, 1915–1918
Parliamentary Papers Cmd 1193: *General annual reports on the British Army (including the Territorial Force) for the period from 1st October, 1913, to 30th September, 1919* (1921)
Parliamentary Papers 1917–1918, III, 327, q. 4383: *Special Report from the Select Committee on the Military Service (Review of Exceptions) Act, 1917* ('Shortt Committee': June 1917)

National Library of Wales
CTB2: Minute books and correspondence, Cardiganshire Appeals Tribunal
CTB3: Appeals files, Cardiganshire Appeals Tribunal

Bodleian Library

Harcourt, Milner MSS

Corporation of London Records Office

COL/SJ/05/006: Minutes of Guildhall Committee, City Appeals Tribunal

Oxfordshire Record Office

BB/xxiv/i/i: Banbury Urban Local Tribunal minute book, 1916–1918
OCA/A.9.4: Oxford Local Tribunal, misc. notes and correspondence, 1916–1918

Centre for Buckinghamshire Studies

DC/10/38/1: Eton Rural Local Tribunal minute book, 1916–1918
DC/13/39/43: Newport Pagnell Local Tribunal register of cases, 1915–1918
DC/14/39/1: Bletchley Urban Local Tribunal minute book, 1915–1918

Warwickshire Records Office

CR1520/59, 62, 64: Warwick District Appeals Tribunal files and clerk's report

Friends' House, London

Temp. MSS 835: T.E. Harvey Papers, Report of the Pelham Committee

Imperial War Museum

Man-power Distribution Board Papers, 1916

Secondary Sources
(place of publication London unless stated otherwise)

Monographs

Adams, R.J.Q. and Poirier, P.P., *The Conscription Controversy in Great Britain, 1900–1918* (1987).

Barnett, L.M., *British Food Policy during the First World War* (1985).

Beaver, S.H., *The Land in Britain* (1943).

Beckett, I.F.W., *The Amateur Military Tradition, 1558–1945* (Manchester, 1991).

Beckett, I.F.W. and Simpson, K. (eds), *A Nation in Arms: A Social Study of the British Army in the First World War* (Manchester, 1985).

Bet-el, I., *Conscripts: The Lost Legions of the Great War* (Stroud, 1999).

Bilton, D., *Hull Pals: The 10th, 11th, 12th and 13th Battalions, East Yorkshire Regiment* (Barnsley, 1999).

Boulton, D., *Objection Overruled* (1967).

Bradbury, J, *Government and County: A History of Northamptonshire County Council, 1889–1989* (Bristol, 1989).

Brazier, R.H. and Sandford, E., *Birmingham and the Great War* (Birmingham, 1921).

Brown, C., *Northampton 1835–1985: Shoe Town, New Town* (Chichester, 1990).

Ceadel, M., *Pacifism in Britain, 1914–1945: The Defining of a Faith* (Oxford, 1980).

Chamberlain, W.J., *Fighting for Peace: The Story of the War Resistance Movement* (1928).

Churchill, R.S., *Lord Derby, 'King of Lancashire': The Official Life of Edward, Seventeenth Earl of Derby, 1865–1948* (1959).

Crick, M., *The History of the Social-Democratic Federation* (Edinburgh, 1994).

Dewey, P.E., *British Agriculture in the First World War* (1989).

Edmonds, J.E., *Military Operations in France and Belgium, 1916*, volume I (1932).

Graham, J.W., *Conscription and Conscience: A History 1916–1919* (1922).

Grieves, K., The *Politics of Manpower, 1914–1918* (Manchester, 1988).

Grigg, J., *Lloyd George: War Leader 1916–1918* (2002).

Harding, J.S., *The Boot and Shoe Industry* (1934).

Harris, P.J., Hartop, P.W. and Buckley, W.H., *Northamptonshire: Its Land and People* (Northampton, 1950).

Hayes, D., *Conscription Conflict* (1949).

HMSO, *History of the Ministry of Munitions* (8 vols, 1921–1922).

——, *Report of the Central Tribunal Appointed under the Military Service Act, 1916* (1920)

——, *Statistics of the Military Effort of the British Empire, 1914–1920* (1922).

Howard, M., *The Continental Commitment* (1972).

Hurwitz, S.J., *State Intervention in Great Britain: A Study of Economic Control and Social Response, 1914–1919* (New York, 1949).

Kennedy, T.C., *The Hound of Conscience: A History of the No-Conscription Movement* (Fayetteville, 1981).

Kirby, D., Thomas, D. and Turner, L. (eds), *Northampton Remembers: Boot and Shoe* (Daventry, 1988).

Lloyd George, D., *War Memoirs of David Lloyd George* (6 vols, 1933–1936).

Maddocks, G., *Liverpool Pals: The 17th, 18th, 19th and 20th Battalions, The King's Own (Liverpool Regiment)* (Barnsley, 1991),

Mansfield, N., *English Farmworkers and Local Patriotism, 1900–1930* (Aldershot, 2001).

Middleton, T.H., *Food Production in War* (Oxford, 1923).

Mitchinson, K.W., *Defending Albion: Britain's Home Army, 1908–1919* (Basingstoke, 2005).

Montgomery, J.K., *The Maintenance of the Agricultural Labour Supply in England and Wales during the War* (Rome, 1922).

Moorehead, C., *Troublesome People: Enemies of War, 1916–1986* (1986).

Rae, J., *Conscience and Politics: The British Government and the Conscientious Objector to Military Service, 1916–1919* (Oxford, 1970).

Robbins, K., *The Abolition of War: The Peace Movement in Britain, 1914–1919* (Cardiff, 1976).

Schwartz, M., *The Union of Democratic Control in British Politics during the First World War* (Oxford, 1971).

Scott, W.H., *Leeds and the Great War* (Leeds, 1923).

Slater. J.G. (ed.), *The Tribunal: Published by the No-Conscription Fellowship, Numbers 1–182* (Kraus reprint, New York, 1970).

Slocombe, I., *The First World War Tribunal in Swindon* (Devizes, Wiltshire Family History Society, 1997).
——, *First World War Tribunals in Wiltshire* (Devizes, Wiltshire Family History Society, 1997).
Stedman, M., *Manchester Pals: The 16th, 17th, 18th, 19th, 20th, 21st, 22nd and 23rd Battalions of the Manchester Regiment* (Barnsley, 1996).
Stone, G.F. and Webb, C., *Bristol and the Great War, 1914–1919* (Bristol, 1920).
Taylor, A.J.P., *Politics in Wartime and Other Essays* (1964).
Turner, W., *Pals: The 11th (Service) Battalion (Accrington) East Lancashire Regiment* (Barnsley, 1998).
Whettam, E.H., *The Agrarian History of England and Wales* (general ed. J. Thirsk): vol. VIII: 1914–1939 (Cambridge, 1978).
Winter, J.M., *The Great War and the British People* (1985).
Wolfe, H., *Labour Supply and Regulation* (Oxford, 1923).

Unpublished theses

Griffin, W.C., *The Northampton Boot and Shoe Industry and Its Significance for Social Change in the Borough from 1800 to 1914* (Northampton, 1968).
Mack, A.R., *Conscription and Conscientious Objection in Leeds and York during the First World War* (York, 1983).
Mitchinson, K.W., *Auxiliary Forces for the Land Defence of Great Britain, 1909–1919* (Luton, 2002).

Memoirs and diaries

Armitage, F.P., *Leicester 1914–1918: The War-time Story of a Midlands Town* (Leicester, 1933).
Barnes, J. and Nicholson, D. (eds), *The Leo Amery Diaries: vol 1, 1896–1929* (London, 1980).
Campbell, P.J., *In the Cannon's Mouth* (1979).
Cartmell, H., *For Remembrance* (Preston, 1919).
Self, R.C. (ed.), *The Neville Chamberlain Diary Letters*, vol. 1 (Aldershot, 2000).

Newspapers, news-sheets and digests

Accrington Observer and Times
Daily Telegraph
Daventry Gazette
Hansard Parliamentary Debates
The Justice of the Peace
Leeds and District Weekly Citizen
Manchester City News
Manchester Guardian
Northampton Chronicle
Northampton Herald
Northampton Independent
Northampton Mercury
Oldham Chronicle

The Times
The Tribunal
Washington Post

Articles, pamphlets and reports

Agriculture and Fisheries, Board of, *Journal of the Board of Agriculture*, October 1916–March 1917.

Beckett, I.F.W., 'The Local Community and the Great War: Aspects of Military Participation', *Records of Buckinghamshire*, vol. XX, 4 (1978), pp. 503–515.

——, 'The Real Unknown Army: British Conscripts, 1916–1918', in Becker, J.J. and Audoin-Rouzeau, S. (eds), *Les sociétés européennes et la guerre de 1914–1918* (Paris, Presses de l'université, Paris-X-Nanterre, 1990), pp. 339–355.

Bibbings, L., 'State Reaction to Conscientious Objection', in Loveland, I. (ed.), *Frontiers of Criminality* (1995), pp. 57–81.

Boot, H.M. and Maindonald, J.H., 'New Estimates of Age- and Sex-specific Earnings and the Male–Female Earnings Gap in the British Cotton Industry, 1833–1906', *Economic History Review*, vol. 61 (2008), pp. 380–408.

Church, P.A., 'The Effect of the American Export Invasion on the British Boot and Shoe Industry, 1885–1914', *Journal of Economic History* (1968), pp. 223–254.

Dewey, P.E., 'Agricultural Labour Supply in England and Wales during the First World War', *Economic History Review*, 2nd Series, vol. 28 (1975), pp. 100–112.

——, 'Military Recruiting and the British Labour Supply during the First World War', *The Historical Journal*, vol. 27, 1 (1984), pp. 199–223.

Douglas, R., 'Voluntary Enlistment in the First World War and the Work of the Parliamentary Recruiting Committee', *Journal of Modern History*, vol. 42 (1970), pp. 564–585.

Ernle, Lord, 'The Food Campaign of 1916–1918', *Journal of the Royal Agricultural Society of England*, vol. 82 (1921), pp. 1–48.

——, 'The Women's Land Army', *Nineteenth Century and After* (1921), pp. 1–16.

Fowler, A., 'The Impact of the First World War upon the Lancashire Cotton Industry and Its Workers', in Wrigley, C. (ed.), *The First World War and the International Economy* (Cheltenham, 2000), pp. 76–98.

——, 'British Textile Workers in the Lancashire Cotton and Yorkshire Wool Industries', Conference paper given at the International Institute of Social History, Amsterdam (2004): www.iisg.nl.

Gregory, A., 'Military Service Tribunals: Civil Society in Action, 1916–1918', in Harris, J. (ed.), *Civil Society in British History* (Oxford, 2003), pp. 177–190.

Grieves, K., 'Military Tribunal Papers: The Case of Leek Local Tribunal in the First World War', *Archives*, vol. 16, 70 (1983), pp. 145–150.

——, 'Total War? The Quest for a British Manpower Policy, 1917–18', *Journal of Strategic Studies*, vol. 9, 1 (1986), pp. 79–95.

——, 'The Recruiting Margin in Britain: Debates on Manpower during the Third Battle of Ypres', in Liddle, P. (ed.), *Passchendaele in Perspective* (Barnsley, 1997), pp. 390–405.

——, 'Lloyd George and the Management of the British War Economy', in

Chickering, R. and Förster, S. (eds), *Great War, Total War* (Cambridge, 2000), pp. 369–387.

Housden, C., 'Kingston's Military Tribunal, 1916–1918', *Occasional Papers in Local History*, no. 2/04 (Centre for Local History Studies, Kingston University, 2004).

Kenefick, W., 'War Resisters and Anti-Conscription in Scotland: An ILP Perspective', in Macdonald, C. and McFarland, E.W. (eds), *Scotland and the Great War* (East Linton, 1999), pp. 59–80.

Lester, H.G., 'British Emergency Legislation', *California Law Review*, vol. 7 (1919), pp. 323–339.

Mornington Hall Ecclesia, *EVIDENCE (extending over half-a-century) that The Conscientious Objection to military Service and the Bearing of Arms is a Denominational Characteristic of the Christadelphian Body of Believers* (1916).

Mountfield, P.R., 'The Footwear Industry of the East Midlands, Part V: The Modern Phase: Northamptonshire and Leicestershire since 1911', *East Midland Geographer*, vol. 4, 1, no. 27 (June 1967), pp. 154–175.

National Union of Boot and Shoe Operatives, *National and Branch Monthly Reports*, January 1916–November 1918.

Osborne, J.M., 'Defining Their Own Patriotism: British Volunteer Training Corps in the First World War', *Journal of Contemporary History*, vol. 23 (1988), pp. 59–75.

Pierce, C., 'A Community of Resistance: The Anti-War Movement in Huddersfield, 1914–1918', in Dockray, K. and Laybourn, K. (eds), *The Representation and Reality of War: The British Experience* (Stroud, 1999), pp. 170–189.

Robbins, K., 'The British Experience of Conscientious Objection', in Cecil, H. and Liddle, P. (eds), *Facing Armageddon* (Barnsley, 1996), pp. 691–706.

Sheail, J., 'The Role of the War Agricultural and Executive Committees in the Food Production Campaign of 1915–1918 in England and Wales', *Agricultural Administration*, vol. 1 (1974), pp. 141–154.

——, 'Land Improvement and Reclamation: The Experiences of the First World War in England and Wales', *Agricultural History Review*, vol. 24 (1976), pp. 110–125.

Simkins, P., 'Kitchener and the Expansion of the Army', in Beckett, I.F.W. and Gooch, J. (eds), *Politics and Defence: Studies in the Formulation of British Defence Policy 1845–1970* (Manchester, 1981), pp. 87–109.

Slocombe, I., 'Recruitment into the Armed Forces during the First World War: The Work of the Military Service Tribunals in Wiltshire, 1915–1918', *The Local Historian*, vol. 30, 2 (2000), pp. 105–123.

Snowden, P., *The Military Service Act Fully and Clearly Explained* (1916).

Spinks, P., '"The War Courts": The Stratford-upon-Avon Borough Tribunal 1916–1918', *The Local Historian*, vol. 32, 4 (2002), pp. 210–217.

Stephen, A., 'The Tribunals', in Bell, J. (ed.), *We Did Not Fight: 1914–1918 Experiences of War Resisters* (1935), pp. 377–392.

Swaysland, E., *Report on American Methods of Boot and Shoe Manufacture* (Northampton, 1906).

Thomson, M., 'Status, Manpower and Mental Fitness: Mental Deficiency in the First World War', in Cooter, R., Harrison, M. and Sturdy, S. (eds), *War, Medicine and Modernity* (Stroud, 1998), pp. 149–166.

Winter, J., 'Military Fitness and Civilian Health in Britain during the First World War', *Journal of Contemporary History*, vol. 15 (1980), pp. 211–244.

Index